NEW WORLD BABEL

NEW WORLD BABEL

LANGUAGES AND NATIONS IN
EARLY AMERICA

Edward G. Gray

PRINCETON UNIVERSITY PRESS   PRINCETON, NEW JERSEY

Copyright © 1999 by Princeton University Press
Published by Princeton University Press, 41 William Street,
Princeton, New Jersey 08540
In the United Kingdom: Princeton University Press,
Chichester, West Sussex

Library of Congress Cataloging-in-Publication Data

Gray, Edward G., 1964–
New World Babel : languages and nations in early America /
Edward G. Gray.
p.   cm.
Includes bibliographical references (p.   ) and index.
ISBN 0-691-01705-0 ((cloth : alk. paper)
1. North America—Languages—History.   2. Indians of North
America—Languages.   3. Language and languages—Philosophy.
4. Language and culture.   I. Title.
P381.N65G73   1999
409′.7—dc21   98-35157

This book has been composed in New Baskerville

Princeton University Press books are printed on acid-free paper
and meet the guidelines for permanence and durability of the
Committee on Production Guidelines for Book Longevity of the
Council on Library Resources

http://pup.princeton.edu

Printed in the United States of America

1   3   5   7   9   10   8   6   4   2

For Mel and Sue

Languages are the pedigree of nations.

—SAMUEL JOHNSON (1773)

Contents

Illustrations

Acknowledgments

I AM grateful to the readers at Princeton University Press and to Laura Murray, all of whom gave invaluable comments and criticism on an early draft of this study. For much-needed remarks about my argument in chapter III, I would like to thank Vicente Rafael, Ives Goddard, and Bernard Bailyn. I am also grateful to Hans Aarsleff for his close and critical reading of chapter IV. For their comments on chapters of the dissertation upon which this book is based, I would like to thank Keith Arbour, Michael Fry, Eric Hinderaker, Lieve Jooken, Jane Kamensky, Karen Ordahl Kupperman, Uta Poiger, and Joan Richards.

Hugh Amory, Philip Benedict, Martha Burns, Catherine Corman, Roy Goodman, Bruce Greenfield, Michael B. Gross, Even Hovdhaugen, Richard John, Alan L. Karras, Dana Leibsohn, Jill Lepore, Galey Modan, Mark Peterson, Rüdiger Schreyer, and Richard B. Sher have all provided greatly appreciated references, ideas, and support of various kinds.

I am grateful to Brigitta van Rheinberg of Princeton University Press for her confidence in the value of this project and for her generous encouragement and advice. For their assistance with illustrations, I would like to thank Susan Danforth and Daniel J. Slive, of the John Carter Brown Library; Jean Rainwater, of the John Hay Library at Brown University; and Beth Carroll-Horrocks and Roy Goodman, both of the American Philosophical Society Library. I am also indebted to Brown University, the Brown history department, the John Carter Brown Library, the Library of the American Philosophical Society, and the J. M. Stuart family for early fellowship support. The entire staff of the John Carter Brown Library—especially my former colleagues Tricia Mighton and Karen De Maria—deserve special thanks for allowing me to become a part of the J.C.B. family.

Two veteran students of early American history have had much to do with this project. Gordon S. Wood directed the dissertation upon which it is based, gave me the freedom to find my own way, and taught me a lesson I will always cherish: history is, in the end, a creative enterprise. Norman Fiering has taught me much more than he would ever admit. I can only hope that in some small way this study lives up to the high standards of scholarship and intellectual honesty to which he shows such rare and appealing devotion.

Jane Kamensky and Uta Poiger have been patient sources of wise counsel on just about everything, and Greg Wallace has endured years of rants and rambles about things scholarly and otherwise. For this, I am deeply in their debt. I would also like to thank the Rutledges, Bosworths, and Grays for their support over the past few years. And Stacey Allison Rutledge—as important to this book's life as its author.

NEW WORLD BABEL

Introduction

WHAT IS the relationship between language and nationhood? The question has preoccupied Americans from Noah Webster to William Safire, both of whom share the conviction that we are how we speak. The cohesion of our society, the clarity of our self-image, the power of our founding ideology are all, in the minds of these men, dependent on our ability to generate and sustain an American idiom. With words, we have the power to remake ourselves, to improve our political and social relationships, and to better our cultural lives.

Behind these assumptions is the Enlightenment idea that words are social conventions. In a departure from the predominant late medieval view that words and things were unified as a matter of divine will, most eighteenth-century theorists came to see words as inventions, arbitrarily assigned by humans to their thoughts. Language no longer merely reflected the divine order of things but instead reflected the mental and social world of speakers. Differences of speech—differences of grammar and syntax, vocabulary, and every other quality that distinguishes one tongue from another—had come to represent much more than superficial linguistic variation. They had become, instead, signatures of human difference of the most profound sort, difference in the very mental and social character of nations.

The idea that in language could be found the sources of national distinction developed concurrently with the idea that some languages were inferior to others. The speakers of such languages, so the reasoning went, had not brought to their tongues the improvements that distinguished the languages of Europe from those of the rest of the world. They had not, that is, through their own creative powers and distinct intellectual energies, crafted tongues able to express the most complex and abstract thoughts. And the reason for this, so most Enlightenment-era theorists assumed, lay in more profound failures, above all the failure to organize and sustain expansive states. This latter operation had brought European nations an accumulation of diverse experiences and ideas, all of which served to expand minds and, in turn, improve speech.

It was this set of assumptions that, for the first time in Western history, made multilingualism a serious social and intellectual problem. Debates about language, usage, and culture were not, of course, new. Since antiquity, Europeans had debated the relative merits of various vernacular tongues, particularly with respect to Greek and Latin. But the idea that linguistic difference corresponded to profound differences in human character—that idea was novel. This study explores the emergence of this understanding of language, and it does so in a context rarely considered relevant to such discussions: North America. The polyglot character of indigenous North America, and its relevance to the colonial expansion of Europe, is something that, until recently, has almost entirely escaped the attention of historians.[1] And yet the presence of a vast array of American Indian languages and their speakers explains why the cultural and social problems associated with linguistic diversity have perhaps never been a more prominent part of American cultural life than they were during the first two centuries of European expansion into North America.

The rise of a distinction between cultivated and unrefined tongues might be understood as the other side of what the sociologist Norbert Elias earlier this century characterized as the "civilizing process."[2] Along with the rise of European notions of social and cultural refinement, and the emergence of distinct "polite" and "plebeian" cultures, came a corresponding tendency to understand the norms of refined societies in opposition to those of "savage" societies—societies separated from the most refined not simply by space but also by time. As Europeans came to regard themselves as "polite" or "refined," so they came to regard other societies as "savage" and "uncivilized."

It is true that such dichotomies were not new to Europeans in the eighteenth century. Patterns of "otherization," or the formulation of various negative types against which Europeans defined themselves— "wild man," "barbarian," "savage," and so forth—were hardly new. But the idea that a person's speech could indicate "savagery" was new. For until the eighteenth century, most European commentators had assumed that language was a divine, primordial endowment over which

---

[1] Two notable exceptions are Stephen Greenblatt, "Learning to Curse: Aspects of Linguistic Colonialism in the Sixteenth Century," in *First Images of America*, ed. Fredi Chiapelli (Berkeley: University of California Press, 1976), vol. 1, 561–80; and Marc Shell, "Babel in America; or, The Politics of Language Diversity in the United States," *Critical Inquiry* 20:1 (Autumn 1993): 103–27. Also see the essays in Edward G. Gray and Norman Fiering, eds., *The Language Encounter in the Americas, 1492–1800* (New York: Berghahn Books, forthcoming). Related themes are treated in Vicente L. Rafael, *Contracting Colonialism: Translation and Christian Conversion in Tagalog Society under Early Spanish Rule* (Ithaca, N.Y.: Cornell University Press, 1988); Louis-Jean Calvet, *Linguistique et colonialisme: Petit traité de glottophagie* (Paris: Éditions Payot, 1974); and Johannes Fabian, *Language and Colonial Power: The Appropriation of Swahili in the Former Belgian Congo, 1880–1938* (Cambridge: Cambridge University Press, 1986).

[2] Norbert Elias, *The Civilizing Process: The History of Manners* and *State Formation and Civilization*, trans. Edmund Jephcott (1939; single-volume English edition, Oxford: Basil Blackwell, 1994).

people themselves had little control. Whatever diversity there was in the world's tongues could not be understood in terms of a simple hierarchy of more or less refined languages. Instead, Europeans understood that diversity as a reflection of primordial events—most significantly, the fall of the Tower of Babel—that destroyed a universal Edenic tongue and left in its place linguistic confusion.

Before the eighteenth century, philosophers of language therefore tended to assume that far from representing an early or "primitive" stage in the development of human language, the languages of non-Europeans were comparable to other vernacular tongues in their powers of expression. There was little sense that the world's languages differed in any profound way, or that their distinctions reflected more than the various stages of decline and deterioration humanity had experienced after Creation.

This perspective informed much missionary activity in the seventeenth-century New World. Christian missionaries regarded language, like other cultural traits, as an impediment to spiritual progress that was essentially superficial. It indicated nothing at all about the nature of different peoples—or their potential for salvation. What a speaker said reflected the world, not the speaker, because words and empirical reality were unified, and this was an almost unwavering matter of faith. For, as Genesis explained, before the Fall, God invited Adam to name all things in nature. These names became one and indistinguishable from those things until the confusion of tongues alienated the natural world from Adam's original and perfect taxonomy. What remained in the aftermath of Babel were thus tongues that vaguely and imperfectly represented reality. What remained, that is, were the corrupted progeny of the language of Eden.

For Puritan missionaries in early New England, the idea that each individual was equipped to recognize his own salvation meant that everyone ultimately had access to the universal language of prayer—the one language with which mortals could communicate with God. But that language was not simply oral utterance, the sort of devil's tongue that allowed humans to curse.[3] Rather, it was the language, encased in mortal speech, that humans communicated in prayer. As Saint Gregory put it, "Men judge a man's heart by his words. God judges words by the heart."[4] The Christian language of the heart transcended all idioms and all cultural barriers. In both an epistemological sense and a cultural sense, it rendered linguistic difference irrelevant.

---

[3] Hence, in *The Tempest*, Caliban says to Miranda and Prospero: "You taught me language; and my profit on't / Is, I know how to curse," (1.2.365–66).

[4] Translated and quoted in Garry Wills, *Witches and Jesuits: Shakespeare's* Macbeth (New York: Oxford University Press, 1995), 95.

While many factors account for the decline of this premodern conception of human speech, prime among them must be the late seventeenth- and early eighteenth-century pursuit of religious toleration. Exhausted by nearly two centuries of brutal religious conflict, increasing numbers of Europeans began to assimilate the idea, formulated most notably by John Locke, that words had no necessary connection to any kind of stable reality—and that any antinomian or fanatical devotion to the Word rested on the flawed assumption that God's word could be known in full. The earlier notion that beneath all the world's tongues lay a universal and perfect Edenic tongue gave way to the idea that all languages reflected the unique social and intellectual experiences of their speakers. In the range of a language's vocabulary, in the elegance and simplicity of its grammar, in its capacity to express thoughts abstracted from diverse experiences—in all these could be seen the collective mental and social powers of its speakers. There was nothing primordial in speech; no necessary connection to an original, perfect tongue. Language was merely an assemblage of utterances, accepted by groups as signifying particular ideas. And because language was shaped by experience and invention, it was opaque, permanently limiting the human capacity to identify truths.

A nation's tongue, therefore, had come to represent a set of mental processes explicable less by primordial events than by the ongoing course of history. And if a nation's history took a progressive path toward refinement and elevation, so, it was assumed, would the speech of that nation reflect this in its refined structure and comprehensive vocabulary. Inspired by this reasoning, philosophers turned to North American Indian language for examples of unrefined or primitive linguistic forms, examples that provided a starting point for a history of the evolution of language.

The notion that language bore the imprint of human development also lay behind the growing eighteenth-century belief that language offered the most accurate perspective on the pasts of peoples without writing. Eighteenth-century natural historians argued that because of its constant utility, language, unlike religion, manners, and morals, required no special acts of collective memory or technological innovation to be sustained over time. For its existence depended not on knowledge but on habit. It was for this reason that Thomas Jefferson and other American antiquaries of his generation turned to American Indian language in their quest to write the history of aboriginal America. Because of its antiquity, because of its capacity to be passed on from generation to generation, and to retain vestiges of its original form through the millennia, it would, these Americans assumed, reveal the lineage of an indigenous American population—an issue of no small significance to a generation of Americans determined to demonstrate the existence of a common human nature.

By 1820, Americans had begun to challenge the Enlightenment assumption that the distinctive qualities of Indian speech resulted from Indians' degraded social and intellectual condition. Drawing on French theorists, one figure in particular, the Philadelphia lawyer and linguist Peter Stephen Du Ponceau, argued that rather than merely representing an inferior stage in linguistic development, American Indian languages represented the epitome of linguistic form. In their capacity to express a myriad of ideas in a single word, Du Ponceau argued, Native American tongues far surpassed any others in eloquence, poetic force, and verbal clarity.

This argument rested on Du Ponceau's belief that the distinctive qualities of American Indian societies bore no immediate relation to the distinct character of American Indian languages. For Du Ponceau, language was distinct from mind; the speaker, distinct from the spoken. Du Ponceau's position emerged out of his Romantic desire to make an exceptional American literary contribution. In the study of American Indian speech, he believed he found the one way for his countrymen to make that contribution. By suggesting that a people's language was a fixed, ancient cultural endowment, over which that people had little control, Du Ponceau also foreshadowed the Romantic idea that language, nation, and race were indistinct.

There is a curious intersection between Du Ponceau's world and that of the missionaries of seventeenth-century New England, an intersection of the sort that makes intellectual history at once frustrating and compelling. For in a certain sense Du Ponceau, borrowing from the Moravian missionary John Heckewelder, implied the same connection between language and culture that dominated seventeenth-century Christian thought. From both perspectives, the possession of language was not a historical fact. It was not an indication of patterns of mental and social growth over time. For both seventeenth-century missionaries and the nineteenth-century Du Ponceau, the speaker could not be comprehended in the spoken. Whatever the expressive powers of a person's speech, they bore no necessary relation to that person's condition.

Babel, far more than the universal and progressive course of linguistic change suggested by eighteenth-century Anglo-American language philosophers is in the end an apt metaphor for describing the Romantic conception of Indian speech: it suggests that different languages are not made by their speakers but rather are given to them by their creator. If for seventeenth-century commentators that creator was God, for Du Ponceau, as for the Romantic nationalists of Europe, it was the mystical ancestry of nations.

CHAPTER I

New World Babel

ACCORDING to Genesis 2, God felled the Tower of Babel as a punishment for human hubris. It was for this reason that Christians have regarded the resulting confusion of tongues as something of a deliberate curse, leaving in its wake a global patchwork of peoples, cultures, and nations without which there would be none of the antagonisms, hatreds, and misunderstandings that made a unified humanity seem like utter fancy. "For when men cannot communicate their thoughts to each other, simply because of difference of language," wrote Saint Augustine, "all the similarity of their common human nature is of no avail to unite them in fellowship. So true is this that a man would be more cheerful with his dog for company than with a foreigner."[1] Genesis had left little doubt that, as the seventh-century encyclopedist Isidorus of Seville observed, "nations have arisen from tongues, not tongues from nations."[2] To conceive of a nation in early modern Europe was thus to conceive of a congruence in language and material culture across a broad expanse of space. "Maps show the borders of states," Leibniz wrote, "but not those of nations, which the harmony of languages more clearly makes evident."[3] The perceived correlation between language and nation was only enhanced with the emergence of perhaps the most revolutionary technology of the early modern era: printing. As much as any more general social or political development, the printing press made possible wide-scale literacy in a select number of vernacular tongues, which in turn became increasingly identified with specific nation-states.[4]

---

[1] Saint Augustine, *The City of God* (Harmondsworth, England: Penguin Books, 1972), book 19, ch. 7.

[2] J. S. Slotkin, ed., *Readings in Early Anthropology* (London: Methuen, 1965), 8. The history of various interpretations of the confusion of tongues is explored in Arno Borst, *Der Turmbau von Babel: Geschichte der Meinungen über Ursprung und Vielfalt der Sprachen und Völker*, 6 vols. (Stuttgart: Hiersemann, 1957–63).

[3] Translated and quoted by Hans Aarsleff in *From Locke to Saussure: Essays on the Study of Language and Intellectual History* (Minneapolis: University of Minnesota Press, 1982), 99 n. 39. On definitions of "nation," see Elie Kedourie, *Nationalism*, 4th ed. (Oxford: Blackwell, 1993), 5–7; and Ernest Gellner, *Nations and Nationalism* (Ithaca, N.Y.: Cornell University Press, 1983), 3–7 and passim.

[4] The effects of printing on national languages are treated in Lucien Febvre and

A similar tendency to associate linguistic and national difference, it should be said, predated Christianity. From Aristotle to Thomas Aquinas and beyond, the primary category in which Europeans placed foreigners and non-Europeans was that of the "barbarian." For the Greeks, the word distinguished true Greek speakers from those who either spoke altogether different languages or spoke vulgarized dialects of Greek. And for the Greeks, the concept had a distinctly ethno-centric cast. As Anthony Pagden has explained, "For the Hellenistic Greeks . . . an inability to speak Greek was regarded not merely as a linguistic shortcoming, for a close association in the Greek mind be-tween intelligible speech and reason made it possible to take the view that those who were devoid of *logos* in one sense might also be devoid of it in another."[5] By the sixteenth century, the idea had changed only in its breadth. Montaigne, for instance, wrote, "Each man calls barbar-ism whatever is not his own practice; for indeed it seems we have no other test of truth and reason than the example and pattern of the opinions and customs of the country we live in."[6] To be a barbarian was thus not merely to speak differently but also to live differently. It was, in essence, to be of another nation.

None of this should obscure the fact that—contrary to the modern nationalist conceit—the boundaries of language and government do-minion almost never match. There are, of course, "national" or domi-nant languages, but these tongues almost never exist to the exclusion of minority languages, much as English now exists in the polyglot United States. Further, these languages achieve dominance because of government policy and economic necessity. And, indeed, it was these factors, along with printing, that meant that by the middle of the eigh-teenth century Europeans could, for the first time, say that Britain was an English-speaking nation; France, a French-speaking one; and Spain, Spanish-speaking—however imaginary and impossible such an ideal may in fact have been.[7]

Henri-Jean Martin, *The Coming of the Book: The Impact of Printing, 1450–1800*, trans. David Gerard (London: Verso, 1990), 319–32.

[5] Anthony Pagden, *The Fall of Natural Man: The American Indian and the Origins of Com-parative Ethnology* (Cambridge: Cambridge University Press, 1982), 16 and passim. Also see Arno Borst, "Barbarians: The History of a Catchword," in *Medieval Worlds: Barbarians, Heretics, and Artists in the Middle Ages*, trans. Eric Hansen (Chicago: University of Chicago Press, 1992), 3–13.

[6] "Of Cannibals," in *The Complete Essays of Montaigne*, trans. Donald M. Frame (Stan-ford, Calif.: Stanford University Press, 1958), 152.

[7] Regarding the nationalist conflation of language boundaries with national borders, one linguist has written, "It has been estimated that there are some four to five thousand languages in the world but only about 140 nation-states. Probably about half the world's population is bilingual and bilingualism is present in practically every country in the

For European observers this perceived congruence between language and nation appeared to have almost no validity when applied to the indigenous nations of North America. From one town to the next, peoples with no obvious difference in manner, dress, or character often spoke mutually unintelligible tongues. Of perhaps more significance, there often appeared to be no dominant tongue or lingua franca to facilitate communication among different Native American towns. This bewildering linguistic landscape stimulated a wonder and confusion like almost nothing else about the New World, but it posed only a partial challenge to inherited explanations for the diversity of the world's languages. Throughout much of the early modern era, Europeans explained the linguistic landscape of the Americas much as they explained that of Europe: a diversity of languages resulted from the failure of societies to preserve an original and perfect God-given tongue. If, as Anthony Grafton has suggested, the European encounter with America stripped classical learning of its "aura of completeness," it did so only in a gradual and partial fashion.[8]

Upon first landing in the West Indies, Columbus concluded that the peoples he had seen were of one nation, sharing as they did a common language. On his second visit, he experienced greater linguistic variation, and by his fourth voyage—which took him to what is now the Costa Rican coast—he had concluded that "although the villages are very close together, each has a different language, and consequently the people of one do not understand those of another, any more than we understand the Arabs."[9] What is striking about this observation is that it came from a man no doubt familiar with polyglot societies. Late

world." Suzanne Romaine, *Language in Society: An Introduction to Sociolinguistics* (Oxford: Oxford University Press, 1994), 33–34. Also see E. J. Hobsbawm, *Nations and Nationalism since 1780: Programme, Myth, Reality* (Cambridge: Cambridge University Press, 1990), 51–63. On the emergence of state-sanctioned languages, see Romaine, *Language in Society*, 34–35. A notable eighteenth-century European attempt to introduce national linguistic uniformity is explored in Michel de Certeau, Dominique Julia, and Jacques Revel, *Une politique de la langue: La Révolution française et les patois* (Paris: Éditions Gallimard, 1975). A work that considers these processes in a colonial context is Louis-Jean Calvet, *Linguistique et colonialisme: Petit traité de glottophagie* (Paris: Éditions Payot, 1974).

[8] Anthony Grafton, *New Worlds, Ancient Texts: The Power of Tradition and the Shock of Discovery* (Cambridge, Mass.: Harvard University Press, 1992), 5. The extensive literature on the impact of the New World on the Old is treated in Karen Ordahl Kupperman's "Introduction" to *America in European Consciousness, 1493–1750*, ed. Kupperman (Chapel Hill: University of North Carolina Press, 1995), esp. 2–5.

[9] *The Four Voyages of Christopher Columbus*, edited by J. M. Cohen (London: Penguin Books, 1969), 299.

medieval and early modern Europe remained a patchwork of distinct languages, dialects, and patois.

In the dominions of the English king alone, no fewer than five mutually unintelligible languages and numerous dialects—of varying degrees of mutual intelligibility—were spoken in the sixteenth century.[10] Indeed, as a general rule, the farther one moved from the power centers of western Europe, the greater the language diversity one was likely to encounter. Writing of the late medieval era, the historian Robert Bartlett has noted, "The interplay of languages was . . . a common and sharply recognizable feature of the frontiers of Latin Europe."[11] The significance of Columbus's remark is thus in the degree of difference it suggested. Native American villages differed in speech not as Spaniards from Portuguese but as Spaniards from Arabs. This degree of linguistic difference appears to have provoked a certain amount of anxiety in Columbus. Rather than accept the possibility that it prevailed across what he hoped to be part of Asia, Columbus concluded that a confusion of tongues was characteristic of "the uncivilized people on the sea-coast but not of those of the interior."[12] The statement suggests that Columbus had doubts that a people in such a state of linguistic disorder could generate the kinds of treasures known to be present in the heart of the Far East. Columbus was not alone in these general perceptions.

Having been sent north from Mexico City to conquer New Mexico and retrieve its rumored riches, Francisco Vásquez de Coronado found little more than hardship. One reason, he explained to his king, was language. "As I have been obliged to send captains and soldiers to many places in this country to find out whether there was anything by which your majesty could be served," he wrote in 1541, "the diversity of languages spoken in this land and the lack of people who understand them has been a great handicap to me, since the people in each town speake their own."[13] Again, we can assume that such a diversity of language was not unfamiliar to the Spanish conquistaders. Throughout the Americas they encountered a patchwork of Indian communities, each speaking distinct mother tongues. In central Mexico, however, an Aztec empire imposed far-reaching imperial institutions through which

[10] William Harrison, *The Description of England*, ed. Georges Edelen (Ithaca, N.Y.: Cornell University Press, 1968), 411–18.

[11] Robert Bartlett, *The Making of Europe: Conquest, Colonization and Cultural Change 950–1350* (London: Penguin Books, 1994), 199.

[12] *The Four Voyages of Christopher Columbus*, 299.

[13] "Francisco Vásquez de Coronado to Charles V," Oct. 20, 1541, in *New American World: A Documentary History of North America*, ed. David B. Quinn (New York: Arno Press, 1979), vol. 1, 431.

Europeans could acquire and disseminate information. Among these was Nahuatl, the language of the Aztec nobility. The tongue served as an imperial lingua franca, which the Spaniards—much like the Aztec nobility themselves—used to extend their colonial authority. Something similar occurred in Peru, where the Inca empire had established Quechua as a language of dominion.[14] In the American Southwest, the far reaches of Aztec influence, however, there was no comparable lingua franca—or at least none that was revealed to Europeans. This is not to say that Europeans found themselves completely unable to communicate with the peoples of North America. The first European to traverse an extensive portion of the continent, Alvar Núñez Cabeza de Vaca, noted that although he and his companions "passed through many and dissimilar tongues [as they traversed the North American Gulf Coast,] our Lord granted us favor with the people who spoke them, for they always understood us, and we them." But that rudimentary understanding did not come from the spoken word: "We questioned them, and received their answers by signs, just as if they spoke our language and we theirs."[15]

With so much linguistic variation, it is no wonder that one of Coronado's henchmen would come to describe isolated groups of native peoples not as "nations" or "tribes" but as "languages." Upon asking his guide who inhabited the Colorado River banks along which he trekked, he learned "by this man that it was inhabited by 23 languages . . . besides others not far off, and that there were besides these 23 languages, other people also which hee knewe not, above the river."[16] What is telling here is that the commentator refers not to towns or nations but to languages, suggesting that in fact this is what his guide referred to—

[14] On the languages of Mexico, see *Hernan Cortes: Letters from Mexico*, ed. Anthony Pagden (New Haven, Conn.: Yale University Press, 1986), 92, 246, 404; and Johannes de Laet, *L'Histoire du Nouveau Monde ou Description des Indes Occidentales. . .* (Leyden: Bonaventura and Abraham, 1640), 153. See also J. Jorge Klor de Alva, "Language, Politics, and Translation: Colonial Discourse and Classical Nahuatl in New Spain," in *The Art of Translation: Voices from the Field*, ed. Rosanna Warren (Boston: Northeastern University Press, 1989), 143–62; Frances Karttunen, "Nahuatl Literacy," in *The Inca and Aztec States 1400–1800: Anthropology and History*, ed. George A. Collier, Renato I. Rosaldo, and John D. Wirth (New York: Academic Press, 1982), 395–417. On Quechua see Shirley Brice Heath and Richard Laprade, "Castilian Colonization and Indigenous Languages: The Cases of Quechua and Aymara," in *Language Spread: Studies in Diffusion and Social Change*, ed. Robert L. Cooper (Bloomington: Indiana University Press, 1982), 118–47; and Bruce Mannheim, *The Language of the Inka since the European Invasion* (Austin: University of Texas Press, 1991).

[15] "The Relations of Alvar Núñez Cabeza de Vaca," in Quinn, *New American World*, vol. 2, 51.

[16] "The Expedition of Hernando de Alarcón," in Quinn, *New American World*, vol. 1, 441.

perhaps an indication of the centrality of language to Native American group identity.

The variation of tongues appeared almost as dramatic in the central and eastern parts of the North American continent as in the Southwest. Father Louis Hennepin, a Recollect missionary who claimed to have traveled in the early 1680s among Dakotan- and Miami-Illinois-speaking peoples in the northern Mississippi valley, remarked that "'tis very strange that every Nation of the Savages of the Northern America should have a peculiar language; for though some of them live not ten leagues one from another, they must use an Interpreter to talk together, there being no universal language amongst them; as one may call the Lingua Franca."[17] Observers had a similar sense about the East Coast. In the late sixteenth century, Thomas Harriot, the official reporter of the Virginia Company, complained that the "language of every [Indian] government is different from any other, and the farther they are distant the greater is the difference."[18] And in 1624 a Dutch observer remarked that the languages of the peoples of the Hudson River valley "vary frequently not over five or six leagues; forthwith comes another language; if they meet they can hardly understand one another."[19] William Wood, a promoter of New England settlement, shared this sentiment. "Every [American] country," he commented, "differ[s] in their speech, even as our northern [British] peoples do from southern, and western from them."[20]

Even those Christians seeking to "normalize" Native Americans, or to see them as in no fundamental way different, could not help but be struck by this state of affairs. In his *History of New France* (1618), for example, the lawyer, historian, and ex-patriot immigrant to New France Marc Lescarbot initially asserted that, as in Europe, "the effects of the confusion of Babel have reached these tribes whereof we speak. . . . For I see that the Patagonians speak another language than the Brazilians, and these otherwise than the Peruvians, and the Peruvians are distinct from the Mexicans; the isles likewise have their peculiar speech: in Florida they speak not as they do in Virginia." But Lescarbot could only conclude that in polyglot Europe there was nowhere near the confusion that appeared to prevail in an America where "every nation

---

[17] Louis Hennepin, *A New Discovery of a Vast Country in America. . .*, ed. Reuben Gold Thwaites (1698; Chicago: A. C. McClurg, 1903), vol. 1, 215.

[18] Thomas Harriot, *A Brief and True Report of the New Found Land of Virginia* (1590; reprint, New York: Dover, 1972), 25.

[19] Nicolaes Van Wassenaer, "Historisch Verhael," in *Narratives of New Netherland, 1609–1664*, ed. J. Franklin Jameson (New York: Scribner's, 1909), 72.

[20] William Wood, *New England's Prospect*, ed. Alden T. Vaughan (1634; reprint, Amherst: University of Massachusetts Press, 1977), 110.

is divided by language; yea in one and the selfsame province languages differ, even as in Gaul the Fleming, the peoples of lower Brittany, the Gascon, and the Basque do not agree."[21]

This linguistic diversity was the source of almost endless frustration for European missionaries. Working in French North America during the early eighteenth century, the Jesuit Father Sébastien Rasles, for example, complained that "each savage tribe has its own special tongue; thus the Abnakis, the Hurons, the Iroquois, the Algonkins, the Illinois, the Miamis, and others, have each their own language." Rasles went to great pains to demonstrate that this was no simple matter of different dialects. He translated a stanza from a sacred hymn into some of these languages to show that few could examine these passages without recognizing "how little resemblance there is between them."[22] Another Jesuit, Father Jacques Marquette, reported to his superiors that in an encounter with a group of Indians in Illinois country, "I spoke to them in six different languages, of which they understood none."[23]

Making matters more confusing for Europeans, in America the geographic limits of tongues were—as they are in most places—ever-changing. One reason was the ongoing creation of pidgins and trade jargons, a process that appears to have accelerated with the arrival of European traders. In the fur-trading regions of the Northeast, for example, broken versions of Huron and Algonquian arose, but pidginized forms of European tongues also emerged as widely used lingua francas. Remembering an experience he had while voyaging in New England in 1623 and 1624, Captain Christopher Levett wrote of "a time the governour was at my house, and brought with himn a salvage who lived about 70 miles from the place which I have made choice of, who talking with another savage thwy were glad to use broken English to express their mind to each other, not being able to understand one another in their language."[24]

Among European observers, there was much disagreement about the precise degree of difference in Native American languages—disagreement that no doubt reflects the fluid meaning of the terms *dialect* and

[21] Marc Lescarbot, *The History of New France*, ed. and trans. W. L. Grant (1612; Toronto: Champlain Society, 1914), vol. 3, 113.

[22] Reuben Gold Thwaites, ed., *The Jesuit Relations and Allied Documents: Travels and Explorations of the Jesuit Missionaries in New France, 1610–1791* (Cleveland: Burrows Brothers, 1900), vol. 67, 147 (hereafter cited as *JR*).

[23] Hennepin, *A New Discovery of a Vast Country in America*, vol. 2, 663. Also see vol. 1, 217.

[24] Christopher Levett, *A Voyage to New England, Begun in 1623 and Ended in 1624* (London: E. Brewster, 1628), 22. Also see Michael Silverstein, "Dynamics of Linguistic Contact," in *Handbook of North American Indians, Vol. 17, Languages*, ed. Ives Goddard (Washington, D.C.: The Smithsonian Institution, 1996), 118–21.

language. In their common usage, these terms describe degrees of mutual intelligibility. Differences in dialect, for instance, are generally understood to afford high degrees of mutual intelligibility, while differences in language are understood to afford low degrees of mutual intelligibility. This appears to have been the assumption of the dissenting New England Puritan Roger Williams when he wrote that in southern New England "there is a mixture of this language North and South, from the place of my abode, about six hundred miles; yet within two hundred miles . . . their dialects doe exceedingly differ; yet not so, but (within that compasse) a man may, [with the aid of Williams's *A Key into the Languages of America*], converse with thousands of Natives all over the Country." Such statements are difficult to evaluate, since it is possible for speakers of very different languages, (say, Italian and Spanish) to grasp each other's meaning, while speakers of the same language who hail from different regions, (say, English speakers from working-class Glasgow and English speakers from working-class Detroit) may have considerable difficulty understanding each other.[25] As it turns out, linguists now describe most of what was spoken in southern New England not as dialects but as distinct—although not unrelated—languages. Massachusett, Narragansett, Mohegan-Pequot, Mahican, and others are all members of the Eastern Algonquian family of languages. And while there was probably some mutual intelligibility afforded by these languages, there is little testimony to suggest that Williams's *Key* actually eased communications in the region.[26]

In colonized regions outside of the Americas, Europeans often found different and in fact less daunting linguistic configurations. In China, for example, the pioneer Jesuit missionary, Matteo Ricci, explained that although the people spoke a wide variety of languages, a logographic writing system transcended differences in the varieties of spoken Chinese. In addition, although "each province hath its owne [language] . . . all hath one common tongue besides, which they call Quonhoa, or the Court Language used in courts and by their learned."[27]

[25] Roger Williams, *A Key into the Language of America*, ed. John J. Teunissen and Evelyn J. Hinz (1643; reprint, Detroit, Mich.: Wayne State University Press, 1973), 84. The general problem of using levels of intelligibility to differentiate languages is treated in John Edwards, *Multilingualism* (London: Routledge, 1994), esp. 23; and Romaine, *Language in Society*, ch. 1. Also see Einar Haugen, "Dialect, Language, Nation," *American Anthropologist* 68:4 (August, 1966), 922–35.

[26] Ives Goddard, "Eastern Algonquian Languages," in *Handbook of North American Indians, Vol. 15, The Northeast*, ed. Bruce Trigger (Washington, D.C.: Smithsonian Institution, 1978), 70–77.

[27] Matteo Ricci, "A Discourse on the Kingdom of China," in Samuel Purchas, *Hakluytus Posthumous, or Purchas His Pilgrimes . . .* (London: Henry Featherstone, 1625–26), vol. 3,

Despite the immense diversity of languages and dialects in China, that
is, a universally understood writing system and a court lingua franca
simplified communications. More important, the writing system facilitated missionary activity for figures like Ricci. The capacity to write
Chinese provided immediate access to literate souls all across China.
Indeed, in the seventeenth century, the universality of written Chinese
captured the imagination of Europeans searching for just such a universal language—a written language that could transcend differences
in human speech.[28] In Africa, too, Europeans who traveled in the north
and along the Atlantic coast found communications to be simpler than
in America—despite the similar abundance of distinct languages. One
writer observed that much like the tribal groups of America, the peoples of sub-Saharan, coastal Africa were widely dispersed into "hun-
dreds of progenies and innumerable habitations." But unlike the native
peoples of North America, they also "use all one kind of language
called by them . . . the noble tongue."[29]

Statistics offer partial confirmation of observers' impressions. The
precise distribution of Native American languages with respect to population is difficult to know. Some regions—California and the northwestern coast, in particular—had an unusually high density of distantly
related and unrelated tongues or language "isolates." Others—the
plains and eastern seaboard among them—reveal far closer genetic
relations among their various dialects and languages. Keeping these
facts in mind, the aggregate numbers are still startling. It has been
estimated that at the time of European contact, between 1,000 and
2,000 distinct, mutually unintelligible tongues were spoken in the
Americas.[30] In all of the Americas, the population on the eve of contact
has recently been estimated at as many as 57,300,000,[31] meaning that

---

384. Also S. Robert Ramsey, *The Languages of China* (Princeton, N.J.: Princeton University Press, 1987).

[28] On the relevance of Chinese to the universal language movement, see Paul Cornelius, *Languages in Seventeenth- and Eighteenth-Century Imaginary Voyages* (Geneva: Librarie Droz, 1965), ch. 2.

[29] "Observations of Africa, taken out of John Leo. . .," in Purchas, *Hakluytus Posthumous*, vol. 2, p. 751. On the problem of language and identity in coastal West Africa, see John Thornton, *Africa and Africans in the Making of the Atlantic World, 1400–1680* (Cambridge: Cambridge University Press, 1992), 184–92. The Philippines lacked a widespread lingua franca, significantly complicating missionary efforts. See Vicente L. Rafael, *Contracting Colonialism: Translation and Christian Conversion in Tagalog Society under Early Spanish Rule* (Ithaca, N.Y.: Cornell University Press, 1988), 20.

[30] Harold E. Driver, *Indians of North America*, 2d ed. (Chicago: University of Chicago Press, 1969), 25.

[31] See "Epilogue," in William M. Denevan, ed., *The Native Population of the Americas in 1492* (Madison: University of Wisconsin Press, 1976), 291.

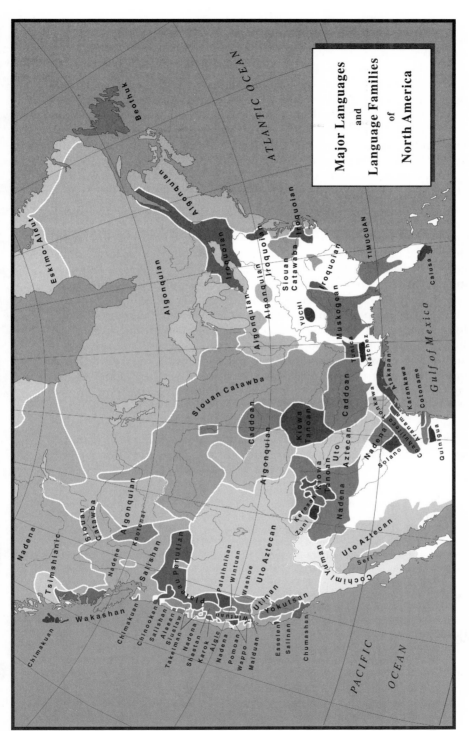

By Mapcraft, from Ives Goddard, "Native Languages and Language Families of North America," to accompany *Handbook of North American Indians, Vol. 17, Languages* (Washington, D.C., 1996); and Harold Driver, "Map 37," in *Indians of North America*, 2d ed. (Chicago, 1969).

for every language group there were an average of 57,300 Indians. On the North American mainland, an area populated by as many as 4,400,000 native people, 329 distinct, mutually unintelligible languages are known to have been spoken during the past five hundred years.[32] Again, the average per capita numbers are staggering: fewer than 14,000 Indians for every distinct tongue, and perhaps even fewer if we accept the possibility that some Native American tongues suffered extinction before they were ever identified by Europeans. By comparison, in the British Isles around the same time, there were nearly 700,000 speakers per language.[33] These facts have remained almost completely absent from historians' discussions, and it is no wonder. Nearly half of the indigenous languages of North America are now extinct, or are verging on extinction.[34]

Although the evidence is scarce, it does suggest that American Indians used linguistic difference to retain some control over local knowledge, cultural inheritance, and political discourse, employing language much as one might employ a secret code. One indication of this practice was simply the persistence of linguistic diversity well after the beginning of European settlement. "The difference of languages, that is found amongst these heathens," noted the North Carolina trader and Indian agent John Lawson in 1709, "seems altogether strange. For it appears, that every dozen miles, you meet with an Indian town that is quite different from the others you last parted withal."[35] Later in the century, the Philadelphia traveler and botanist William Bartram emphasized that this kind of diversity was not merely a matter of dialect. While traveling in the Chattahoochee River valley, he observed, one could very easily encounter two Indian towns that "almost join each other, yet speak two languages, as radically different perhaps as the Muscogulge's

---

[32] On the number of North American languages, see Ives Goddard, "Introduction," in *Handbook of North American Indians, Vol. 17, Languages*, 3. There are considerable discrepancies in the estimated indigenous population of North America before European contact. But even the largest number, eighteen million, leaves slightly less than thirty-three thousand Indians per language. See John D. Daniels, "The Indian Population of North America in 1492," *William and Mary Quarterly* 49:2 (April 1992): 300.

[33] For population estimates, see Colin McEvedy and Richard Jones, *Atlas of World Population History* (New York: Facts on File, 1978), 49, 105. On the different languages of England, see Charles Barber, *The English Language: A Historical Introduction* (Cambridge: Cambridge University Press, 1993), 65–66 and passim. On Iberian languages, see Philippe Wolff, *Western Languages, AD 100–1500*, trans. Frances Partridge (London: World University Library, 1971), 173–84.

[34] Goddard, "Introduction," 3.

[35] John Lawson, *A New Voyage to Carolina* (1709; reprint, Chapel Hill: University of North Carolina Press, 1967), 233.

and Chinese."[36] There thus appears to have been little movement among Native Americans toward a crystallization of tongues—something, as will become apparent, Europeans associated with civilization or social refinement.

Another indication that language served to mark kin group identity was the frequent refusal of Indians to engage in diplomatic negotiations in any language but their own. As one eighteenth-century observer noted of a group of Iroquois diplomats, "Most of them understood English, though they will not speak it when they are in treaty." John Lawson explained that "the most powerful nation of these [North Carolina Indians] scorns to treat or trade with any others (of fewer numbers and less power) in any other tongue but their own."[37]

Related to this is what appeared to Europeans to have been profound linguistic bias and prejudice among some Indian groups. The French Jesuit Joseph François Lafitau recalled that "the other Iroquois make fun of the [Cayuga and Seneca] and say they speak badly."[38] Elsewhere, John Lawson remarked that "difference of speech causes jealousies and fears amongst [Indians], which bring wars, wherein they destroy one another." Likewise, Lawson concluded, had it not been for this language variation, Christians would not have "settled America so easily."[39] Instead of loosely bound societies, they would have found a formidable, unified nation, much as existed in Europe. Lawson was suggesting that the entire conquest owed something to the perceived linguistic prejudices of native peoples. From the Indians' perspective, however, it may very well have been a connection between language distinction and small-scale, kin identity that allowed for the preservation of cultural autonomy and political power.

Multilingualism and the use of language as a cultural or social marker are virtually universal in polyglot societies. A familiar example is the practice of using some government-sanctioned dominant lan-

---

[36] *Travels of William Bartram*, ed. Mark Van Doren (New York: Dover, 1955), 362.

[37] Witham Marshe, "Journal of the Treaty . . . at Lancaster, Pennsylvania, June, 1744," *Collections of the Massachusetts Historical Society*, 1st ser., 7 (1800): 180; Lawson, *A New Voyage*, 233. James H. Merrell touches on this in *The Indians' New World: Catawbas and Their Neighbors from European Contact through the Era of Removal* (Chapel Hill: University of North Carolina Press, 1989), 147–48. Also see Michael K. Foster, "On Who Spoke First at Iroquois-White Councils: An Exercise in the Method of Upstreaming," in *Extending the Rafters: Interdisciplinary Approaches to Iroquoian Studies*, ed. M. K. Foster, J. Campisi, and M. Mithun (Albany: State University of New York Press, 1984), 183–207.

[38] Joseph François Lafitau, *Customs of the American Indians Compared with the Customs of Primitive Times*, ed. William N. Fenton and Elizabeth L. Moore (1724; Toronto: Champlain Society, 1977), vol. 2, 264.

[39] Lawson, *A New Voyage*, 239.

guage (English, for example) in public situations, while retaining a regional dialect or ancestral language (such as Spanish in the United States) for more intimate, local interactions. These practices can indicate deference to a dominant language, but they can also indicate sociopolitical choice, insofar as they affirm traditional identities, patterns of thought, and social ties. Ethnolinguists have identified similar processes among multilingual indigenous peoples in South America. As one scholar has written of peoples of the northwestern Amazon basin, in oral exchanges "each individual initially speaks in his own father-language . . . in order to assert his tribal affiliation and identification."[40] We can conjecture that something similar occurred in early American diplomatic councils: bilingual Native American speakers used their nation's tongue as a way of affirming group allegiance in the presence not only of Europeans but also of members of their own and other kin groups. We might even say that a tongue was to tribal groups what a crest was to European aristocratic families or clans: a sign of shared ancestry, shared traditions, and common memories. Such uses of language may have led European observers to believe there was a greater variation among dialects than there in fact was. They also may have led them to believe Indian bilingualism was less widespread than it was.

Europeans were not struck just by the variety of tongues they encountered in North America. Of equal significance was their wonder at the seeming absence of any clear congruence of language difference and differences of manners or morals. The Dutch geographer and director of the Dutch West India Company, Johannes De Laet, observed that Indians "being divided into many nations and people differ much from one another in language though very little in manners."[41] In New Netherland, all the things that Europeans believed differentiated nations—clothing, food, the shape of weapons, the manner of building homes and boats—appeared to serve no such purpose at all. Language alone marked one people apart from another. Elsewhere, the entire notion of a "nation," defined by shared material culture, social habits, and language, did not appear to fit with the facts in America. Henri Joutel, a member of LaSalle's fateful 1684 expedition to find the mouth of the Mississippi River, explained that for the Cenis, in what is

[40] Arthur P. Sorenson Jr., "Multilingualism in the Northwest Amazon," *American Anthropologist* 69:6 (1967): 678. Also Jean Jackson, "Language Identity of the Columbian Vaupés Indians," in *Explorations in the Ethnography of Speaking*, ed. Richard Bauman and Joel Sherzer (Cambridge: Cambridge University Press, 1974), 50–64. Useful introductions to the matters of language choice and multilingualism can be found in Romaine, *Language in Society*, 33–64, and Edwards, *Multilingualism*, 83–88. Also relevant is Clifford Geertz, *The Interpretation of Cultures* (New York: Basic Books, 1973), esp. 241–43.

[41] Johannes de Laet, "New World," in Jameson, *Narratives of New Netherland*, 57.

now eastern Texas, "the word Nation, is not to be understood . . . to denote a people possessing a whole province, or vast extent of Land." Rather, for them "Nations are no other than a parcel of Villages, dispers'd for the space of twenty or thirty leagues at most, which compose a distinct People or Nation; and they differ from one another rather in Language than in manners, wherein they are all much alike."[42] It was precisely this paradox—of shared material culture among peoples differing sharply in their speech—that challenged inherited explanations for linguistic difference.

Medieval and Renaissance writers generally assumed that in felling the Tower of Babel, God transformed the world from a place unified by a single language to one divided into seventy-two distinct mother tongues, scattered across the globe and correlating with seventy-two distinct nations. This deep and lasting reprimand brought with it the burden of reunifying humanity in the community of God through the universal language of prayer—an imperative that, as we will see, was very much central to the early modern Christian missionary impulse.[43] By almost any measure, the plurality of American tongues made the seventy-two post-Babel tongues seem an impossibly small and trivial number. Writing in the middle of the seventeenth century, in an effort to disprove the widely held view that the American Indians were descendants of one of the ten lost tribes of Israel, Hamon L'Estrange observed that "they say that at the confusion of tongues, there were 72 languages, but the Americans have 700 and more."[44] With such seeming linguistic anarchy, L'Estrange argued, it was no wonder that those who searched found Indian words that resembled Hebrew words. But the question was, What explained this apparent inconsistency in biblical knowledge? Why were there so many more languages in the world than allowed for by the biblical account?

There is little evidence that in the sixteenth and seventeenth centuries Europeans understood the linguistic diversity of America—or anywhere else—to be the result of fundamental racial difference. That is, they did not conclude that this diversity indicated something fundamentally nonhuman or innately different about American Indians. Instead, the broad variety of American languages was for many merely evidence of the failure of Native Americans to heed the divine mandate of repentance, salvation, and unification. Writing to promote the

---

[42] Henri Joutel, *A Journal of the Last Voyage Perform'd by Monsr. de la Sale, to the Gulph of Mexico. . . .* (London: A. Bell, 1714), 114.

[43] See Hermann J. Weigand, "The Two and Seventy Languages of the World," *Germanic Review* 17:4 (1942): 241–60.

[44] Hamon L'Estrange, *Americans, no Jewes, or Improbabilities that the Americans are of that race* (London: Henry Seile, 1652), 60.

settlement of Virginia, Robert Johnson explained, "It is recorded that when the pride of earthlie men, in the race and progenie of Noah, began to aspire and sought to clime the Celestial throne; it so highly provoked the Majestie of God, that . . . he subverted their devices and proud attempt, infatuating their understanding by confounding their tongues." To emerge from that confusion was, for Johnson, to emerge from savagery and paganism. Hence, "the sundrie nations of America: which as they consist of infinite confused tongues and people, that sacrifice their children to serve the divel" were ripe for the civilizing effects of Christianity.[45] For Johnson, the Christians of the world had transcended and ameliorated the confusion of tongues. The heathens had not.

Another explanation for America's linguistic diversity, and one that would become common in the eighteenth century, was that of Hugo Grotius, a seventeenth-century Dutch jurist and an inventor of natural-law theory. In an essay challenging Johannes De Laet's theory of Indian origins, Grotius set out to prove that far from emanating from a single source during some distant age, America's indigenous population emanated from different places sometime after the birth of Christ. This was plainly indicated, Grotius argued, by the residual diversity of American tongues—a diversity, he argued, that originated in Jerusalem. In parts of America, however, there was simply too much language variation to be attributed to the small number of ancestral Hebrew peoples Grotius identified in the Bible. In Florida, for example, it appeared that "individual families framed a vocabulary specially for themselves." Hence, although the parent tongues may have had diverse origins, something about the New World led even these tongues to experience a sort of linguistic fission. For Grotius, this state of affairs resulted from the absence of "a common government." With no central authority, there was nothing to impose uniformity on a people; nothing, that is, that could lead them—by necessity or coercion—to devise shared patterns of speech, with the jarring result that families, let alone larger tribal groups, spoke in sharply differing ways. This explanation was consistent with Grotius's pursuit of an alternative moral order, shaped not so much by God's active will as by natural laws, or those irrefutable principles—initiated by God but, much as might be the case with certain mathematical propositions, true regardless of God's will—that allow for human harmony in a world of cultural diversity. For Grotius, what made humans different was their varying ability to identify natural laws

---

[45] Robert Johnson, *The New Life of Virginia* (1612), in *Tracts and Other Papers, Relating Principally to the Origin, Settlement and Progress of the Colonies. . .*, comp. Peter Force (Washington, D.C.: Peter Force, 1836), vol. 1, no. 7, pp. 7–8.

and to implement institutions that facilitated the operation of those laws. The failure to recognize laws of nature could result in the kind of cultural atomization he believed to be present in Florida.[46]

If Native Americans appeared unable to introduce the political structures that would bring greater uniformity to the American linguistic landscape, so too did they at times appear to lack the very conceptual foundation necessary for forming distinct cultural and ethnic identities. Beyond identifying with a specific kin group, Indians often seemed unaware of any more comprehensive categories of identity. Indeed, for some commentators, what was remarkable about the peoples of America—what made them both praiseworthy and pitiable—was precisely this: a failure to distinguish themselves from other cultures and ethnicities.

In what was no doubt meant as a critical appraisal of his own fractious Puritan society, Roger Williams remarked that while the English may categorize the peoples of America in terms of general racial rubrics such as "Natives, Salvages, Indians, Wild-men, Abergeny men, Pagans, Barbarians, Heathen," the Indians had no such terms. "I cannot observe," Williams explained, "that they ever had (before the comming of the English, French, or Dutch amongst them) any Names to difference themselves from strangers, for they knew none; but two sorts of names they had and have amongst themselves." Those names were the general ones, "Nínnuock, Ninnimissinnûwock, Eniskeetompaúwog, which signifies men, folke, or people." Beyond these all-inclusive names, there were the highly exclusive ones "peculiar to severall Nations, of them amongst themselves, as, Nanhigganéuck, Massachusêuck, Cawasumsêuck, Cowweséuck, Quintikóock, Qunnipiéuck, Pequttóog, & c." Any sense of ethnic or racial difference, Williams insisted, came from the English themselves: "They have often asked mee, why wee call them Indians, Natives, & c. And understanding the reason, they will call themselves Indians, in opposition to English, & c."[47] For Williams, the failure of Native Americans to formulate identities more comprehensive than kin-based, or familial, identity, was no failure at all. Instead, it reaffirmed the possibility that people could live as one unified creation, bound by a common humanity and unburdened by the arbitrary distinctions that Englishmen imposed on the peoples of America.

In a world in which the notion of chaos was all but inadmissible, it is not surprising to find scattered intellectuals attempting to identify

---

[46] Hugo Grotius, *On the Origin of the Native Races of America*, ed. Edmund Goldsmid (Edinburgh: Privately Published, 1884), 17. Also see Joan-Pau Rubiés, "Hugo Grotius's Dissertation on the Origin of the American Peoples and the Use of Comparative Methods," *Journal of the History of Ideas* 52:2 (April–June, 1991): 221–44.

[47] Williams, *A Key into the Language of America*, 84–85.

some sort of order in the American linguistic landscape. This meant attempting to classify American tongues with respect to other languages of the world. Until late in the eighteenth century, the predominant means of doing this involved evaluating words for traces of ancestral relations. For most of the medieval and early modern eras, this sort of analysis rested on the Christian assumption that all languages were descended from the same original language given by God to Adam.

It is therefore not coincidental that the most frequent classificatory assertion was that American Indian speech was somehow descended from Hebrew—an argument that served to reinforce the widely held view that America was peopled by one of the ten lost tribes of Israel. Thomas Thorowgood, the chief seventeenth-century English advocate of this theory, explained that "very many of [the Indians'] words are like the Hebrew."[48] But Thorowgood well knew that a few etymological parallels did not demonstrate the Hebrew origins of Indian speech. As his chief critic, Hamon L'Estrange, later argued, "If a man have a minde to trifle away time, he may now and then hit upon some words . . . that may agree in sound and sense with some of ours in Europe."[49] Anticipating this criticism, Thorowgood articulated an ingenious defense, revealing for what it says about the prevailing understanding of language change and the European understanding of American Indian society.

As most Christians understood it, language change was a process of degradation and decay—whether attributable to a single act of divine retribution or to human negligence and social dissipation. In either case, speech grew further alienated from an original, perfect tongue. A number of questions about this process, however, remained unanswered. The most important among these concerned the timing of language decay. How long would it take for one vulgar offspring to emerge from a parent tongue? In his response to L'Estrange's criticism, Thorowgood proposed that it was only a matter of several generations: "'Tis fit then to consider, that in all nations, in two or three ages there is a great alteration in their Tongues." Hence, "our Saxon ancestors translated the Bible into English as the Tongue then was, but of such antique words and writing, that few men now can read and understand it." With "such suddaine change of language universally, wee need not wonder, that so little impression of the Hebrew tongue remains among them . . . but wee may marvaile rather, that after so many yeares of most grosse and cursed blindnesse, and having no commerce, nor converse with other Nations, that any the least similitude thereof should be left."[50]

---

[48] Thomas Thorowgood, *Jewes in America, or, Probabilities that the Americans are of that Race* (London: T. Slater, 1650), 15.

[49] L'Estrange, *Americans, No Jewes*, 60.

[50] Thorowgood, *Jewes in America*, 16.

Another proponent of the Hebrew origins hypothesis was Antoine Laumet de La Mothe, Sieur de Cadillac, the commander of French military forces at Michilimackinac, on Michigan's Upper Peninsula. In a memoir written near the end of the seventeenth century, Cadillac listed an array of cultural practices that in his mind were common to both the native peoples of the upper Great Lakes and the original tribes of Israel. The fact that the languages of the region bore no discernible relation to an ancestral Hebrew tongue did not, Cadillac argued, refute his claims but instead reflected the overall delinquencies of Indian societies. "A language that is badly taught," he explained, "rusts and perishes completely, as everything else does in the course of time."

There was, however, another reason to accept the Hebrew origins hypothesis, similar to the one Grotius put forth to explain the plurality of tongues in Florida: "There is no cause for surprise, that we find so many different languages among the Indians," since there were in Jerusalem "men of every tribe under the sun. . . . It may be conjectured from this that the Jews . . . introduced a diversity of languages into their books which the inhabitants of the New World may have allowed to fall into disuse."[51] While the original languages may have gone extinct, the practice of tolerating the coexistence of different languages was, in Cadillac's view, an Israelite habit that persisted in North America.

Greek and Latin were also often thought to be parent languages of the languages spoken in America. Roger Williams acknowledged that while some Indian words suggested a Hebrew origin, "I have found a greater affinity of their language with the Greek tongue."[52] Thomas Morton, author of the 1632 "New English Canaan," explained to his readers that after endeavoring "by all wayes and meanes that I could to find out from what people or nation, the Natives of New England might be conjectured originally to procede, and by continuance and conversation amongst them, I attaned so much of their language [that I]" and "those of good judgment" had concluded that "the Natives of this country, doe use very many wordes both of Greeke and Latine, to the same signification that the Latins and Greeks have done."[53] Again, like Thorowgood, Morton confronted the improbable historical distance that seemed to separate Indian languages from their supposed

[51] Antoine Lamoth Cadillac, *The Western Country in the Seventeenth Century: The Memoirs of Antoine Lamoth Cadillac and Pierre Liette*, ed. Milo Milton Quaife (New York: Citadel Press, 1962), 59–60.

[52] Williams, *A Key into the Language of America*, 86.

[53] Thomas Morton, *The New English Canaan* . . . (1632), in Force, *Tracts and Other Papers*, vol. 2, no. 5, p. 15. Also see Jean de Léry, *A History of a Voyage to the Land of Brazil* . . . , trans. Janet Whatley (1578; reprint, Berkeley: University of California Press, 1990), 177; and *Jesuit Relations*, vol. 15, 155.

parent tongues. For him, the explanation was pidginization—at the time, understood in the normative sense as a form of language decay. "I know not for this is commonly seene where 2 nations traffique together," he explained, "the one endeavouring to understand the others meaning makes the both many times speak a mixed language, as is approved by the Natives of New England, through the covetous desire they have, to commerce with our nation, and wee with them."[54] Commerce, in other words, had the effect of corrupting languages, leaving them ever more dissipated versions of the original. The argument is almost identical to Thorowgood's.

For both commentators, an original and universal language of Eden had long since given way to corrupted versions of the same. The reason was that most tongues were unwritten and, as such, unstable, with nothing to protect them from the corrosive effects of historical change. The one idiom secured from such effects, early modern scholars generally held, was Latin. Through the Middle Ages, as the various derivative dialects of Latin came to be the spoken tongues of the nonliterate, its original written form nonetheless survived in all its purity among the literate. Unwritten tongues—such as those spoken in most of the Americas—could thus be expected to suffer a sort of entropy. Hence, Cadillac explained, "If at the time of the Caesars all Latin documents had been destroyed, and afterwards no one had been able to write in that language, it is plain that its use would have become so corrupted and changed that if those who spoke it originally were to talk to men of the present age they would not understand one another at all."[55] In addition, as an artifact of the Roman Empire, learned Latin was used in the farthest reaches of Europe, making it the ideal tongue for transcontinental institutions such as the Catholic Church, an institution dependent upon easy communication across national and linguistic boundaries.[56] Other languages, so scholars assumed, had no such fortune. They changed and developed as a consequence of invention, decay, corruption, infestation, or contamination by imitation, commerce, and conquest. In his 1668 work *An Essay towards a Real Character and a Philosophical Language*, John Wilkins, a founder of the English movement to construct a perfect, universally comprehensible language and a founding member of the Royal Society, explained that, for language, "every change is a gradual corruption."[57] In addition to commercial

---

[54] Morton, *New English Canaan*, 17.

[55] Cadillac, *The Western Country in the Seventeenth Century*, 59.

[56] Walter J. Ong, *Orality and Literacy: The Technologizing of the Word* (1982; reprint, London: Routledge, 1988), 112–15.

[57] John Wilkins, *An Essay Towards a Real Character and a Philosophical Language* (1668; facsimile reprint, Menston, England: Scolar Press, 1968), 8.

interchange and cultural imperialism, the corruption of tongues could be caused by "that affectation incident in some eminent men in all ages, of coining new words, and altering the common forms of speech, for greater elegance" or "the necessity of making other words, according as new things and inventions are discovered."[58] This notion that language change was essentially a matter of infiltration and corruption was entirely compatible with assumptions about American linguistic diversity: without imperial states or other institutions to impose standards of discourse, linguistic anarchy seemed inevitable. There was little sense that language variation could be deliberate or political.[59]

The notion that pidginization or language differentiation of any sort represents some form of decline or overall "corruption" of an original, ideal form has almost no currency among modern linguists. Instead, language change is generally regarded as indicative of the inherent tension between the immutable process of historical adaptation and the social need to maintain some degree of linguistic familiarity. As the Russian linguist Roman Jakobson put it, "The spirit of equilibrium and the simultaneous tendency toward its rupture constitute the indispensible properties of that whole that is language."[60] It was, however, with the opposite conviction—that languages could be understood as corrupted descendants of a single, perfect, God-given tongue—that Christian missionaries came to the New World. And it was the struggle to reconcile that conviction with vexing barriers to oral and written communication that occupied those missionaries almost without end.

[58] Ibid., 6. For an analysis of seventeenth-century theories of language change, see D. C. Allen, "Some Theories of the Growth and Origin of Language in Milton's Age," *Philological Quarterly* 28:1 (January 1949): 5–16.

[59] Modern explanations for the dominance of certain tongues tend to focus less on the actions of governments and individuals than on socioeconomic imperatives. See, for example, Carol Myers Scotton, "Learning Lingua Francas and Socioeconomic Integration: Evidence from Africa," in Cooper, *Language Spread*, 63–94. For an explanation that emphasizes cultural factors, see Benedict Anderson, *Imagined Communities: Reflections on the Origin and Spread of Nationalism*, rev. ed. (London: Verso, 1991), ch. 5. The notion that the emergence of dominant tongues owed something to deliberate government policy, however, still has considerable support. See the important study by Johannes Fabian, *Language and Colonial Power: The Appropriation of Swahili in the Former Belgian Congo, 1880–1938* (Cambridge: Cambridge University Press, 1986).

[60] A. R. Keiler, ed., *A Reader in Historical and Comparative Linguistics* (New York: Holt, Rinehart and Winston, 1972), 137. On language change, see Jean Aitchison, *Language Change: Progress or Decay?* (Cambridge: Cambridge University Press, 1991); and James Milroy, *Linguistic Variation and Change: On the Historical Sociolinguistics of English* (Oxford: Blackwell, 1992).

CHAPTER II

Language and Conversion

THE EARLIEST European ventures to the New World owed as much to the intense Christian desire to combat paganism as they did to any purely economic or military objectives. The rhetoric of conquest was thus often couched in terms of religious warfare: "Your highnesses decided to send me, Christopher Columbus, to see these parts of India and the princes and peoples of those lands and consider the best means for their conversion . . . and your highnesses as Catholic princes and devoted propagators of the holy Christian faith have always been enemies of the sect of Mahomet and of all idolatries and heresies."[1] When the language was not openly militant, it often resonated with chiliastic visions of a renewed holy kingdom under God. As the late sixteenth-century English geographer and promoter of colonization Richard Hakluyt urged the explorer Sir Walter Ralegh, "Up then, go on as you have begun, to leave posterity an imperishable monument of your name and fame, such as age will never obliterate. For to posterity, no greater glory can be handed down than to conquer the barbarian, to recall the savages and the pagan to civility, to draw the ignorant within the orbit of reason, and to fill with reverence for divinity the godless and the ungodly."[2] There was also the ever-present idea among members of dissident religious groups that in America lay the only real possibility for a return to a pure and original godly community, untainted by the cancerous decay and corruption thought to be so thoroughly absorbed by European society. The Indians, in this version of the missionary impulse, were less barbarians and savages than the innocent children of nature, ripe for Christianity of a sort not possible in the morally corrupt communities of the Old World.[3] These various justifications for spiritual conquest were made all the more urgent by fierce antagonism between Protestants and Catholics—an antagonism

[1] *The Four Voyages of Christopher Columbus*, ed. J. M. Cohen (London: Penguin Books, 1969), 37.

[2] *The Original Writings and Correspondence of the Two Richard Hakluyts*, ed. E. G. R. Taylor (London: Hakluyt Society, 1935), vol. 2, 368. See also Bernard Sheehan, *Savagism and Civility: Indians and Englishmen in Colonial Virginia* (Cambridge: Cambridge University Press, 1980), ch. 5.

[3] J. H. Elliott, *The Old World and the New, 1492–1650* (Cambridge: Cambridge University Press, 1970), 25.

that grew in the latter sixteenth and seventeenth centuries as the Roman Catholic Church fought to counter the global advance of Protestantism.[4]

This often bloody and long-lasting confessional conflict resulted in remarkably uniform experiences for competing missionary orders. In the case of almost every sixteenth- and seventeenth-century missionary initiative in the Americas, early idealism was short-lived. For Catholic missionary orders in particular, the desire to achieve for themselves the status of spiritual leaders or "fathers" often met with resistance, and resulted not so much in any replication of a harmonious church hierarchy as in a series of compromises that allowed Native American Catholicism to bear as much the imprint of indigenous cultures as the ideals and ambitions of the Catholic Church's overseas representatives.[5] Something similar occurred among the Protestant missions in New England. As we shall see in the next chapter, early confidence gave way not so much to compromise as to outright conflict and a significantly less hopeful approach to Indian conversion. Forced to go beyond the relatively simple languages of trade and diplomacy, all Christian missionaries found themselves encumbered by an unexpected range of communication problems. And these problems grew more involved as missionaries struggled to establish deeper levels of understanding among converts. As a result, missionaries found themselves with a task not unlike that of the modern semiotician: to identify and codify the range of spoken and unspoken strategies of communication available to themselves and to Indians.

If Protestants and Catholics shared a similar desire to extend their faiths—and encountered similar obstacles—differences in doctrine meant that early initiatives often differed in fundamental ways. This is perhaps nowhere more evident than in northeastern North America

---

[4] On this tension in North America, see James Axtell's *The Invasion Within: The Contest of Cultures in Colonial North America* (New York: Oxford University Press, 1985).

[5] This phenomenon has been of particular interest to historians of colonial Latin America. See, for instance, Kenneth Mills, *Idolatry and Its Enemies: Colonial Andean Religion and Extirpation, 1640–1750* (Princeton, N.J.: Princeton University Press, 1997); and Nancy M. Farriss, *Maya Society under Colonial Rule: The Collective Enterprise of Survival* (Princeton, N.J.: Princeton University Press, 1984), ch. 10. For New France, the phenomenon is less well studied, but still suggestive is Axtell's *Invasion Within*, ch. 5. Also see Daniel K. Richter, *The Ordeal of the Long House: The Peoples of the Iroquois League in the Era of European Colonization* (Chapel Hill: University of North Carolina Press, 1992), ch. 5; and Natalie Zemon Davis, *Women on the Margins: Three Seventeenth-Century Lives* (Cambridge, Mass.: Harvard University Press, 1995), 123–28. For a comprehensive survey of American Indian Catholicism, see Christopher Vecsey's two volumes, *On the Padre's Trail* (Notre Dame, Ind.: University of Notre Dame Press, 1993), and *The Paths of Kateri's Kin* (Notre Dame, Ind.: University of Notre Dame Press, 1997).

during the seventeenth century. In what is now southern New England, Protestants of a particularly zealous variety set out to save Indian souls, while to the north and west—in regions adjoining the St. Lawrence River and the northern Great Lakes—another sort of missionary worked to bring Indians into the Catholic Church. These two groups of missionaries—the one, a small handful of committed Puritan ministers, and the other, a larger and better-funded group of French Catholic missionaries, most of whom were Jesuits—understood the Word, and the communication of the Word, in very different ways. This was not a fundamental difference in linguistic philosophy. There is little reason to believe that any of these Europeans dissented from the prevalent late medieval view that language was a gift from God, and that its variations could be explained by human failings. This difference was, rather, in the understanding of how the written and spoken word ought to serve the larger goal of transmitting divine wisdom and saving souls.[6]

The first Catholic missionaries to establish a significant presence in the colony the French called *La Nouvelle France* were members of the Recollect order. They approached their mission with the intent not simply of baptizing native peoples or cleansing them of their pagan beliefs but rather of completely reforming their way of life. Doing so meant inducing Indians to live in settled, agricultural communities, composed of families founded on monogamous marriage, governed by French law, and presided over by local magistrates and Catholic clergy. Although the Recollects initially focused their efforts on relatively sedentary Huron groups, they had limited success. One reason was that they were never able to bring more than a small handful of missionaries to New France, and these were all but powerless in the face of both a much larger and often militant Huron population, and French fur traders—people whose livelihoods militated against efforts to reform Huron life. Far from benefiting from a Huron community removed to Quebec and settled among the meager French settlement—one of the Recollects' original goals and one that presumed Indians would become French farmers through social osmosis—these French agents were best served by an Indian population dependent on the burgeoning fur trade. By 1625 the general failure of the Recollect missions, and the risk of admonishment from a Crown desiring favorable relations with the Catho-

---

[6] My interpretation here relies in part on Walter J. Ong, *The Presence of the Word: Some Prolegomena for Cultural and Religious History* (New Haven, Conn.: Yale University Press, 1967).

lic Church, compelled the French viceroy in Canada to invite the Jesuits to establish their first major mission in New France.[7]

The Jesuits tended to be more pragmatic. They initially set out not to transform the Indians' way of life but simply to catechize and to baptize receptive Indians, with the intent of later instituting more far-reaching reforms. This seemingly less intrusive approach was partly the result of Jesuit experience in India and the Far East, regions where the sheer magnitude of existing military and political structures made any kind of wholesale transformation of pagan life utterly impossible. And the approach proved valuable in North America, where Jesuits often found themselves in positions of weakness with respect to native populations. During the initial decades of the Jesuit mission, missionaries commonly lived within native communities, at great distances from European settlements, and almost entirely at the mercy of their Indian flock for the basics of life. They were, in a certain sense, captives. Food, protection, shelter—for all these things they depended on the goodwill of the Indians. As a matter of principle, the Recollects had refused to live among pagans. When they established missions, they usually did so on the edges of Huron villages, and, as outsiders, they were required to pay for any sustenance they might need. The Jesuits, in contrast, generally accepted the necessity of living among the unconverted in order to be embraced by Indian families and, in turn, given food, shelter, and protection.[8]

As part of efforts to curb this dependency, Jesuit missionaries often resorted to surreptitious or Machiavellian means to gain power within native communities—much as they had done in Asia. They would, for instance, interrupt the flow of desired trade goods, particularly guns, to any but those Indians willing to be baptized. They also made agreements with local traders that Christianized Indians were to receive favorable trading terms—something that benefited traders by assuaging administrative fears that the Christianization process was inhibited by

---

[7] Bruce G. Trigger, *Natives and Newcomers: Canada's "Heroic Age" Reconsidered* (Montreal: McGill–Queen's University Press, 1985), 200–203.

[8] On the social relations between French missionaries and Indians, see Axtell, *Invasion Within*, ch. 4. Also see Denys Delâge, *Bitter Feast: Amerindians and Europeans in Northeastern North America, 1600–1664* (Vancouver: University of British Columbia Press, 1993), ch. 4; Trigger, *Natives and Newcomers*, 251–59; and Cornelius J. Jaenen, *Friend and Foe: Aspects of French-Amerindian Cultural Contact in the Sixteenth and Seventeenth Centuries* (New York: Columbia University Press, 1976), ch. 2. The larger point here, that supposed Jesuit tolerance for Native American culture was more the result of necessity than of any sense of cultural relativism, has been made by Neal Salisbury. See his "Religious Encounters in a Colonial Context: New England and New France in the Seventeenth Century," *American Indian Quarterly* 16:4 (Fall 1992): 506.

trade.[9] A perhaps more insidious form of the same impulse was the Jesuit habit of using scientific and technological knowledge to demonstrate mystical powers superior to those of traditional native shamans. In a 1635 report to their superiors, Jesuits explained that they were able to capture Indians' interest with so simple an object as a "lodestone, into which [the Indians] looked to see if there was some paste" that held the stone to other objects. Nothing, however, appeared to inspire awe in this Huron audience in the same way as writing, "for they could not conceive how, what one of us, being in the village, had said to them, and put down at the same time in writing, another, . . . far away, could say readily on seeing the writing. . . . All this serves to gain their affections, and to render them more docile when we introduce the admirable and incomprehensible mysteries of our Faith."[10] Any underhanded tactics employed by Jesuits ultimately reflected the precariousness of their position with respect to Indian societies. They were engaged in a constant balancing act, struggling to exercise some degree of control over the lives of native peoples, while in a position of decided material and military weakness. In the early decades of their mission, force was almost never on their side.

While Jesuits may have found effective strategies for coercing Indians into accepting the sacraments, they faced daunting obstacles when their goals involved more profound levels of indoctrination. To allow those Indians who had been baptized to realize the benefits of grace, Jesuits, much like ordinary priests, had to provide them with a spiritual education. This meant, of course, finding a way to communicate abstract Christian concepts, and since it proved impractical to teach Indians the French language on any large scale, Jesuits found themselves with the single and rather passive option of having to learn Native American languages.[11] For, as their critic Marc Lescarbot understood it,

[9] Delâge, *Bitter Feast*, 166–70; and Axtell, *Invasion Within*, 100–102. For instances of Jesuits employing similar practices in China, see Jonathan Spence, *The Memory Palace of Matteo Ricci* (New York: Penguin Books, 1983), 132–61. The Jesuit use of writing as a means of impressing the Indians with their "shamanic" power is treated by James Axtell in "The Power of Print in the Eastern Woodlands," in *After Columbus: Essays in the Ethnohistory of Colonial North America* (New York: Oxford University Press, 1988), 86–99. A contrasting view is offered by Peter Wogan, "Perceptions of European Literacy in Early Contact Situations," *Ethnohistory* 41:3 (Summer 1994): 407–29. Also see the relevant discussion in Adriano Prosperi, "The Missionary," in *Baroque Personae*, ed. Rosario Villari (Chicago: University of Chicago Press, 1995), 160–94.

[10] *JR*, 8:113. Also Louis Hennepin, *A New Discovery of a Vast Country in America. . .*, ed. Reuben Gold Thwaites (1698; Chicago: A. C. McClurg, 1903), vol. 1, 260.

[11] Victor Egon Hanzeli, *Missionary Linguistics in New France: A Study of Seventeenth- and Eighteenth-Century Descriptions of American Indian Languages* (The Hague: Mouton, 1969), ch. 4; and Axtell, *Invasion Within*, 81–83. Margaret J. Leahey, "'To Hear with My Eyes':

"In order to teach [the Indians] usefully and attain to their speedy conversion, and nourish them with a milk not bitter to them, they must not be overloaded with unknown tongues, since religion does not consist therein." For this reason, the Indians' own tongues were preferable to French for instructing "these poor savages, whose salvation must above all things be sought, and [by] the shortest road thereto."[12] To this end, Recollects and Jesuits produced grammars, dictionaries, prayer books, and catechisms in various indigenous languages. But, significantly, they were never able to do this on a large scale. Although Jesuits had asked for a printing press in 1665, the request was never granted.[13] No doubt reflecting increased government scrutiny of the Jesuits for their tolerance of indigenous ways, and restrictive church and state policies with respect to the dissemination of printed matter, the absence of a printing press in New France inhibited missionary activity in the most dramatic fashion. Without printing facilities, works such as Sagard's *Dictionaire de la langue huronne* (1632) or the many treatments of Native American speech in Jesuits' *relations* had to be published in France and were rarely circulated in America. As a consequence, newly arrived missionaries depended on the handwritten grammars and vocabularies of their predecessors to aid their language studies.[14]

In addition to this limitation, and the sheer diversity of North American languages, few obstacles frustrated French missionaries so much as the scarcity of willing translators and language instructors. There were traders who had some knowledge of American languages, but given the corrupt and immoral qualities missionaries generally attributed to these figures, they hardly seemed like suitable conduits for Christian truths. "So only one method remained," Jesuits reported to their superiors, "to learn it from the . . . natives, not by lessons, but by constant practice." Perhaps because they perceived the language barrier as a defense against European cultural intrusion, Indian teachers proved impatient and uninterested. They would provide nothing "unless their stomachs were first liberally crammed," and "being very impatient of even a short delay, would often be distracted and drawn away from one

---

The Native Language Acquisition Project in the 'Jesuit Relations'" (Ph.D. diss., Johns Hopkins University, 1991), is a valuable exploration of Catholic missionaries' efforts to learn American Indian speech.

[12] Marc Lescarbot, *History of New France*, ed. and trans. W. L. Grant (1612; Toronto: Champlain Society, 1914), vol. 3, 125–26.

[13] *JR*, 49: 167; Hanzeli, *Missionary Linguistics in New France*, 50.

[14] The publication history and censorship of the *Jesuit Relations* is discussed in Lawrence C. Wroth, "The Jesuit Relations from New France," *Papers of the Bibliographical Society of America* 30 (1936–37): 110–49.

Devant. coram me, aent. ethieont. coram te. neste mets pas
x ...moy. ennonchien askeontax. aller devant. ohentoutest tese.
aller au devant de glg. Kyatrandihon.
Devenir. voy les verb. en. et Aton in gram. v. Rad.

Deuil. pauur etre induil. Astaron. etreyeuf. Atonneaskya.
Deviner. arendio. yanne. Deviner. chi atoen. jay deviné
chi yaetoen. user de superstition pr deviner. Kg atoxyi.

x developper q. c. agennondiaskayan. in cp.

Devoir. per mod potentialem experiment. si mutant per vous
bien ou mal fait.

Diable. oKi ondechonronnon. yoy. Aki.

Diacre. ond. harihgayasendik hatsihenstatsi. Nhachenk.

Diarrée. voy flux de venue.

Diettes, la f. Entoutieti. jeûner.

Dieu. Dig. hayendio.

Diffamer. atehenz, v atehenchaz. arihondati. arihontiensenni.

Different. ya arihgennon. 2. ch differentes. ya Kirihgennon.

Differer. andiseyan s. f. differer. andisegatandi. R

Difficile. andoron. vonk ron ronde. s. Atendoronxyandi. trouuer
difficile q. c. satendoronKyandik il as tu de la peine a cela?

Digerer. Atekyichiai. voy. consumer.

Digue. chaussée. ocha.

Diminuer. aeniesti. aeniestandi. R. arihyasKyati. voy. petit.

Diner. voyez. Repas. Atsataion.

Dire. 8n.g. o v in vru nisi in pret. Aton. in vru tu in pres. et imps.
ihon. in fut. et Aors. Dire deglg. ent. ond. iit ichit. istak ichitak. isa
iont, je parle de toy. aeren imprieffe Kond. ihoeven. j la dit cela
endoton v Atendoton imprie raconter dire avec glg. suivre la voix
atendaienton. entendre dire Aronen.

by earnest inquiry about any subject."[15] As another Jesuit explained, "It is a strange thing to find oneself in a country where it is necessary to learn without a teacher, without books, and without rules, at an age already mature, a language which has no likeness to ours."[16] Book learning, the knowledge of grammar and vocabulary, the use of Latin and Greek—all could assist in the learning of European languages. But missionaries found no such aids in America. The only means of acquiring these languages was use and rote memorization under the tutelage of the Indians themselves. For Jesuits, many of whom had served as teachers of Latin in their native France, to find themselves abandoned to the whims of Indian teachers must have been to experience the deepest humiliation and confusion. The notion that one must learn fundamentals from students before even an elementary lesson could be taught meant that far from the sort of generally accepted superiority enjoyed by a Jesuit schoolmaster, Jesuit missionaries were at once the pupils and the spiritual fathers of their Christian charges. This instructional relationship represented a total reversal of the usual channels of authority in Jesuit education. Overcoming such psychological obstacles did not, however, ensure successful language learning.[17]

Father Sébastien Rasles, writing in the early eighteenth century, explained that "at least, after five months . . . , I succeeded in understanding all [the Indians'] terms; but that did not enable me to express myself to their satisfaction. I had still much progress to make before catching the form of expression and the spirit of the language, which are entirely different from the spirit and form of European languages."[18] Even with the grammars and dictionaries that had accrued by the end of the seventeenth century, this missionary faced serious difficulties. Rasles explained that "Father Chaumonot, who lived fifty years among the Hurons, composed a Grammar of that language which is very helpful to those who come without experience to that mission. Nevertheless a missionary is fortunate if he can, even with this aid, express himself elegantly in that language after ten years of constant study."[19]

While communication on even the simplest level was difficult, the communication of abstract religious concepts proved a source of particular frustration. Time and again, French missionaries complained that the Native American lexicon was not fit for Christian discourse.

---

[15] *JR*, 2:219–21.

[16] Ibid., 39:103.

[17] Hanzeli, *Missionary Linguistics in New France*, ch. 3; Axtell, *Invasion Within*, 75–76. On Jesuits' education see also John W. O'Malley, *The First Jesuits* (Cambridge, Mass.: Harvard University Press, 1993), esp. ch. 6.

[18] *JR*, 67:143.

[19] Ibid., 67:147.

Father Pierre Biard, a Jesuit missionary among the Micmac in Nova Scotia, explained to his superior in 1612 that although one of his fellow missionaries understood the Indians' language "better than anyone else here, is filled with earnest zeal, and every day takes a great deal of trouble to serve as our interpreter, . . . as soon as we begin to talk about God he feels as Moses did,—his mind is bewildered, his throat dry, his tongue tied."[20] The words, indeed the holy concepts, did not seem to exist. "All [the Indians'] conceptions are limited to sensible and material things," Biard explained, and "there is nothing abstract, internal, spiritual, or distinct." There were, that is, none of the same words for soul, for salvation, grace, and dozens of other Christian ideas, unrelated to the material world. Biard further observed that "they will name to you a wolf, a fox, a squirrel, a moose, and so on to every kind of animal they have, all of which are wild, except the dog; but as to words expressing universal and generic ideas, such as beast, animal, body, substance, and the like, these are altogether too learned for them."[21] Almost thirty years later, missionaries among the Huron reported a similar problem. Father Jean de Brébeuf—known for imposing upon himself "many voluntary mortifications: disciplines every day, and often twice each day; very frequent fasts; haircloths, and belts with iron points; vigils which advanced far into the night"[22]—explained to his superiors that the Huron "can not say simply, Father, Son, Master, Valet, but are obliged to say one of the three, my father, thy father, his father." The result of this, he continued, is that "we find ourselves hindered from getting them to say properly in their language, *In the name of the Father, and of the Son, and of the holy Ghost.*" The significance of this problem, Brébeuf well knew, could be monumental, for the closest approximation he could derive in the Huron tongue was "*In the name of our Father, and of his Son, and of their holy Ghost.*" Put this way, the Holy Trinity appeared to lack the singularity and universality Christians assumed it to possess. Brébeuf also explained that it was nearly impossible to teach a people to say *Our Father who art in Heaven,* "who have [no generic father] on earth." Furthermore, the entire notion of "Heaven" was a problem, since "to speak to them of the dead whom they have loved, is to insult them. A woman, whose mother had died a short time before, almost lost her desire to be baptized because the command, *Thou shalt honor thy Father and thy Mother,* had been inadvertently quoted to her."[23]

[20] Ibid., 2:9.
[21] Ibid., 2:11; 2:221; 3:193–95; 10:117. Also see Hennepin, *A New Discovery,* 2:467–68.
[22] *JR,* 34:183.
[23] Ibid., 10:119–21.

To compensate for these perceived lexical failings, Jesuits often resorted to theatrical or gestural embellishment. This too, however, could bring ridicule and undermine missionaries' moral authority. Father Biard explained, "We are compelled to make a thousand gesticulations and signs to express to them our ideas, and thus to draw from them the names of some of the things which cannot be pointed out to them. For example, to think, to forget, to remember, to doubt." He continued, "To know these four words, you will be obliged to amuse our gentlemen for a whole afternoon at least by playing the clown; and then, after all that, you will find yourself deceived, and mocked anew."[24] The sort of humiliation involved in such experiences proved almost as disconcerting as did the Indians' own improvised performances. "As sometimes they could not make me understand their conceptions," the Recollect Father Gabriel Sagard noted, "they would explain them to me by figures, similitudes, and external demonstrations, sometimes in speech, and sometimes with a stick, tracing the object on the ground as best they could, or by a movement of the body; and they were not ashamed to make very unseemly movements in order to be able the better to make me understand by means of these comparisons."[25] It was one thing to learn a language through long-ordained methods of grammatical instruction—that is, to learn a language by beginning with the most systematic and rule-bound sort of rigor that had been applied in Latin instruction for centuries. It was altogether another to abandon those expedients for the seemingly disorderly and unscripted ways of Native teachers—ways that not only defied the cautious and obedient practices of Jesuit instructors but also overturned the hierarchical Jesuit ethos of obedience. Because of the North American language barriers, missionaries found themselves in the awkward position of having to defer to their flock. In French America, obedience was no simple patriarchal equation whereby children obeyed fathers. Rather, it was all give-and-take, with fathers often as dependent on their children as their children were on them.

Catholic missionaries' anxiety about the need for gesture and theatrics, it should be said, was very different from the widespread Calvinist suspicion of superficial dramatization or needless verbal embellishment —both of which, according to much early modern moral thought, found their most extreme and troubling expression in the theater, an institution believed to encourage the uneducated to defy conscience. Public spectacles, plays, processions, and orations were often an inte-

[24] Ibid., 2:11.
[25] Gabriel Sagard, *The Long Journey to the Country of the Hurons*, ed. George M. Wrong and trans. H. H. Langton (1632; Toronto: Champlain Society, 1939), 73.

gral—if controversial—component of Jesuit pedagogy. When the parameters of such performances could be carefully governed, they
served to prepare students for roles as oracles of the church; at the
same time, they provided a readily disseminated form of public moral
instruction—and a form that, because figural or symbolic, could, its
teachers presumed, transcend language barriers. This was not merely
because they presented tales of piety and virtue through symbols and
performance, but also because the act of speaking from a script was,
much like uttering a prayer one did not understand, to affirm one's
implication in a sublime patriarchal power structure that may not have
been fully comprehensible to the layperson. In New France these sorts
of spectacles proved of special import, in part, no doubt, because they
allowed missionaries to communicate without a perfect grasp of local
languages. In his *relation* for the year 1640, Father Paul Le Jeune, the
superior of the Jesuit mission to New France (and a former Huguenot), explained how members of the Society of Jesus embellished a
play honoring France's newborn prince in such a way that it would also
serve to instruct Indians in the virtues of Christian belief: "We had the
soul of an unbeliever pursued by two demons, who finally hurled it into
a hell that vomited forth flames; the struggles, cries, and shrieks of this
soul and of these demons, who spoke in the Algonquin tongue, pene-
trated so deeply into the hearts of some of [the Indians], that a Savage
told us, two days afterward, that he had been greatly frightened that
night by a very horrible dream." That dream, in which the Indian confronted "a hideous gulf whence issued flames and demons" was, for Le
Jeune, added evidence that drama furthered the cause of the church.[26]

It was not just in seeing such spectacles that Indian souls were saved.
Indeed, some Jesuits appeared to assume that acting itself, or really any
sort of mimetic behavior that followed the prescription of the church,
was an indication that a soul was being saved. Another Jesuit superior,
Father Jérôme Lalemant, asserted that since solemn processions had
been unknown in America before the recent arrival of Europeans, the
perfect replication of them by Indian children could only be evidence
of the growth of Christianity in New France: "A few days ago, a small
band of these little innocents was observed marching in order; one
bore a Cross, another a banner, others candlesticks made in the Savage
fashion or naturally formed. Some sang, while others walked two by
two, as they had seen us do. All this teaches us that Christianity is
becoming founded and established among these peoples."[27]

The notion that faith could be expressed in a purely mimetic fashion

---

[26] *JR*, 18:87. Also see 28:251; 36:149; 37:95; 44:103; 51:145, 147.
[27] Ibid., 32:225.

is indicative of the common Roman Catholic belief that the communication of doctrine was legitimate because behind it lay the authority of the church. The power of the medium, thus, had everything to do with the moral authority behind the message. And one was admitted to the early modern Catholic Church not so much because one grasped the small particulars of the creed but because one recognized the superior moral authority that lay behind the words and gestures of the priesthood. This sort of thinking explains why Catholic missionaries so often emphasized that what was to be learned from their words and deeds was not the logic of belief or the literal content behind symbolic expressions of faith, but the objective truth that behind such expressions lay the authority of God. As Father Sébastien Rasles emphasized to a group of Abenaki, "All these words that I have just explained to you are not human words; they are the words of the Great Spirit. They are not written like the words of men, upon a [wampum belt], on which a person can say everything that he wishes; but they are written in the book of the Great Spirit, to which falsehood cannot have access."[28] The implication of Rasles's point was that lay faith required no ownership or personal, heartfelt understanding of the Word, but instead could rest on a general sense of the righteousness of a priest's words—a sense inspired by certainty that from the pope himself to the lowliest missionary lay a continuum through which divinity expressed itself. To assimilate a priest's words, that is, was to give one's self over to the powers of a papal hierarchy, in the service of God. What this meant was that words could function much as a charm might: they could inspire thoughts and feelings without any concurrent sense of their literal meaning.[29]

This thinking was actually similar to what might be termed a Native American semiotics. One Iroquois diplomat, according to an account related by Father Le Jeune "made . . . a number of presents, according to the custom of the country, in which the term 'present' is called 'the word,' in order to make clear that it is the present which speaks more

[28] Ibid., 67:187.

[29] On the relation of the Word to words, see Keith Thomas, *Religion and the Decline of Magic: Studies in Popular Beliefs in Sixteenth- and Seventeenth-Century England* (London: Penguin Books, 1991), 69–71; Jane Kamensky, *Governing the Tongue: The Politics of Speech in Early New England* (New York: Oxford University Press, 1997), ch. 1; David D. Hall, *Worlds of Wonder, Days of Judgement: Popular Religious Belief in Early New England* (New York: Knopf, 1989), 202; Garry Wills, *Witches and Jesuits: Shakespeare's* Macbeth (New York: Oxford University Press, 1995), 95–96; Lucien Febvre, *The Problem of Unbelief in the Sixteenth Century: The Religion of Rabelais*, trans. Beatrice Gottlieb (Cambridge, Mass.: Harvard University Press, 1982), 255–60; and Davis, *Women on the Margins*, 77. More generally, see S. J. Tambiah, "The Magical Power of Words," *Man* 3:2 (June 1968): 175–208; and Ong, *The Presence of the Word*, esp. 262–86.

forcibly than the lips."[30] For this diplomat, what mattered was not literal meaning but symbolic meaning. Beyond this, by referring to a present as "the word," one did not mean that the "present" was in fact verbiage but that it should have all the weight and authority Christians attached to the written word. It seems probable that Jesuits would have taken advantage of such fluidity in the relationship between words and things. Perhaps they even appropriated the Indians' "the word" for their own "Word." For if transposing God's Word into the form of a gift or present facilitated its more ready acceptance, there is good reason to believe Jesuits would have done so. Jesuits had been in the habit of assigning to their own words and actions strictly symbolic significance, something that was acutely evident in the practice of systematic equivocation or "mental reservation."

Facing possible execution for heresy, Jesuit missionaries in Protestant nations often did what persecuted religious minorities have always done. They engaged in what amounted to conscious acts of equivocation by revealing only part of what they knew to be true, or by making statements that had more than one possible meaning. What distinguished this practice from the obviously immoral and unchristian act of telling a lie, according to casuists, was the fact that it did not represent a deliberate distortion or abandonment of truth. Rather, it represented only a partial expression of truths known in their fullness by the speaker. And this practice was acceptable if it served the higher purpose of defending the church. It was no doubt a sense that such mental reservation could be morally defensible that allowed Jesuits to justify to themselves the manipulation of Indian religious beliefs in order to supplant traditional spiritual leaders.[31]

The Jesuit embrace of figural modes of expression is also consistent with the more general Jesuit reliance on vision as an avenue into the pagan soul. To use images in the conversion process was to privilege the sublime effects of the medium over the message. Indeed, pictures seemed uniquely equipped to capture the limitless power of divinity. Father Le Jeune remarked, "Heretics are very much in the wrong to condemn and to destroy representations." Having established this through his own experience, and the relative failure of mere speech to convey the imponderable pain of damnation, Le Jeune requested from his Parisian supporters painted images of "three, four, or five demons

[30] *JR*, 21:47.
[31] Johann P. Sommerville, "The 'New Art of Lying': Equivocation, Mental Reservation, and Casuistry," *Conscience and Casuistry in Early Modern Europe*, ed. Edmund Leites (Cambridge: Cambridge University Press, 1988), 159–84. Also Perez Zagorin, *Ways of Lying: Dissimulation, Persecution, and Conformity in Early Modern Europe* (Cambridge, Mass.: Harvard University Press, 1990).

tormenting one soul with different kinds of tortures,—one applying to
it the torch, another serpents, another pinching it with red-hot tongs,
another holding it bound with chains."[32] As might be expected, judgment and damnation were subjects that, for Jesuits, seemed especially
suited to the visual image. In 1666, Claude Allouez explained that in a
bark chapel he constructed were hung "various pictures, as of Hell and
of the universal judgment, which furnish me themes for instruction
well adapted to my hearers."[33] Writing several years later, another Jesuit
explained that in his chapel was kept a rendering of Judgment Day, "in
the upper part of which the parents were glad to be shown the place
that their baptized children would occupy; while below they saw with
horror, the torments suffered by the devil." So eager were the Indians
to pray before these pictures "that many children used to come bare-
foot through the snow, over nearly a quarter of a league's distance."[34]
Finally, Jacques Bigot, missionary among the Abenaki, observed that
"the most natural picture that I place before their eyes, to make them
fear the flames of hell, is that representing the fire in which their enemy, the Iroquois, is burning them . . . , I add that these torments are
nothing in comparison with those of hell."[35]

While the Jesuits were inventive in their strategies for affecting souls,
as linguists they actually tended to be rather rigid in their assumptions.
When they complained that native peoples lacked the words needed to
convey Christian abstractions, they were as much asserting seeming indigenous linguistic failures as they were registering a profound intellectual dilemma of their own. Aside from the simple fact that Jesuits were
often dependent on Indians for both sustenance and translation, their
intensive training in classical language and literature was almost useless
in North America. Indeed, little that they brought from Europe prepared them to learn Native American languages. And in the minds of
some, far from continuing their Old World role as teachers of language, Jesuits in New France had the wholly novel position of being
inventors of language. As Father Lafitau explained, seventeenth-century missionaries had "to make a more individual and much more

[32] *JR*, 11:89.
[33] Ibid., 50:299.
[34] Ibid., 56:135.
[35] Ibid., 62:135. Also see François-Marc Gagnon, *La Conversion par l'image: Un aspect de la mission des Jésuites auprès des Indiens du Canada au XVIIe siècle* (Montréal: Les Éditions Bellarmin, 1975); and Margaret J. Leahey, "Iconic Discourse: The Language of Images in Seventeenth-Century New France," in *The Language Encounter in the Americas, 1492–1800*, ed. Edward G. Gray and Norman Fiering (New York: Berghahn Books, forthcoming). A treatment of French Catholic reliance on representation in art and literature is Henry Phillips, *Church and Culture in Seventeenth-Century France* (Cambridge: Cambridge University Press, 1997), ch. 2.

painful study to draw from the very depths of these languages, as it were, a new language, which serves to make known to the Indians, matters pertaining to God and abstract truths."³⁶ But perhaps their greatest obstacle was the view that Latin provided the grammatical standard, through which all contemporary languages ought to be understood.

Most missionaries who came to New France had, from the very beginning of their educations, been immersed in Latin, having been forced to speak it at Jesuit colleges and teach it at Jesuit grammar schools. As a consequence, Jesuit missionaries tended to privilege lexical over grammatical meaning. That is, they assumed that changes in meaning, as so often is the case with Latin, were primarily the result of inflection—that is, the addition of prefixes and suffixes which in themselves do not constitute meaningful units of speech. The result of this thinking was an unending struggle to transmit linguistic knowledge in the readily familiar forms of classical language textbooks—that meant identifying declensions and verb conjugations, much as one would do when studying Greek or Latin. Writing in 1660, one missionary working in the northern Great Lakes region proudly explained that he and his colleagues had an advantage over those working in other areas because "the languages of all those nations being Algonkin or Montagnais or Abnaquiois, we are ready on the instant to give them succor, since we arranged all the principles of those Tongues exactly according to those of Greek and Latin."³⁷

The impetus for applying a European grammatical standard to American tongues, it should be emphasized, was only indirectly related to the conversion process. Jesuits were little interested in teaching Indians the grammatical interstices of their own languages. Rather, efforts to codify Indian tongues according to a Latin standard had no other purpose than to facilitate language teaching among the Jesuits themselves—and, in turn, liberate missionaries from their dependence on Indian teachers. For the one subject every Jesuit missionary could be assumed to have mastered was Latin grammar. Indeed, in the mind of the founder of the order, Saint Ignatius of Loyola, this was the foundation of all education: "The order to be observed in the subjects [taught in Jesuit colleges] is that a solid foundation should be laid in the Latin language before the liberal arts, in the liberal arts before scholastic theology, and in scholastic theology before positive theol-

³⁶ Joseph François Lafitau, *Customs of the American Indians Compared with the Customs of Primitive Times*, ed. William N. Fenton and Elizabeth L. Moore (1724; Toronto: Champlain Society, 1977), vol. 2, 264.

³⁷ *JR*, 46:71. Also Hanzeli, *Missionary Linguistics in New France*, 33 and passim.

ogy."[38] And Latin instruction began with the study of Latin grammar. To be the student of Jesuits was thus to build one's understanding of the order of the universe upon one's understanding of the order of the Latin language. One came to know things through words, not the other way around.[39]

For Puritans, the opposite was generally the case. One came to know words through things. As with so much seventeenth-century Reform ideology, this notion depended in part on a caricature of Jesuit learning as formulaic, theory-bound, and totally unrelated to ordinary experience—all of which, it was assumed, served to inhibit the recognition of divine truths. Puritan antagonism toward this scholastic pedagogy inspired something of a pedagogical revolution, motivated mostly by growing evangelical demands on a Calvinist ministry besieged by apostles of counterreform. To make language learning more expeditious was, in the minds of these Reformers, to expand the authority of Scripture while diminishing that of a corrupt Catholic clerical hierarchy. And the way to do this was by allowing students to study their own tongues before embarking on the more arduous task of learning a wholly alien language. As perhaps the most influential advocate of this new approach to language learning, the Czech pedagogue and Moravian missionary Jan Amos Comenius asked, "Who can be ignorant how much easier it is to learne a language by use among those that speake it, [than] in the schools where it is hardly learned in many yeares?"[40] John Dury, another Continental pedagogue who, like Comenius, had been exiled to England at the height of the Counter-Reformation, explained in his *The Reformed School* of 1651 that "the teaching of words, is no further usefull then the things signified thereby are familiar to the Imagination; and that the teaching of Rules before the Materiall sense of the words is known, or before the formall coherence of things which their construction is to represent in a sentence, can be apprehended; is wholly preposterous and unprofitable to the memory."[41] That is, there

[38] *St. Ignatius and the Ratio Studiorum*, ed. Edward A. Fitzpatrick (New York: McGraw-Hill, 1933), 73.

[39] François de Dainville, *L'Éducation des Jésuites (XVIe–XVIIIe siècles)* (Paris: Les Editions de Minuit, 1978), 188.

[40] Jan Amos Comenius, *A Reformation of Schooles, Designed in Two Excellent Treatises . . .* (1642; facsimile reprint, Menston, England: Scolar Press, 1969), 7. Comenius's presence in England is discussed in Hugh Trevor-Roper, "Three Foreigners: The Philosophers of the Puritan Revolution," in *Religion, the Reformation, and Social Change* (London: Macmillan, 1967), 237–93; and Christopher Hill, *Intellectual Origins of the English Revolution* (Oxford: Clarendon Press, 1965), 100–109.

[41] John Dury, *The Reformed School and the Reformed Library Keeper* (1651; facsimile reprint, Menston, England: The Scolar Press, 1972), 48.

is no point in presenting students with terms of vocabulary that are unrelated to their immediate experience. To do so is to make language learning needlessly tedious and, in turn, to delay recognition of the majesty of divine creation.

It is worth noting that Comenius modeled one of his most widely known pedagogical treatises, *Jannua linguarum reserata* (published in 1631, simultaneously in Latin, German, French, and English and used at Harvard College by both English and Indian students), after another *Jannua linguarum* published in Spain in 1611 by Irish Jesuits at Salamanca. That work, which consisted of Latin passages alongside Spanish passages, was also devised to expedite the learning of Latin but was a decided departure from the Jesuit norm, which presumed the memorization of the parts of speech, declensions, and conjugations prior to any actual use of Latin. Nevertheless, a prefatory note by Luys de Valdivia, S.J., a missionary in India, indicates that there was some sense within the Jesuit order that a new and more efficient approach to the teaching and learning of foreign languages was desirable.[42]

The primary goal of Comenius, Dury, and their mostly Puritan supporters was by no means to elevate the vernacular tongues to the prominence of Latin. Rather, it was to shorten the route to complete comprehension of the Scripture. Perhaps the culminating expression of this movement was the complete abandonment of the Latin grammatical standard as a component of language instruction. In 1653, John Wallis, professor of geometry at Oxford, published his *Grammatica Linguae Anglicanae*, the first significant attempt to formulate a grammar of the English language that deferred entirely to observations about English itself. For Wallis, those who deferred to the Latin standard "introduce many useless principles concerning the cases, genders, and declensions of nouns, and the tenses, moods, and conjugations of verbs . . . and many other like things, which are all together alien to our language, and thus the confusion and obscurity they create are greater than the clarification they afford."[43]

In Puritan New England, this utilitarian pedagogical ethos was evident in the fact that Puritans did not much trouble themselves with diagramming indigenous tongues according to a Latin grammatical

---

[42] See G. A. Padley, *Grammatical Theory in Western Europe, 1500–1700: Trends in Vernacular Grammar I* (Cambridge: Cambridge University Press, 1985), 339–41. On Comenius at Harvard, see Robert F. Young, *Comenius in England* (Oxford: Oxford University Press, 1932), 61; and Samuel Eliot Morison, *Harvard College in the Seventeenth Century* (Cambridge, Mass.: Harvard University Press, 1936), vol. 1, 354.

[43] Translated and quoted in Richard Foster Jones, *The Triumph of the English Language: A Survey of Opinions Concerning the Vernacular from the Introduction of Printing to the Restoration* (Stanford, Calif.: Stanford University Press, 1953), 290.

model. For instance, Roger Williams's *A Key into the Language of America* (1643), designed to assist users in learning the Narragansett tongue, was no schematic breakdown of the Narragansett lanugage. Rather, much like a traveler's phrase book, *A Key* is organized purely according to familiar concepts and subjects likely to concern any English user of the volume. Chapters include "Of Salutation," "Of Eating and Entertainment," "Concerning Sleepe and Lodging," "Of Buying and Selling," and "Of Sicknesse." Each of these consists of a series of Narragansett terms, arrayed next to appropriate English terms and embellished with Williams's observations about indigenous culture. As Williams explained the form of his book, "A Dictionary or Grammar way I had consideration of, but purposely avoided, as not so acommodate to the Benefit of all, as I hope this forme is."[44] This approach has the effect of rendering *A Key* less a linguistic tract than an ethnographic one, designed above all to introduce readers to the Narragansett people. But it is also indicative of the widely held Puritan notion that language would become familiar only when associated with familiar things. Experience and utility rather than grammatical abstraction, so Williams appears to have believed, would lead to a greater familiarity not only with the Narragansett tongue but also with the speakers of that tongue.

Aside from bringing to America a distinct background with respect to language, Puritan missionaries brought an ethos that differed from that of the Jesuits in other significant ways. They never came to America, for instance, with the sole purpose of Christianizing Indians. Those who did prozelytize among Indians did so as a subordinate activity to their primary service to specific English congregations. When ministers left their congregations to preach to Indians, even for short periods, they were obliged to find substitute ministers, an especially difficult proposition in colonies to which few English ministers were eager to emigrate.[45] A shortage of trained and willing missionaries was compounded by difficulties of obtaining material and financial resources. The few ministers inspired to adhere to the charter of the Massachusetts Bay Colony to "wynn and incite the Natives . . . [to] the knowledge and obedience of the onlie true God and Savior of mankinde" found themselves confronting a mostly indifferent white population and looking to the mother country for critical financial support. Only in the middle of the seventeenth century, after the modest successes of the Mayhew family at Martha's Vineyard and of John Eliot on the main-

---

[44] Roger Williams, *A Key into the Language of America*, ed. John J. Teunissen and Evelyn J. Hinz (1643; reprint, Detroit, Mich.: Wayne State University Press, 1973), 90.

[45] Axtell, *Invasion Within*, 220.

Sh: Twisse

A KEY into the
LANGUAGE
O F
AMERICA:
O R,

An help to the *Language* of the *Natives*
in that part of AMERICA, called
NEW-ENGLAND.

Together, with briefe *Observations* of the Cu-
ftomes. Manners and Worships, &c. of the
aforefaid *Natives*, in Peace and Warre,
in Life and Death.

On all which are added Spirituall *Observations*,
Generall and Particular by the *Authour*, of
chiefe and fpeciall ufe (upon all occafions,)to
all the *English* Inhabiting thofe parts;
yet pleafant and profitable to
the view of all men :

BY ROGER WILLIAMS
of *Providence* in *New-England*.

LONDON,
Printed by *Gregory Dexter*, 1643.

Title page from Roger Williams's *A Key into the Language of America* (London, 1643). Courtesy of the John Carter Brown Library at Brown University.

land, were they able to reassure patrons that the American missions deserved support.[46]

These kinds of concrete difficulties no doubt reinforced the widespread English sense that American tongues were especially difficult to learn. With such meager resources, there was little incentive for the English to labor at the often frustrating process of learning the Indians' language. "Their language is hard to learn," William Wood wrote in 1634, "few of the English being able to speak any of it, or capable of the right pronunciation, which is the chief grace of their tongue."[47] In his tribute to the ministers of New England, *Magnalia Christi Americana*, published at the beginning of the eighteenth century, Cotton Mather wrote of John Eliot's efforts to interpret and employ words "long enough to tire the patience of any scholar in the world; they are Sesquipedalia Verb [Interminable Words], of which their linguo is composed; one would think they had been growing ever since Babel unto the dimensions to which they are now extended." Mather asked his readers to notice the number of letters in "this one word, *Nummatchekodtantamooongenunnonash*, when he is done, for his reward, I'll tell him it signifies no more in English than *our lusts*; and if I were to translate, *our loves*, it must be nothing shorter than *Noowomantammooonkanunonnash*." Making matters worse, Mather explained, there was not "the least affinity to, or derivation from any European speech that we are acquainted with." So alien and difficult did Mather find the language of the native people of Massachusetts that "once, finding that the Dæmons in a possessed young woman understood the Latin, and Greek, and Hebrew languages, my curiosity led me to make trial of this Indian language, and the Dæmons did seem as if they did not understand it." The evil spirits, Mather implied, were baffled by this Indian tongue; and this meant to Mather that the divine spirits he imparted to these Indian words could penetrate the girl's soul and give it the power to overcome the evil within.[48]

Beyond the practical difficulties of second-language acquisition, any desire to acquire Indian language was inhibited by the common belief that translation insinuated an air of mystery and spiritual power be-

[46] Nathaniel B. Shurtleff, ed., *Records of the Governor and Company of the Massachusetts Bay in New England* (Boston: William White, 1853–54), vol. 1, 17. Francis Jennings, *The Invasion of America: Indians, Colonialism, and the Cant of Conquest* (Chapel Hill: University of North Carolina Press, 1975), 243; and Alden T. Vaughan, *New England Frontier: Puritans and Indians, 1620–1675*, 3d ed. (Norman: University of Oklahoma Press, 1995), ch. 9.

[47] William Wood, *New England's Prospect*, ed. Alden T. Vaughan (1634; reprint, Amherst: University of Massachusetts Press, 1977), 109.

[48] Cotton Mather, *Magnalia Christi Americana; or, The Ecclesiastical History of New England* . . . (1852; reprint, New York: Russell and Russell, 1967), vol. 1, 561–62.

tween ministers and their Indian listeners. John Eliot explained that although he and his fellow Christians aspired to preach to the Indians in their own tongue, "wee began in [English,] an unknowne tongue to them, partly to let them know that this duty in hand was serious and sacred."[49] Further complicating matters, Indians too seemed to have recognized the power of a "private" language to control and shape social relations. They are "not a little proud that they can speak the English tongue," wrote William Wood, "using it as much as their own when they meet with such as can understand it, [and] puzzling stranger Indians, which sometimes visit them from more remote places, with an unheard language."[50] Reflecting on what might have been a similar phenomenon, in 1628, the Dutch Reverend Jonas Michaelius observed, "It . . . seems to us that [the Indians] rather design to conceal their language from us than to properly communicate it, except in things which happen in daily trade." Perhaps expressing frustrations about Indians' refusal to give over control of this crucial source of indigenous power, Michaelius belittled the trade jargon Indians used to communicate with Europeans as "a made-up, childish language; so that even those who can best of all speak with the savages, and get along well in trade, are nevertheless wholly in the dark and bewildered when they hear the savages talking to themselves."[51] The peoples whom Michaelius sought to convert, we can conjecture, recognized that in their language lay protection from European cultural intrusion. To inhibit language acquisition was to provide a critical defense against intrusions into local spiritual life.

After the initial decades of colonization, English missionaries, quite unlike their Jesuit counterparts, were generally not dependent on Indians for basic protection and sustenance. Instead, they usually lived in or near English settlements and received compensation from their Puritan congregations. There was therefore less incentive to accommodate Indian ways of life. For some Englishmen, for instance, Indian speech was a problem that only needed to be eliminated. In much the way that the English viewed Welsh or Gaelic, many of them came to regard Algonquian tongues as inferior languages that merely interfered with the process of Native American acculturation.[52] These were the

---

[49] John Eliot, *The Day Breaking, If Not the Sun-Rising of the Gospell with the Indians in New England* (London: Fulk Clifton, 1647), 2.

[50] Wood, *New England's Prospect*, 110.

[51] J. Franklin Jameson, ed., *Narratives of New Netherland, 1609–1664* (New York: Scribner's, 1909), 128.

[52] Victor Edward Durkacz, *The Decline of the Celtic Languages: A Study of Linguistic and Cultural Conflict in Scotland, Wales, and Ireland from the Reformation to the Twentieth Century* (Edinburgh: John Donald, 1983), ch. 1; and Vivian Salmon, "Missionary Linguistics in

initial advocates of English-language instruction for Indian children. Writing to the Massachusetts governor, John Winthrop, in 1632, Edward Howes explained, "I conceive it sufficient to teach the Indian children only to read English and to know none other, because they may not imagine there is the same confusion of tongues amonge Christians as there is amonge them."[53] Michaelius hoped to do the same in New Amsterdam. "Although it would be attended with some expense," he wrote, "we ought, by means of presents and promises, to obtain children, with the gratitude and consent of their parents, in order to place them under the instruction of some experienced and Godly schoolmaster, where they may be instructed . . . to speak, read and write in our language." This was to be the foundation for missionary activity in New England in the eighteenth and nineteenth centuries: teach Indian children English so that they would be equipped to function as translators and go-betweens, in turn sparing Englishmen from having to learn Indian languages. In seventeenth-century New England, however, there proved to be little support for such root and branch reeducation.[54]

What initially seemed like a more efficient method, and the one that Puritan missionaries applied most fervently before King Philip's War—which broke out in 1675—was to make the Word of God available to native peoples in their own languages. In keeping with the Puritan quest to make the Word the possession of all believers, this meant much more than merely preaching in Indian tongues. It meant making the liturgy and the Bible available in the local language. In giving Indians access to the Word, Puritan missionaries assumed they were making possible the slow and labored preparation required for entry into the Congregational Church—a Calvinist church founded on a demonstrated relationship with divine spirit. This, however, involved yet another problem, one that the Catholic missionaries of New France had little confronted: Indian literacy.

As Experience Mayhew explained to a group of Narragansetts in 1713, "If they would learn to read [the Bible], this would teach them how to know and serve the only true God, that so they might be happy; and that the English were willing to teach them, if they would consent to it." On the same mission, Mayhew explained to a group of Mohegans that the Bible "belongs unto the Indians as well as unto English men, and they should learn to read it, that so they may know the only

---

Seventeenth Century Ireland and a North American Analogy," *Historiographia Linguistica* 12 (1985): 321–49.

[53] *The Winthrop Papers*, ed. Allyn B. Forbes (Boston: Massachusetts Historical Society, 1943), vol. 3, 77.

[54] Jameson, *Narratives of New Netherland*, 129; Axtell, *Invasion Within*, 182–86, and ch. 8.

true God, and learn to serve him."[55] This claim rested on the Puritan assumption that salvation and church membership came only to those able to develop a personal understanding of God's Word, an assumption that owed much to Reformers' tireless accusations that the Catholic laity experienced the liturgy in a purely rote and mimetic fashion— a state of affairs, Protestants often assumed, that owed much to the continued primacy of Latin in the Roman Catholic Church. In an early expression of this view, the sixteenth-century English Bible translator William Tyndale derided Roman Catholic praying as "a false kind of praying, wherein the tongue and lips labor . . . but the heart talketh not with God."[56] Such prayer, in the minds of Reformers like Tyndale, was no better than a charm. It was the empty gesture of conjurers and magicians speaking the devil's language and keeping from the faithful the only language with which they could communicate with God: the heartfelt language of prayer. For Puritans, Catholic prayer provided a sort of antithetical ideal against which to model a seemingly more knowing expression of faith. Such an expression could be neither received nor conveyed in the ambiguous form of signs, symbols, or gestures— media that, by their figural form, were assumed to inadequately convey God's word. Indeed, to present God's word in media other than print was merely to continue the alienation of the believer from God. It was to insert an obstacle between believers and Scripture in its least fluid—and truest—form: the printed form. What this meant was that for Puritan missionaries, in contrast to Catholic missionaries, the first objective was not to administer the sacraments but to make the Indians self-sufficient inquirers after grace. It was, that is, to make them literate.[57]

It is one of the more remarkable phenomena of life in early New England that what was perhaps the most literate culture in the world merged with cultures that, until the arrival of Europeans, were without writing.[58] This state of affairs, historians have begun to recognize, had profound and often destructive consequences. Judging from the often lukewarm and occasionally downright murderous reception of literate

---

[55] John W. Ford, ed., *Some Correspondence between the Governors and Treasurers of the New England Company in London and the Commissioners of the United Colonies in America . . . between the Years 1657–1712 to Which Are Added the Journals of the Rev. Experience Mayhew* (London: Spottiswoode, 1896), 99, 106.

[56] William Tyndale, *Expositions and Notes*, ed. H. Walter (Cambridge: Cambridge University Press, 1849), 80.

[57] Ong, *The Presence of the Word*, 262–86.

[58] On the high literacy rates in seventeenth-century New England, see Kenneth Lockridge, *Literacy in Colonial New England: An Enquiry into the Social Context of Literacy in the Early Modern West* (New York: Norton, 1974), 46 and passim; Hall, *Worlds of Wonder, Days of Judgement*, ch. 1.

Indians by their own communities, native peoples saw in the capacity to read a far-reaching threat to their own traditions and ways of life.[59] But in seeing literacy as a threat, they betrayed a keen, if ambivalent, awareness of the power of print. Roger Williams noted that the Narragansetts had no "books, nor letters, and conceive their Fathers never had; and therefore they are easily perswaded that the God that made English men is a greater God, because hee hath so richly endowed the English." Revealing his own interest in acquiring support for Christianization in New England, Williams continued, "But when they heare that about sixteen hundred yeeres agoe, England and the Inhabitants thereof were like unto themselves, and since have received from God, Clothes, Books, & c. they are greatly affected with a secret hope concerning themselves."[60] Whatever Williams's ambition in writing these lines, there is reason to believe what he said. Native Americans were, it is clear, impressed by the powers of the written word. As early as 1632, Thomas Morton reported that "a salvage made this request to mee. That I would let his sonne be brought up in my howse, that hee might be taught to read in [the Bible]: which request of his I granted; and he was a very joyfull man to thinke, that his sonne should thereby (as hee said) become an Englishman; and then hee would be a good man."[61] Whether or not the particular father to which Morton referred wanted his son to "become an Englishman" or simply to learn to read, we do not know. But what is clear is that he regarded literacy as integral to his son's education—a remarkable development, coming as it did only a few years after the initial European settlement of Massachusetts Bay.

In accord with their pragmatic educational philosophy, the Puritans taught Indians to read in an entirely phonetic fashion. In part, this had

[59] Jill Lepore, "Dead Men Tell No Tales: John Sassamon and the Fatal Consequences of Literacy," *American Quarterly* 46:4 (December 1994): 479–512. For a compelling exploration of the introduction of alphabetic writing in central Mexico, see Serge Gruzinski, *The Conquest of Mexico: The Incorporation of Indian Societies into the Western World, Sixteenth–Eighteenth Centuries,* trans. Eileen Corrigan (Cambridge, England: Polity Press, 1993), 51–69.

[60] Williams, *A Key into the Language of America,* 85.

[61] Thomas Morton, "New English Canaan; or, New Canaan, Containing an Abstract of New England" (1632), reprinted in Peter Force, comp., *Tracts and Other Papers Relating Principally to the Origin, Settlement, and Progress of the Colonies in North America* (Washington, D.C.: Peter Force, 1836), vol. 2, no. 5, p. 35. See also *Winthrop Papers,* vol. 5, 146, 150; Ford, *Some Correspondence between the Governors and Treasurers,* 111, 126. Experience Mayhew, *Indian Converts, or Some Accounts of the Lives and Dying Speeches of a Considerable Number of Christianized Indians . . .* (London: J. Osborn and T. Longman, 1727), 3–4, 63, 68, 140. On Native American literacy in New England, see Kathleen Joan Bragdon, "'Another Tongue Brought In': An Ethnohistorical Study of Native Writings in Massachùsett" (Ph.D. diss., Brown University, 1981), ch. 3.

to do with who was learning what. Rather than missionaries seeking familiar principles with which to understand alien tongues, New England missionaries simply sought to introduce literacy, and this could be achieved through phonetics. As John Eliot described the process, "I taught our Indians first to lay out a word into syllables, and then according to the sound of every syllable to make it up with the right letters, viz. if it were a simple sound, then one vocall made the syllable; if it were such a sound as required some of the consonants to make it up, then the adding of the right consonants either before the vocall, or after it or both. They quickly apprehended and understood this epitomie of the Art of Spelling, and could soon learn to read."[62] The process Eliot describes was one of simply transposing familiar words and phrases into a purely phonetic alphabet, not one of learning an entirely new language—something Eliot did, and something for which he eventually composed a grammar of the Massachusett language.

The Indian experience of literacy is difficult to assess, in part because of the ambiguities of the very idea of "literacy." It has long been the habit of scholars to approach literacy as a historical problem (something achieved) rather than as an anthropological one (something practiced). When understood in the latter sense, literacy becomes less important for what it reveals about the ordering of consciousness, or the evolution of mind, than for what it says about the ways cultures deploy symbol systems. In this latter light, the Native American tendency to privilege oral communication over written or graphic forms of communication becomes not "illiteracy" but "nonliteracy." As one historian has written, nonliteracy arises "not from an ignorance but from an absence of texts."[63] The introduction of texts by Puritan missionaries thus does not necessarily mean that the Indian societies of southern New England became "literate" societies, or societies that—like Puritan ones—assigned superior powers of truthfulness to the printed word. Indeed, it appears that oral and textual knowledge came together in complex ways in early New England. In their study of Massachusett texts written by native Massachusett speakers, Ives Goddard and Kathleen Bragdon observe that, given the

---

[62] John Eliot, *The Indian Grammar Begun* (Cambridge, Mass.: Marmaduke Johnson, 1666), 4.

[63] Brian Stock, *The Implications of Literacy: Written Language and Models of Interpretation in the Eleventh and Twelfth Centuries* (Princeton, N.J.: Princeton University Press, 1983), 8. Also see the essays in Brian V. Street, ed., *Cross-Cultural Approaches to Literacy* (Cambridge: Cambridge University Press, 1993); and Jonathan Boyarin, ed., *The Ethnography of Reading* (Berkeley: University of California Press, 1993).

amount of knowledge these writings assume, they "are more appropriately viewed as aids to memory" than as literal representations of thought and feeling.[64]

If this was the broad nature of Massachusett literacy, on a more specific level, some Indians came to associate the ability to read with salvation. Explaining the nature of his conversion experience, the Indian schoolmaster Monequassun wrote, "When I did teach among the Indians, I was much humbled because I could not reade right, and that I sinned in it . . . and I feared how should my wife and child be clothed, if I spend my time in learning to reade; but then God was merciful to me, and shewed me that Word."[65] This association of providence with literary talents served English ministers as well: they understood that although they may not have sufficient mastery over Indian tongues for perfect communication, the divine will would ensure that whatever the limitations of speech, the spirit of God's word would be communicated. "Though the Indian tongue be very difficult, irregular, and anomalous," explained William Leverich, "and wherein I cannot meet with a verb substantive as yet, nor any such Particles, as Conjunctions, & c. . . . , yet I find God helping, not onely my selfe to learne and attaine more of it in a short time, [than] I think I could or did of Latine, Greek, or Hebrew, in the like space of time, when my memory was stronger, and when all known rules of Art are helpfull to fasten such notions in the mind of the learner; but also the Indians to understand me fully (as they acknowledge)."[66]

This is a far cry from the ruminations of Jesuits, struggling to master the subtleties of Huron or Abenaki in order to convey the will of God and the church—ruminations that reflect what must be the crucial distinction between Jesuit and Puritan language philosophies. If for Jesuits words were meaningful in direct proportion to their capacity to inspire obedience, for Puritans they were meaningful only insofar as they captured and conveyed an underlying divine spirit. Martin Luther conveyed this idea when he wrote, "Languages are in place of scabbards, in which the sword of Spirit, namely, the word of God, is kept sheathed. They are the ark, or the secret repositories, which preserve this noble treasure locked up in it. . . . They are the cells ever ready,

[64] Ives Goddard and Kathleen J. Bragdon, *Native Writings in Massachusett* (Philadelphia: American Philosophical Society, 1988), vol. 1, 19.

[65] John Eliot and Thomas Mayhew Jr., *Tears of Repentence: Or, a Further Narrative of the Progress of the Gospel amongst the Indians* (London: Peter Cole, 1653), 17.

[66] [The Reverend Henry Whitfield,] *Strength Out of Weaknesse Or, a Glorious Manifestation of the Further Progress of the Gospel among the Indians of New England* (London: John Blague, 1652), 22.

from which the worthy preacher brings forth the Gospel bread."[67] This was no mere theological abstraction. John Eliot recalled that a Christian Indian had explained that "while hee was praying, one of his fellow Indians interrupted him, and told him, that he prayed in vaine, because Jesus Christ understood not what Indians speake in prayer, he had bin used to heare English man pray and so could well understand them, but Indian language in prayer hee . . . was a stranger to it." When asked whether this was in fact true, whether "Jesus Christ did understand, or God did understand Indian prayers," the minister explained that "Jesus Christ and God by him made all things, and makes all men, not onely English, but Indian men, and if hee made them both . . . then he knew all that was within man and came from man, all his desires, and all his thoughts, and all his speeches, and so all his prayer."[68] The specific language of prayer was thus unimportant. What mattered in Eliot's mind was the sincerity and depth of feeling that lay behind that language. This was evident, Eliot's Indian flock appears to have assumed, in what the Bible said about translation. In a letter purportedly written by sixteen Natick Indians to Eliot, the writers explained that translation "is approved of in scripture in the primitive times as in 1. Corinthians.14.27.28. that if one speak in an unknown tongue another should interpret."[69]

However Puritans and Jesuits may have differed in their linguistic practices, one distinction loomed larger than all others, and that was their different criteria for membership in the two churches. For the latter, acceptance of the sacraments, some knowledge of doctrine, and recognition of clerical moral authority were of primary importance. For the former, it was ultimately the experience of divine grace that afforded entry into a new, pure church, and the validity of this experience had to be judged by church members according to the standards of Scripture. This made literacy a chief precondition for church membership. And while communicating Catholic doctrine posed unique and vexing problems, they were problems that paled in comparison with the demands of creating and disseminating the Bible in an Indian language. For it was perhaps this burden more than any other that ultimately distinguished the spread of Christianity in Puritan New England from

---

[67] Quoted by Peter Albinus, "A Treatise on Foreign Languages and Unknown Islands," in Edmund Goldsmid, trans. *On the Origin of the Native Races of America* . . . (Edinburgh: Privately Printed, 1884), 61.

[68] Eliot, *The Day Breaking*, 4. Also see Eliot, *A Further Account of the Progress of the Gospel amongst the Indians of New England*. . . (London: John Macock, 1660), 30; and Eliot and Mayhew, *Tears of Repentence*, 7.

[69] Ford, *Some Correspondence between the Governors and Treasurers*, 75.

that in Catholic New France. Indeed, it was just this burden that John Eliot took upon himself in the middle of the seventeenth century, in the heroic endeavor of translating the entire Bible into the Massachusett language. Such a project raises all sorts of questions about the process of translation, the nature of the Word, and the power of print in seventeenth-century New England. But it also offers insight into Puritan ideas about knowledge, mind, the soul, and their relation to language.

CHAPTER III

The Burden of Translation

Jesus nampoohuk kah wuttinnuh, Wunamuhkut kuttinth; kuttumma woske-
tomp neekit nompe, wutch waàbe matta woh naumoo wuttahsootamóonk
God. John 3:3[1]

THIS PASSAGE is from the first complete Bible printed in the Western
Hemisphere, the first complete Bible printed in a non-European tongue
for evangelical purposes, and the first printed Bible for which an entire
phonetic writing system was devised. This particular Bible preceded
even the first complete Irish Bible by twenty-two years and was preceded in the Anglo-American world by only English- and Welsh-
language Bibles. In addition to being unprecedented at the time of its
initial printing in 1663, this Bible, in the Natick dialect of the Massachusett language, would remain the only complete Bible in an indigenous New World tongue until 1862, when missionaries translated the
Old and New Testaments into Western Cree.[2]

The Massachusett Bible was created at a place unique for being both
on the fringes of the Protestant world and the location of one of the
most radical utopian experiments in English history. In the middle of
the seventeenth century, at a time when England was without a king;
when the Puritan ideal of a nation governed by saints seemed at hand;
when religious extremists formerly banished to the New World were
returning to the Old; when millennial visions of the imminent reign of
Christ on earth inspired all sorts of utopian plans for Christian renewal
and purification—at this moment the Congregationalist minister John
Eliot undertook to create a new kind of Christian polity among the

---

[1] *Mamusee Wunneetapanatamwe Up-Biblum God* (Cambridge, Mass.: Marmaduke Johnson, 1663).

[2] The publication dates of the world's Bibles can be found in, *The Book of a Thousand Tongues*, ed. Eugene A. Nida (1939; revised ed., London: United Bible Societies, 1972), 475–76, 484–94, and passim. Eliot's actions as Bible maker, have been overshadowed by fierce debate about his character. His sobriquet, "the apostle to the Indians," has been alternately affirmed as indicative of his earnest spirit, and assailed as so much White propaganda. The former view is generally associated with Alden T. Vaughan, *New England Frontier: Puritans and Indians, 1620–1675*, 3d ed. (Norman: University of Oklahoma Press, 1995), while the latter has been associated with Francis Jennings, *The Invasion of America: Indians, Colonialism and the Cant of Conquest* (Chapel Hill: University of North Carolina Press, 1975), esp. 233.

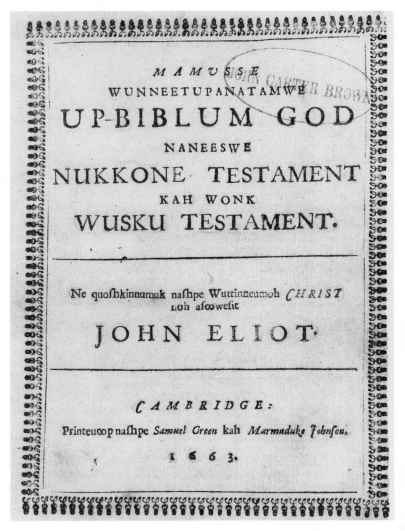

Title page from John Eliot's Massachuset Bible (Cambridge, Mass., 1663). Courtesy of the John Carter Brown Library at Brown University.

native peoples of Massachusetts. In his more sanguine moments, Eliot hoped this New World polity would come to envelop the Old, preparing the way for a New Jerusalem governed by the "Fifth Monarch," or Christ himself. While awaiting the Second Coming, this new political order would be governed not by a single monarch or any common law but by a series of elected judicial boards whose duty was to interpret and institute the ultimate and final body of law: Scripture. "The Written Word of God," Eliot explained, "is the perfect Systeme or Frame of Laws, to guide all the Moral actions of man, either towards God or man." And Eliot assumed that the Indians, innocent of the insidious and corrupting habits of the English—and possibly even descendants of one of the ten lost tribes of Israel—would be the ideal subjects for such a utopian experiment. Having been governed by no law—godly or otherwise—they were free from prejudice regarding moral order and therefore free to make an easy transition to government by Scripture. Eliot even went so far as to proclaim that the Word of God would become the Indians' "only magna charta, for government, laws, and all conversation."[3] It was as part of his broader efforts to achieve this new political order that Eliot undertook to translate the Bible. For him, the Bible was to be the legal foundation for the sort of society the founders of the Massachusetts Bay Colony were failing to establish: a model Christian community upon which all of England would need to found its reforms if the millennial dreams of the age were to be realized.[4]

Eliot's thorough embrace of biblical prophecy explains more than his reason for producing a Massachusett-language Bible. It also explains his guiding assumptions as a translator and linguist, particularly his unflagging confidence that the Massachusett tongue was a suitable conduit for Christian ideas. This confidence was reinforced by Eliot's

[3] John Eliot, *The Christian Commonwealth: Or, The Civil Policy of the Rising Kingdom of Jesus Christ* (London: Livewell Chapman, 1659), 35; *John Eliot and the Indians, 1652–1657: Being Letters Addressed to Rev. Jonathan Hanmer of Barnstaple, England*, ed. Wilberforce Eames (New York: Adams and Grace Press, 1915), 7. Also see Richard W. Cogley, "John Eliot and the Origins of the American Indians," *Early American Literature* 21:3 (Winter 1986/87): 210–225; and Eliot, "Learned Conjectures," in Thomas Thorowgood, *Jewes in America, or Probabilities that those Indians are Judaical, made more probable by some additionals to the former conjectures* (London: H. Brome, 1660), 1–27.

[4] On Eliot's millennialism, see James F. Maclear, "New England and the Fifth Monarchy: The Quest for the Millennium in Early American Puritanism," *William and Mary Quarterly*, 3d ser., 32:2 (April 1975): 223–60; James Holston, "John Eliot's Empirical Millenarianism," *Representations* 4 (Fall 1983): 128–53, and *A Rational Millennium: Puritan Utopias of Seventeenth-Century England and America* (New York: Oxford University Press, 1987), ch. 3; Timothy J. Sehr, "John Eliot, Millennialist and Missionary," *Historian* 46:2 (February 1984): 187–203; and Theodore Dwight Bozeman, *To Live Ancient Lives: The Primitivist Dimension in Puritanism* (Chapel Hill: University of North Carolina Press, 1988), ch. 8. Changes in Eliot's millenarianism after the Restoration are explored in Richard W. Cogley, "John Eliot and the Millennium," *Religion and American Culture: A Journal of Interpretation* 1:2 (Summer 1991): 227–50. A more general treatment of Interregnum millennialism of the sort Eliot is usually associated with is Bernard Capp, *The Fifth Monarchy Men: A Study in Seventeenth-Century English Millenarianism* (Totowa, N.J.: Rowman and Littlefield, 1972).

First page of Genesis, the Eliot Bible (Cambridge, Mass., 1663).
Courtesy of the John Carter Brown Library at Brown University.

sense that Massachusett represented a critical barrier to latent Old World immorality and depravity. Eliot assumed that he himself would be able to transcend that barrier without communicating corrupt thoughts through translation. His views on this literary act were very different from our own. We commonly assume that translation entails the transfer of systems of representation, hierarchies of power, or codes of authority. The act of committing Massachusett to Roman characters, and committing the Bible to Massachusett, might thus be understood as a process of give-and-take that created new contexts within which Europeans and non-Europeans worked out political relations.[5] But for a figure like Eliot, such processes would have been alien. For him, language did not shape knowledge; instead, knowledge shaped language. Hence, he let it be known that not just the Indians themselves but the "Indian language might be sanctified by the translation of the Holy Scriptures into it."[6] He assumed truths to be universal, and this meant that while the process of translation may affect the form of knowledge, it did not affect its underlying Christian substance. It was for this reason that Eliot could expect to be forgiven for errors in his translation: "No doubt there be many defects in the work, but the Lord is mercyfull to pitty our weaknesses, and to bless our poor indeavours, for the good of their soules, who are glad to heare the WORD of GOD, speaking in their own language to them."[7]

What ultimately mattered in Eliot's world were not the distinct qualities of a given tongue but what he imparted to that tongue as translator. God made the apostles "able to minister the New Testament, not of the letter, but of the spirit. For the letter killeth, but the spirit giveth life" (2 Cor. 3:6). The letter is of the flesh; the spirit is of God. Quakers took this ideal to the extreme of valuing silence above carnal speech or the dead letter. Eliot's own apostolic ambitions made such views impossible, but the freedom and enthusiasm with which he made the Word the Indians' Word suggest that, for Eliot, words were vessels within which the universal language of faith resided, and it is that language that God hears. That language is transparent, collapsing the distance between the soul and its professions. To present the Bible in Massachusett was thus to present universal truths that transcend the confu-

---

[5] The literature on the politics of translation is vast. Several treatments that emphasize its relation to colonialism are Walter Mignolo, *The Darker Side of the Renaissance: Literacy, Territoriality, and Colonization* (Ann Arbor: University of Michigan Press, 1994); J. Jorge Klor de Alva, "Language, Politics, and Translation: Colonial Discourse and Classical Nahuatl in New Spain," in *The Art of Translation: Voices from the Field*, ed. Rosanna Warren (Boston: Northeastern University Press, 1989), 143–62; Vicente L. Rafael, *Contracting Colonialism: Translation and Christian Conversion in Tagalog Society under Early Spanish Rule* (Ithaca: Cornell University Press, 1988), esp. ch. 1; and David Murray, *Forked Tongues: Speech, Writing, and Representation in North American Indian Texts* (Bloomington: Indiana University Press, 1991), esp. ch. 1.

[6] Quoted in Wilberforce Eames, "Bibliographic Notes on Eliot's Indian Bible and on His Other Translations . . . ," in *A Bibliography of the Algonquian Language*, ed. James Constantine Pilling (Washington, D.C.: Government Printing Office, 1891), 131.

[7] Quoted in Wilberforce Eames, "Discovery of a Lost Cambridge Imprint: John Eliot's *Genesis*, 1655," *Publications of the Colonial Society of Massachusetts* 34 (1937–42): 11.

An Eliot Bible, in an early binding, and thought to have been owned by Roger Williams. Photo by Brooke Hammerle. Courtesy of the Brown University Library.

sions of worldly utterance. And truths came not only from the ideas represented in the words of the Bible but also from the spirit behind those words, the spirit that Eliot himself imparted to them as he laboriously committed them to the printed page. Eliot's was thus not so much an intellectual labor, driven by philological and linguistic concerns, as it was a labor of faith, driven by a fevered pursuit of a millennial kingdom under God, a kingdom of all peoples that would first flower in the uncorrupted New England wilderness. This Bible kingdom was to be above and beyond linguistic difference—it was to be a kingdom wholly unified by the universal language of faith.[8]

John Eliot came to Massachusetts in 1631 after earning a B.A. at Cambridge and serving as an assistant to the radical Puritan minister and educational reformer Thomas Hooker. After arriving in the colony, he rose to become minister to the congregation at Roxbury and began spreading the Word among the native peoples of the region. These two activities consumed the man until his death in 1690. Through his missionary work, Eliot was fulfilling an imperative issued by the Crown to the New England Company as a condition for the privilege of settling New England: to Christianize the heathen Americans. Few, however, had either the will or the resources to fulfill the company's mandate. Aside from the general inability of the New England ministry to combine evangelical activities with ministerial duties, the vast majority of ordinary Whites tended to be downright hostile to the Indian population, regardless of its religious inclinations. Eliot's chiliastic zeal, however, compelled him to establish nineteen "praying towns," or settled communities of Christian Indians, in which he hoped to achieve his ultimate goal: a polity "wholly governed by the Scriptures in all things both in Church and State."[9] While these communities were more akin to refugee camps—inhabited by those Indians who survived the onslaught of pathogens and White settlers but lacked the desire or the capacity to retreat to the north and west—than the utopian villages Eliot sought to make them, it is nonetheless clear that Eliot was singular in his belief that he could fashion his beleaguered flocks into model biblical polities. His correspondence reveals a ceaseless quest for provisions of all sorts.[10] For such basic necessities as clothing and blankets,

---

[8] The influence of millenarianism and religious radicalism more broadly on seventeenth-century language philosophy is treated in Hugh J. Ormsby-Lennon, "From Shibboleth to Apocalypse: Quaker Speechways during the Puritan Revolution," in *Language, Self, and Society: A Social History of Language*, ed. Peter Burke and Roy Porter (Cambridge, England: Polity Press, 1991), 72–112; Hugh Ormsby-Lennon, "Nature's Mystick Book: Renaissance *Arcanum* into Restoration Cant," in *Secret Texts: The Literature of Secret Societies*, ed. Marie Mulvey Roberts and Hugh Ormsby-Lennon (New York: AMS Press, 1995), 24–96; and Nigel Smith, *Perfection Proclaimed: Language and Literature in English Radical Religion, 1640–1660* (Oxford: Clarendon Press, 1989).

[9] Eliot in Henry Whitfield, *The Light Appearing More and More towards the Perfect Day* (London: John Bartlet, 1651), 23.

[10] With the restoration of Charles II, the "New England Company for the Promoting and Propagating of the Gospels of Jesus Christ in New England," became the "Society or Company for the Propagation of the Gospel in New England and the parts adjacent." Both entities were, and remain, generally referred to as the "New England Company," which should not be confused with the "New England Company for a Plantation in Massachusetts Bay," incorporated in the 1620s, and the predecessor of the "Massa-

Eliot relied almost entirely on donations from England. Aside from the practical difficulties of communicating his needs to supporters in England, however, Eliot struggled with commissioners of the Massachusetts Bay Company who had discretionary authority over funds sent from England. Eliot's radical theology would test his relations with these local officials as they struggled to mute the more extreme expressions of Puritan radicalism, lest they face intrusions by an English government sensing danger and sedition in such marginal theological initiatives.[11] The best way available for them to compel Eliot to quiet his radical designs was by controlling the purse strings. It was perhaps for this reason that while Eliot was optimistic about "religion . . . gaineing hand," in Indians' institutional affairs such as "church estate, and . . . ecclesiastical polity," what progress the Indians did achieve they did so "but slowly" and only with Eliot's guiding hand, "not according to theire owne motions."[12] Given the range of obstacles Eliot faced, and his desire to save his Indian flock from European intrusions, it was perhaps inevitable that Eliot would direct his own energies toward equipping the praying towns to sustain their own churches. And this meant, of course, providing Massachusett-speaking people with access to Scripture.

By most accounts, Eliot began imagining a Massachusett-language Bible as early as 1647, but he actually undertook the project between the years 1654 and 1657, a period of severe illness. Fearing imminent death, he concluded that an Indian-language Bible was urgently needed if the Christian Indians were to maintain their progress toward a new kingdom under God after his passing.[13] By late 1659, Eliot had completed a draft of the Massachusett Bible and was prepared to seek the linguistic and editorial council of both Puritan and Indian as he finalized the manuscript for publication. Finally, in 1661 the Cambridge,

---

chusetts Bay Company"—the corporate entities that financed the early New England settlements, and whose affairs were managed primarily by magistrates residing in New England—figures who, it should be added, had discretionary authority with regard to funds generated in England by the New England Company. See William Kellaway, *The New England Company, 1649–1776: Missionary Society to the American Indians* (London: Longmans, 1961).

[11] See, for instance, Eames, *John Eliot and the Indians*, passim.

[12] Ibid., 21–22.

[13] Eliot expresses fears about not living to complete his translations in Henry Whitfield, *Strength Out of Weaknesse; Or, a Glorious Manifestation of the Further Progress of the Gospel among the Indians in New England* (London: John Blague, 1652), 7. Also see Rev. Richard Baxter to Eliot, Jan 20, 1656/7, in, "Some Unpublished Correspondence of the Rev. Richard Baxter and the Rev. John Eliot, 'The Apostle to the American Indians,' 1656–1682," F. J. Powicke, ed., in *Bulletin of the John Rylands Library, Manchester*, 15:1 (January 1931): 156.

Massachusetts printers Samuel Green, Marmaduke Johnson, and their Indian helper, a Nipmuck called James Printer, had completed a run of some two hundred copies of the New Testament; by 1663 they had begun what would become a run of over one thousand copies of the entire Massachusett Bible.[14] As was the case w   the printers worked with native Algonquian speakers-—in ,s.   tably Printer, employed at the Cambridge press until 1707—who served as linguistic mediators between Eliot and the printers, as well as between the printers and Indian readers. Although Eliot was the prime translator of the work, it was still very much a collaborative labor.[15]

However critical the Indian-language Bible was to his overall goals, it is clear that Eliot assumed Indian Christianity would be possible only after a complete reformation of the Indians' way of life, and this was reflected in his priorities as a missionary: "That which I must now most follow, is, first the spreading of the Gospel into more remote places. . . . the second thing attended, is the civilizing of [the Indians]. . . . The third thing is the Printing of the Bible in their Language."[16] For Eliot, although the peoples of Massachusetts were free of the corrupting habits and ideas so rife in the Old World, it remained the case that their natural virtues were "drowned in theire wild, and rude manner of liveing." It was this manner of living that left Indians without what Puritans assumed to be the central and distinctive quality of Puritan societies: settled patriarchal family lives. Eliot and his financial supporters assumed that without this, and with instead migratory habits and a kin-based social order, the propagation of the gospel would always founder amid socioeconomic instability, and a church of the elect—or recipients of some form of divine grace—would have been impossible. "By [agri]culture, order, government, and religion they begin to be furbished up, and drawn forth unto some good imployments," Eliot

---

[14] Vaughan, *New England Frontier*, 276–79. For the printing history of Eliot's "Indian Library," see George Parker Winship, *The Cambridge Press, 1638–1692: A Re-examination of the Evidence Concerning the Bay Psalm Book and the Eliot Indian Bible . . .* (Philadelphia: University of Pennsylvania Press, 1945), ch. 10; and Kellaway, *The New England Company*, ch. 6.

[15] While little attention has been given to the collaborative nature of such Christian religious texts, the idea that much Native American writing was in fact collaborative has been explored in depth. See Hertha D. Wong's *Sending My Heart Back across the Years: Tradition and Innovation in Native-American Autobiography* (New York: Oxford University Press, 1992); and Mary Louise Pratt's "Arts of the Contact Zone," in *Profession* (1991), 33–40; and "Criticism of the Contact Zone: Decentering Community and Nation," in *Critical Theory, Cultural Politics, and Latin American Narrative*, ed. Steven M. Bell, Albert H. LeMay, and Leonard Orr (Notre Dame, Ind.: University of Notre Dame Press, 1993), 83–102.

[16] Quoted in Eames, "Bibliographic Notes," 131.

wrote, "and by Gods blessing I hope they will be in these civile respects raised to forme good improvements."[17]

Given the depth of the social and spiritual transformation Eliot sought to achieve, it is perhaps surprising that the one element of Indian culture he made virtually no effort to transform was language. Part of the reason for this, as we have seen, was Eliot's belief that the Indian-European language barrier was valuable insulation against impure European cultural intrusion. But for somebody committed to the supreme authority of the written Bible, this position depended on a certain confidence in the Massachusett language and its speakers. Indeed, however difficult the language was to learn, Eliot wrote virtually nothing to suggest that he saw in American languages anything inherently deficient or unsuited for conveying Christian knowledge; nor did he complain that his Indian students and interpreters lacked his knowledge of Christianity, and therefore were unable to translate abstract theological terms. In a certain sense, this thinking did not set Eliot apart from mainstream Protestantism. "I wish," Martin Luther wrote in 1520, "that, at the same time as he 'elevates' the sign or sacrament openly before our eyes . . . [the priest] would do it in the vernacular, whatever that may be, in order that faith may be the more effectively awakened. For why should it be permissible to celebrate mass in Greek, Latin, and Hebrew, but not in German or any other language?"[18] What did distinguish Eliot was his unwavering determination to apply this doctrine to a language with no known European lineage.

Massachusett is one of eighteen distinct, mutually unintelligible Eastern Algonquian languages—the family of languages that dominated coastal regions of eastern North America, from present-day North Carolina to the Canadian Maritime Provinces. The variant of Massachusett dialect along the Atlantic coast north of Boston appears to have differed from what was spoken at the town of Natick, which in turn seems to have been different from dialects spoken in northern Rhode Island, Cape Cod, and Martha's Vineyard. The exact degree of difference among these dialects, as well as between these and the dialects of the other major languages of southern New England—the Narragansett and Mohegan-Pequot languages—is unclear.[19] And, as we have seen, there is no necessary correlation between levels of intelligibility and

[17] Eliot to Hanmer, Aug. 29, 1654, in Eames, *John Eliot and the Indians*, 21.

[18] *Martin Luther: Selections from His Writings*, ed. John Dillenberger (New York: Anchor Books, 1962), 288.

[19] Ives Goddard, "Eastern Algonquian Languages," in *Handbook of North American Indians, Vol. 15, The Northeast*, ed. Bruce Trigger (Washington, D.C.: Smithsonian Institution, 1978), 70–77.

degrees of structural or morphological difference. Much of this is a matter of pronunciation, which is often socially or culturally determined. It is nonetheless clear that the seeming linguistic confusion of the region raised doubts about the value of a Massachusett Bible among those financing Eliot's missions.

Some feared that Eliot's translation, which as far as anyone could tell was more faithful to the Natick dialect than any other, would have too small an audience to justify its cost. Writing in 1655, shortly after Eliot had completed a catechism for his Natick group, the Massachusetts Bay Company commissioners explained that while they never forbade him to translate Scripture, they advised that he do so in such a fashion that "the Indians in all partes of New England might share in the benefitt; which wee feare they can not soe well doe by what you have alreddy printed."[20] This was an imperative Eliot never fulfilled, and it explains much of the resistance that appeared through the years to his translating the Bible. Around the time the Massachusett Bible first appeared in print, Eliot's friend Richard Baxter wrote him from England, asking, "How far your Indian Tongue extendeth; how large or populous the Country is that useth it (if it be known); and whether it reach only to a few scattered Neighbours, who cannot themselves convey their Knowledge far, because of other Languages."[21] Baxter had evidently heard of the confusions that seemed to plague the American linguistic landscape, but, as might be expected, Eliot was confident that his friend's concerns were unfounded. "By an eminent providence of God, the extent [of Massachusett] is very large, though not without some variation of dialect, yet not such as hindereth a ready understanding of each other. And all p'ts wch receive the word of God, and pray, doe readyly understand the Bible, and catechisme, and other books." There was, in Eliot's view, enough mutual intelligibility among the languages of southern New England to facilitate the dissemination of Scripture. But of even more importance, Eliot recognized the possibility that through his endeavors "these books will be a meanes to fix, and extend this language."[22] However idealistic he may have been about the unifying language of faith, it is clear that Eliot was aware of the significant unifying powers of one mediating technology, namely, print. For he antici-

---

[20] *Acts of the Commissioners of the United Colonies*, ed. David Pulsifer, in *Records of the Colony of New Plymouth, in New England* (Boston: W. White, 1859), vol. 2, 140.

[21] Richard Baxter to Eliot, Nov. 30, 1663, *Reliquiæ Baxterianæ: or, Mr. Richard Baxters narrative of the most memorable passages of his life and times* (London: T. Parkhurst et al., 1696), 296.

[22] Eliot to Baxter, 20th of April, 1669, in Powicke, ed. "Some unpublished correspondence of the Rev. Richard Baxter . . . ," in *Bulletin of the John Rylands Library* 15:2 (July 1931): 454.

pated what appears to have actually occurred: the Massachusett library would come to mute dialectical variation in the region.[23]

In Eliot's world, the translator's capacity to impart to the printed page the proper pious spirit depended on a single, almost undisputed truth: the world's languages were corrupted versions of an original, perfect tongue. What made that tongue perfect was the absence of any disparity between sign and signified, and it was the possibility that such a tongue could be resurrected that inspired so many seventeenth-century universal language schemes, all designed to aid in the discovery of divine design. Perhaps the most common assumption behind these schemes was that a perfect language would bear some sort of innate connection to that to which it referred. In "Of an Universall Language," penned in 1661, a young Isaac Newton observed that "the dialects of each language [are] soe divers and arbitrary [that] a generall language cannot bee so fitly deduced from them as from ye natures of things themselves wch is ye same in all nations and by which all language was at ye first composed."[24] Only a language derived directly from the true nature of things could be a universal language because it was only such natures that could be grasped by all of God's children. The quest to discover such a language was closely related to the apocalyptic fever of the age, for very much integral to the quest to reunite humanity under pure biblical law was the desire to reunite humanity under a single, perfect, and universally understood tongue. And it was in these two inseparable goals that Puritan educational reform and proselytization found common ground. Both were founded on a broader desire to prepare the way for a new millennium by demolishing the cultural barriers that separated nations. This meant, above all, countering the ill effects of Babel.

There was little sense among Eliot's contemporaries that the story of Babel was at all apocryphal. Henry Edmundson explained in the epistle dedicatory of his 1655 Lingua linguarum, "As it is observed by our great Advancer of Learning, the main business of mankind, besides the doing of Gods will, . . . is the redeeming himselfe from those curses which he gained by his sin [such as] the curse in the Confusion of Tongues at Babell, which is repaired by Arts, Learning, and Languages."[25] The same sentiment was expressed by the latitudinarian

---

[23] Kathleen Joan Bragdon, "'Another Tongue Brought In': An Ethnohistorical Study of Native Writings in Massachusett" (Ph.D. diss., Brown University, 1981), 26–27.

[24] Ralph W. V. Elliott, "Isaac Newton's 'Of an Universal Language,'" *Modern Language Review* 52:1 (January 1957): 13.

[25] Henry Edmundson, *Lingua Linguarum: The Naturall Language of Languages* . . . (1655; facsimile reprint, Menston: Scolar Press, 1970), "Epistle Dedicatory [1]." On the desire to remedy Babel among seventeenth-century language reformers, see James Knowlson,

bishop John Wilkins in his *Essay towards a Real Character and a Philosophical Language*, which appeared in 1668: "Besides that most obvious advantage which would ensue, of facilitating mutual *Commerce*, amongst the several Nations of the World, and the improving of all *Natural knowledge*," a perfect language "would likewise very much conduce to the spreading of the knowledge of *Religion*."[26] Another of Eliot's contemporaries, the natural philosopher and eventual governor of the New England Company Robert Boyle, wrote that since the ambition of the builders of the Tower of Babel—to provide humanity with an easy road back to Eden—was contrary to the will of God, "he made use of that very conspiracy, that brought them together, to effect that which they conspired to prevent; so that now the remotest parts of the inhabited world are but the colonies of *Babel*, whose scattered architects have indeed made themselves a name, but upon a quite contrary account than they intended or expected."[27]

Eliot embraced a parallel position. In keeping with the Puritan preference for revelation, he articulated his linguistic views in a far more orthodox manner than Wilkins, Newton, Boyle, and others identified with the new natural theology, or the view that one served God equally by studying his works as by studying his word. In a letter to Richard Baxter, Eliot made it known that while he applauded the overall aims of the universal language movement, he believed that rather than some newly discovered tongue, which for him amounted to a temporary expedient, the English nation ought to seek truth through the true language of Jerusalem: "Why may we not make ready for Heaven in this Point, by making and fitting [Hebrew], according to the rules of the Divine artifice of it, to express all imaginable Conceptions and Notions of the Mind of Man in all Arts and Sciences? . . . Were this done, all schools would teach this Language, and all the World, especially the Commonwealth of Learning, would be of one."[28] Eliot's reference to

---

Universal Language Schemes in England and France, 1600–1800 (Toronto: University of Toronto Press, 1975), esp. 9–10; Robert Markley, *Fallen Languages: Crises of Representation in Newtonian England, 1660–1740* (Ithaca, N.Y.: Cornell University Press, 1993), 69–70 and passim; and Arno Borst, *Der Turmbau von Babel: Geschichte der Meinungen über Ursprung und Vielfalt der Sprachen und Völker*, 6 vols. (Stuttgart: Hiersemann, 1957–63), vol. 3, passim. Also see Tony Davis, "The Ark in Flames: Science, Language and Education in Seventeenth-Century England," in *The Figural and the Literal: Problems of Language in the History of Science and Philosophy, 1630–1800*, ed. Andrew E. Benjamin, Geoffrey N. Cantor, and John R. R. Christie (Manchester: Manchester University Press, 1987), 83–102.

[26] John Wilkins, *An Essay towards a Real Character and a Philosophical Language* (1668; facsimile reprint, Menston, England: Scolar Press, 1968), "Epistle Dedicatory [5]."

[27] Robert Boyle, *The Works*, ed. Thomas Birch (London: W. Johnson et al., 1772), vol. 2, 417–18.

[28] Eliot to Baxter, Aug. 6, 1663, in *Reliquiæ Baxterianæ*, 294.

the "Divine artifice" of Hebrew is indicative of his overall conception of language. Far from being unified in substance and content, language is a mere vessel for divine truths; it is, to put it differently, merely symbolic. Only in the case of Hebrew, the single tongue to precede the fall of Babel, can language be regarded as unified in both form and content, and therefore absent any disparity between signifier and signified.

Eliot's interest in Hebrew was by no means unique in its day. Since the early Renaissance, Jewish students of the cabala—a series of writings from A.D. 1200 that purportedly contained ancient mystical wisdom—had formulated a theory of textual exegesis that involved analysis not only of the rhetorical dimensions of Hebrew writing but also of the nonrhetorical elements—those that might be conveyed through the shape of a given letter, syntax, punctuation, and the placement of numbers. Robert Fludd, a member of the English College of Physicians and a leading English cabalist, attempted to prove in his *Utriusque cosmi, maioris scilicet et minoris, metaphysica, physica* (1617–21) that, as the true divine tongue, Hebrew possessed no quality or formal characteristic that could be regarded as conventional. Rather, in every respect the language contained divine encryption.[29]

The general sense that, as the original tongue, Hebrew somehow retained underlying mystical meanings was not just the stuff of theosophists and mystics. During the Elizabethan period, magical charms often contained Hebrew characters, and the apocalyptic mood of the latter civil war era revived interest in Hebrew, as Puritans struggled to identify the sources and symptoms of the Second Coming. In the late 1640s, Parliament even acted to acquire a collection of Hebrew-language texts from Italy, and through the 1650s some of the same Fifth Monarchy Men with whom Eliot has been associated propagated the notion that the purest, most ready expression of the Word was to be found only in its uncorrupted Hebrew form. After struggling to translate passages from the Book of Daniel, William Aspinwall, a Fifth Monarchist ideologue (who had emigrated to Massachusetts but made a triumphal return to England during the Interregnum), concluded that only in the original Hebrew, "which concise forme of speech is peculiar only to the Pen-men of Scripture," could perfect understanding be achieved.[30] It was no doubt similar reasoning that explains the

---

[29] Fludd and the hermetic-cabalist tradition are treated in Frances A. Yates, *The Rosicrucian Enlightenment* (London: Routledge, 1972), ch. 6 and passim. Also see Nicholas Hudson, *Writing and European Thought, 1600–1830* (Cambridge: Cambridge University Press, 1994), 21–26.

[30] William Aspinwall, *An Explication and Application of the Seventh Chapter of Daniel* (London: Livewell Chapman, 1654), 4. On the use of Hebrew characters in charms, see Keith Thomas, *Religion and the Decline of Magic: Studies in Popular Beliefs in Sixteenth- and Seven-*

prominence of Hebrew-language studies in the seventeenth-century Harvard College curriculum.[31]

Although some may have regarded Hebrew as a remedy for the confusion left in the wake of Babel, for Puritans a Bible in any language was only as good as one's capacity to extract truths from that Bible. And doing that depended on the art of thinking. For all their bizarre millenarian fantasies, for all their literalism with regard to Scripture, Puritans—even those of Eliot's fanatical strain—regarded themselves as fully rational beings, able to systematically and methodically achieve understanding. Among the Puritan clergy, there was less inspiration and gross enthusiasm than labored exegesis in their preparation for a new millennium. Hence, for Indians to engage with Scripture in a reasoned way, they needed to learn the arts of rational thought and communication. It is "one of my chief cares and labours," Eliot wrote, "to teach [the Indians] some of the Liberal Arts and Sciences, and the way how to analize, and lay out into particulars both the Works and Word of God; and how to communicate knowledge to others methodically and skillfully."[32] To a Puritan student, this would have meant assimilating the basics of classical learning: rhetoric, logic, Latin, and probably Hebrew and Greek. And for those Indian students either sent to Harvard or schooled by Puritan tutors (in preparation for later matriculation at Harvard), there would have been the added burden of instruction in English. But this immersion in classical education was rarely successful as Indian students fell victim to disease and homesickness. The preferred approach to Indian education—at least for Eliot—was to establish Indian-language schools, staffed by Indian teachers, in the various praying towns of southeastern New England.[33]

For use in these schools, Eliot prepared a series of textbooks, including the *Logick Primer*, printed in 1672 and designed to familiarize Indian students with the art of—as Eliot perhaps narrowly defined it—"the laying of sentences together to make up a Speech."[34] Logic itself

teenth-Century England (London: Penguin Books, 1991), 213, 275. The promotion of Hebrew during the Interregnum is treated in Nigel Smith, "The Uses of Hebrew in the English Revolution," in *Language, Self, and Society: A Social History of Language*, ed. Peter Burke and Roy Porter (Cambridge, England: Polity Press, 1991), 51–71. Also relevant is David S. Katz, *Philo-Semitism and the Readmission of the Jews to England, 1603–55* (Oxford: Clarendon Press, 1982), ch. 2.

[31] Samuel Eliot Morison, *Harvard College in the Seventeenth Century* (Cambridge, Mass.: Harvard University Press, 1936), vol. 1, 200–207.

[32] Quoted in Eames, "Bibliography," 174.

[33] James Axtell, *The Invasion Within: The Contest of Cultures in Colonial North America* (New York: Oxford University Press, 1985), 182–84.

[34] John Eliot, *The Indian Grammar Begun: or, An Essay to Bring the Indian Language into Rules* . . . (Cambridge, Mass.: Marmaduke Johnson, 1666), 5.

had been discovered by heathen Greeks and Romans, demonstrating that like all the communicative arts, it was a divine gift to which God offered equal access to all. For, as Perry Miller has written, "The authority of logic was divine no matter who employed it."[35] In providing the Indians with this means for exposing and communicating scriptural truths, Eliot was merely introducing them to that gift. It was a universal and transcendent tool, and therefore one with the power to overcome the imperfections that the confusion of tongues had wrought upon humanity. As the educational reformer John Dury wrote in a work published in the mid–seventeenth century, "Without their subordination unto [the classical] Arts and Sciences, [languages] are worth nothing towards the advancement of our Happiness."[36] That is, language, whether Latin or Massachusett, was of no use without rhetoric, grammar, and, most of all, logic—the arts that enabled verbal artifice to become truth.

To the extent that Puritan logic was at all distinctive, it was indebted primarily to the Huguenot rhetorician and logician Petrus Ramus, after whose hugely popular logic texts Eliot modeled his own Indian-language logic. Ramus worked in a reformist spirit similar to that of Comenius and other Continental educational reformers, arguing for a selective approach to the classical arts of communication in order to facilitate, above all, a less cumbersome approach to Bible studies than that suggested by pure Aristotelian logic. Underlying much of the Ramist impulse was a desire to eliminate from classical logic and rhetoric any presupposition that knowledge could be invented rather than revealed or discovered. The popularity—in the Puritan world—of this reform is difficult to grasp without recognizing the general absence in the late sixteenth and early seventeenth centuries of a modern, experimental scientific ethos, and the predominance of an alternative ethos in which semantic disputes were not dismissed as petty but were regarded as the very essence of learning. While Puritan educational reform was to play a major part in the emergence of a new inductive science, its early initiatives with respect to dialectic or logic came less as attempts to overturn the syllogistic, classical approach to inquiry than simply as efforts to revise that approach in such a way that it was more consistent with Calvinism. That meant making it conducive to the rapid and personal assimilation of scriptural truths.[37]

[35] Perry Miller, *The New England Mind: The Seventeenth Century* (Cambridge, Mass.: Harvard University Press, 1939), 112.

[36] John Dury, *The Reformed School and the Reformed Library Keeper* (1651; facsimile reprint, Menston, England: Scolar Press, 1972), 47.

[37] On the connection between seventeenth-century millenarianism and the rise of experimental science, see Charles Webster, *The Great Instauration: Science, Medicine and Reform, 1626–1660* (London: Duckworth, 1975); and Margaret C. Jacob, "Millenarianism

The chief and guiding revision promoted by the Ramists rested on the basic point that rhetoric and logic were not necessarily complementary arts. There was, among humanist logicians as well as numerous bands of religious dissenters, both Catholic and Protestant, the increasing sense that criteria for the truthfulness of a proposition need not include the degree to which it was eloquent. For Ramus—and for Puritans who, like Eliot, had been exposed to his teachings at seventeenth-century Cambridge—the traditional Aristotelian distinction between logic and rhetoric rested on the assumption that truths were discovered by intellectuals, who then sought to communicate them to a broader public. Such a division in the nature of learned discourse rested on the notion that truth could be obtained only through the highest levels of intellectual discourse, and that therefore a separate art was needed to render those truths intelligible and convincing to those not functioning at such a level. In the view of reform-minded Christians, such thinking made no sense. It implied that insofar as truths were the result of the liberal arts of logic and rhetoric, they were not divine—an impossibility for any right-living Christian. Such thinking merely secured the privileged place of the clerical establishment. For classical logic to be useful as a means of biblical exegesis, that is, it would have to be freed from the premise that truths were arrived at through discourse, and made consistent with the premise that truths were revealed in Scripture. The revisions proposed by the Ramists were, in essence, aimed at securing for logic the task of stripping away superfluity and embellishment in order to bring forth the Word in its plainest form. And while the popularity of Ramism in higher education waned in England after the 1620s, it remained influential at Harvard and among those Calvinist ministers and schoolmasters whose objective was more immediate access to scriptural knowledge. The Ramist impulse should not be mistaken for a desire to somehow simplify or vulgarize the way to truth. Puritans wanted to make the art of thinking more consistent with their assumptions about knowledge and its origins, but they in no way wanted to privilege the possession of truth over the art of thinking. To do so would have been to give over biblical exegesis to enthusiasts and fanatics, inclined to eschew the true and divinely sanctioned way to knowledge: logic. For Indian teachers, ministers, and church members to possess the art of logic was thus for them to possess the capacity to think like Puritans by coming to Christian knowledge through deliberate and orderly reasoning from biblical

and Science in the Late Seventeenth Century," *Journal of the History of Ideas* 37:2 (April–June 1976): 335–41. Also see Christopher Hill, *Intellectual Origins of the English Revolution* (Oxford: Clarendon Press, 1965).

text—an ability Puritans generally took to be indicative of divine grace.[38]

While Eliot's primary reason for translating the Bible and creating an Indian-language logic text and Christian primer was to make Indians pious and self-sustaining believers, it is clear that at some level this objective went unfulfilled. The Christian Indians of Natick and elsewhere were to a large extent dependent on Eliot not only for material sustenance but also for communication with the English-speaking world. In itself, this had certain benefits for Eliot, not the least of which was that it allowed him some control over the influx of potentially damaging English impieties. But, not surprisingly, it also created serious problems for both Eliot and his Indian converts. None was more critical or far-reaching than the problem of establishing the validity of Native American salvation experiences. Among English speakers, this was always a difficult enough proposition, but when torturous interrogation and personal narrative had to be conducted entirely through interpreters, it became next to impossible.[39]

Anticipating criticism on these grounds, Richard Mather, Cotton Mather's grandfather, rhetorically asked, "How shall we know that the [Indian] Confessions here related, being spoken in their Tongue, were indeed uttered by them in such words, as have the same signification and meaning with these that are here expressed, for we have only the testimony of one [interpreter] to assure us of it?"[40] How, Mather

---

[38] On Puritan Ramism, see Miller, *The New England Mind*, ch. 5; and John Morgan, *Godly Learning: Puritan Attitudes towards Reason, Learning and Education, 1560–1640* (Cambridge: Cambridge University Press, 1986), 105–12. More general treatments of Ramism are Wilbur Samuel Howell, *Logic and Rhetoric in England, 1500–1700* (Princeton, N.J.: Princeton University Press, 1956), ch. 4; Walter J. Ong, *Ramus, Method, and the Decay of Dialogue* (Cambridge, Mass.: Harvard University Press, 1958); Hugh Kearney, *Scholars and Gentlemen: Universities and Society in Pre-Industrial Britain, 1500–1700* (Ithaca, N.Y.: Cornell University Press, 1970), ch. 3; and Anthony Grafton and Lisa Jardine, *From Humanism to the Humanities: Education and the Liberal Arts in Fifteenth- and Sixteenth-Century Europe* (Cambridge, Mass.: Harvard University Press, 1986), ch. 7. On the relationship between Ramism and Puritan conceptions of language, see Charles Feidelson Jr., *Symbolism and American Literature* (Chicago: University of Chicago Press, 1953), 83–94. My interpretation here and throughout this chapter has also been influenced by David D. Hall, *Worlds of Wonder, Days of Judgement: Popular Religious Belief in Early New England* (New York: Knopf, 1989), ch. 1, esp. page 25.

[39] Although the question has generated a vast historical literature, there remains little consensus about the degree to which Indian conversions were bona fide. For overviews of these debates, see Richard W. Cogley, "John Eliot in Recent Scholarship," *American Indian Culture and Research Journal* 14:2 (1990), 77–92; and Alden T. Vaughan's introduction to the third edition of his *New England Frontier*, esp. lv–lix.

[40] John Eliot and Thomas Mayhew Jr., *Tears of Repentence: Or, a Further Narrative of the*

wanted to know, could he be sure that what he was hearing from the lips of the interpreter accurately represented the Indian confessor's truest sentiments? To allay such fears, Eliot developed a special set of rhetorical strategies. Speaking of one confessor, he explained "that he spake so plain to his understanding . . . because I had advised him, and so all the rest, to express themselves in the most plain and familiar words and expressions they could, for my more easie and perfect understanding."[41] In the end, however, the only guarantee of accuracy was the reputation of the interpreter. As Mather continued, Indian confessions were as trustworthy as their interpreter's "integrity and faithfulness." A figure of good character would never "utter a falsehood in any matter whatever, and much less so many falsehoods, & that in such a publick manner, in the view of God and the World, as he must needs have done if he have coyned these confessions of his own head, and have not to his best understanding truly related them in our Tongue, according as they were uttered by them in theirs."[42]

For Eliot, this matter had far-reaching implications. Both local magistrates and investors in his mission expected returns in the form of demonstrated Indian conversions for their indulgence of Eliot's schemes. It was thus inevitable that Eliot would find himself struggling to assure New England Company officials that although there may have been inaccuracies in his translations, the spirit he conveyed was true. "When I had read this Confession," he explained to the governors of the New England Company, "I said, because the Lord hath said, that in the mouth of two or three witnesses, every Truth shall be established; therefore I desired that the rest of the Interpreters might attest unto this which I had read." The witnesses did not assure the church fathers that Eliot's translations had been flawless. But they did indicate that, in spirit, Eliot's words accurately reflected the Indians' feelings. One explained, "So far as I discern, I doubt not of the truth of what Mr. Eliot hath delivered, and for that which he hath now uttered, though some things the Indian hath added more than he spake in private, and some things left out, and some things otherwise placed, yet for the substance of his present confession, it is the same with that which he delivered in private, where we did carefully try all things."[43] What sustained Eliot's mission was thus a combination of trust and faith: trust in Eliot's sin-

---

Progress of the Gospel amongst the Indians (London: Peter Cole, 1653), p. 5 of Richard Mather letter.

[41] John Eliot, *A Further Account of the Progress of the Gospel amongst the Indians of New England* . . . (London: John Macock, 1660), 45.

[42] Eliot and Mayhew, *Tears of Repentence*, p. 6 of Richard Mather letter.

[43] Eliot, *A Further Account*, 45.

cerity as an interpreter and faith that whatever the precise terms of a confession, it was ultimately the underlying spirit of godliness that indicated salvation. One way for Indians to express that spirit was through gesture and movement. For the body, it was assumed, did not lie. As Richard Mather explained, "Though they spake in a language, of which many of us understood but little, yet we that were present that day, we saw them, and we heard them perform the duties mentioned [the meditation of Jesus Christ], with such plenty of tears trickling down the cheeks of some of them, as did argue to us that they spake with much good affection, and holy fear of God, and it much affected our hearts." Indeed, so earnest did the Indians' performances appear that Mather found no credibility in the assertion that "in these things they were acted [on] and led by that spirit which is wont to breath amongst Indians, the Spirit of Satan, or of corrupt Nature, but that herein they had with them another Spirit," the benevolent and all-knowing divine spirit.[44] For Mather, Eliot, and other Puritan workers in the fields of idolatry and paganism, the glow of salvation showed itself not only in precise and rational discourse but also in the gestures and physical expression of the professor. It was precisely this sort of non-spoken communication—in which little that was worldly insinuated itself between the worshiper and his or her professions—that Puritans would come to associate with a primitive or uncorrupted church. With this in mind, in the early eighteenth century Cotton Mather asked what it was about praying Indians that "will assure us that *prayer* is one of their devotions?" He found the answer in his grandfather Richard's account of Indian prayer in the age of Eliot. They pray, Cotton relays to the reader, "'without a form, because from the heart'; which is," Mather added, "as I remember, Tertullian's expression concerning the prayers in the assemblies of the Primitive Christians; namely *sine monitore quia de pectore* (without a formula, because from the heart)." Such was the mode of discourse in the original church of saints. "It is evident," Mather continued, "that the primitive Christians had no stated *liturgies* among them; that no *forms of prayers* were in their time imposed upon the ministers of the gospel." But of most consequence for those not equipped with English modes of worldly discourse, "even about the platform of prayer given us by our Lord," it was the opinion of some that "'our Lord therein taught, not what words we should use in prayer, but what things we should pray for.'" Indian preaching had a similar primitive quality. But it was not pure, pagan primitivism, because its spirit came from the pious. Their preaching "has much of

[44] Eliot and Mayhew, *Tears of Repentence*, page 9 of Mather letter.

Eliot, and therefore you may be sure much of *Scripture,* but perhaps more of the *Christian* than of the *scholar* in it."[45]

Mather's analysis would seem to confirm that in the minds of some Puritans, anyway, whatever Eliot may have set out to do to bring the Indians into the fold of English modes of education and communication, the success of Indian conversion was judged according to an ideal, primitive Christianity of a sort that branded the heart as much as the mind. This was also a Christianity in which faith was so pure, in which conviction was so complete and unyielding, that the rhetorical arts of persuasion would be rendered almost obsolete.[46] One might even imagine Eliot uttering John Bunyan's lines: "My dark and cloudy words they do but hold / The Truth, as Cabinets inclose the Gold."[47] This kind of thinking is evident in Cotton Mather's point that Eliot took "delight in speaking to the Almighty God" no less than he did in "speaking of him." Mather contrasted this habit with a portrayal of a group of Jesuits who once "made a no less profane than severe order, 'that no man should speak of God at all.' "[48] Mather's hyperbole should not obscure the critical point that the Puritan ministry sought to transcend mere speech. To deliver the Word was to move the heart in the most profound and basic way. It was to rise above words in order to reach that transcendent and universal faculty that allowed all listeners to receive the doctrinal knowledge needed to prepare the heart for holy grace.

The impulse to render the Bible in vernacular tongues was, much like the desire to comprehend the Word in its original Greek or Hebrew, part of a broader Reformist impulse to reduce Scripture to its purest, most immediate and primitive form. It was, that is, part of a broader seventeenth-century impulse to make the meaning of the Word more readily obtainable and affecting by stripping away the accumulated layers of perversion imposed by a corrupt and decadent church. This was an ideal, however, that engendered lasting and often fierce controversy.[49] Indeed, Bible translation, let alone the act of inventing a pho-

---

[45] Cotton Mather, *Magnalia Christi Americana; or, The Ecclesiastical History of New England* (1852; reprint, New York: Russell and Russell, 1967), vol. 1, 569. On Puritan primitivism see Bozeman, *To Live Ancient Lives,* esp. 32–50.

[46] For a related discussion see Charles Cohen, *God's Caress: The Psychology of Puritan Religious Experience* (New York: Oxford University Press, 1986), 82 n. 18.

[47] John Bunyan, *The Pilgrim's Progress,* ed. N. H. Keeble (Oxford: Oxford University Press, 1984), 4.

[48] Mather, *Magnalia Christi Americana,* 1:532.

[49] Stephen Greenblatt, *Renaissance Self-Fashioning: From More to Shakespeare* (Chicago: University of Chicago Press, 1980), ch. 2; Michel de Certeau, "L'Idée de traduction de la Bible au XVIIème siècle: Sacy et Simon," *Recherches de Science Religieuse* 66:1 (1978): 73–91;

netic alphabet, had a long and eventful history by the time Eliot undertook his own translation. In 1532, before the vernacular Bible had become common, Sir Thomas More complained that in the first English-
language translation of the New Testament the translator, William Tyndale, "changed . . . the common known words [with] the intent to
make a change in the faith."[50] In More's mind, Tyndale did so deliber-
ately and surreptitiously, using the act of translation to conceal the
manipulation of pure and original biblical truths. Similar complaints
about Bible translations were not at all unknown in seventeenth-century England. In 1644, for instance, the House of Commons moved to
suppress faulty foreign translations, an action that had support through
the 1650s. The fevered impulse to disseminate Scripture always en-
tailed the risk that evangelical publishing would become an end in
itself, leading to careless translation and damaging corruption of the
Word. Writing in 1659, William Kilburne decried the proliferation of
unscrupulous Bible printers and translators, calling upon Parliament to
ensure "that such printers only, as have heretofore discharged themselves with the greatest care and conscience . . . be hereafter autho-
rized, and permitted to print the Bible."[51]

While there is little evidence to suggest that anyone questioned the
accuracy of Eliot's printed translations, the general diminution of chiliastic enthusiasm that came with the restoration of Charles II in the
spring of 1660 did have an impact on Eliot's plans. In the spring of
1662, the Massachusetts General Court ordered the condemnation and
destruction of Eliot's *The Christian Commonwealth*, a work that described
the sort of polity Eliot sought for the Christian Indians. Although Eliot
wrote the book in the early 1650s, at the height of Interregnum exhil-
aration, it was published in England in 1659 and appeared in Massa-

George Steiner, *After Babel: Aspects of Language and Translation* (New York: Oxford University Press, 1975), 245; and Stephen Prickett, *Words and* The Word: *Language, Poetics and
Biblical Interpretation* (Cambridge: Cambridge University Press, 1986), ch. 1.

[50] From Thomas More's *Confutation of Tyndale's Answer* (1532), excerpted in *Transla-
tion/History/Culture: A Sourcebook*, ed. André Lefevere (London: Routledge, 1992), 71.
Also see Christopher Hill, *The English Bible and the Seventeenth-Century Revolution* (London:
Penguin Books, 1993), esp. 15. The politics of Bible translation in the age of Tyndale are
treated in Gillian Brennan, "Patriotism, Language, and Power: English Translations of
the Bible, 1520–1580," *History Workshop* 27 (Spring 1989): 18–36. See also William Fulke,
A Defence of the Sincere and True Translations of the Holy Scriptures into the English Tongue
(London: H. Bynneman, 1583).

[51] William Kilburne, *Dangerous Errors in Several Late Printed Bibles: To the Great Scandal,
and Corruption of Sound and True Religion* (Finsbury, 1659), reprinted in W. J. Loftie, *A
Century of Bibles, or, The Authorised Version from 1611 to 1711* (London: Basil Montagu Pickering, 1872), 49. Also see Charles Ripley Gillett, *Burned Books: Neglected Chapters in British
History and Literature* (New York: Columbia University Press, 1932), vol. 1, 25–26.

chusetts two years later. The timing could hardly have been worse. At the very moment that Massachusetts officials were striving to normalize relations with the king and a new Parliament, Eliot's openly anti-monarchical work set precisely the wrong tone. Fearing retribution, the General Court of Massachusetts banned Eliot's book and demanded that its author submit to the court a signed recantation.[52] The fate of *The Christian Commonwealth* was not altogether unlike the impending fate of Eliot's Bibles. In another act of censorship, copies of the Massachusett Bible met their end during the cataclysmic flurry of vengeance and brutality that has come to be known as King Philip's War.

The immediate instigation of the war was the execution of three Indians convicted by a Plymouth, Massachusetts, court of murdering the interpreter, missionary, and sometime Indian assistant to Eliot, John Sassamon. The Wampanoag leader, Metacom, or King Philip, as he was known to the English, allegedly responded to the execution with a call for vengeance; in the spring of 1675, he led an attack against the English town of Swansey. This, in turn, brought indiscriminate retaliation by whites against all Indians in southern New England, Christian or otherwise. The ensuing cycles of often genocidal violence left the region devastated in almost every respect. The Indian population of southeastern New England was nearly wiped out, and one in ten English males were either killed or taken captive. Perhaps none fared worse than the Christian Indians of Natick. Despite Eliot's desperate efforts to protect them from their neighbors, the community suffered almost unending attacks by both marauding whites and allies of Metacom. In the winter of 1676, with the support of provincial authorities, Eliot took the desperate measure of removing most of the Natick group to the protected isolation of Deer Island in Boston Harbor. Lacking adequate food and shelter, however, many of them died of starvation and disease.[53]

Given the level of destruction and violence brought by the war, it is perhaps not surprising that the Eliot Bibles did not fare well. According to some Dutch missionaries, seeking a copy several years after the war's end, an aged Eliot told them that "in the late Indian war all the

---

[52] This incident is summarized by Bozeman, *To Live Ancient Lives*, 264–65.

[53] On King Philip's War, see Douglas Leach, *Flintlock and Tomahawk: New England in King Philip's War* (New York: Norton, 1966); Russell Bourne, *The Red King's Rebellion: Racial Politics in New England, 1675–1678* (New York: Atheneum, 1990); and Jenny Hale Pulsipher, "Massacre at Hurtleberry Hill: Christian Indians and English Authority in Metacom's War," *William and Mary Quarterly*, 3d ser., 53:3 (July 1996): 459–86. The latter emphasizes the impossible predicament of the Christian Indians. For an exploration of the social psychology of the war, see Jill Lepore, *The Name of War: King Philip's War and the Origins of American Identity* (New York: Knopf, 1998).

Bibles and Testaments were carried away and, burnt or destroyed."[54] This is a remarkable quote, in light of the fact that over one thousand of these books had been circulating in an area populated by forty-five hundred native Massachuset speakers at the very most.[55] But the quote is more tantalizing than telling. It indicates that these books were threatening to someone; perhaps even more broadly, it tells us that someone objected to the entire notion that the Word should be the Indians' Word. It does not, however, tell us who was so threatened.

There is good reason to believe that the Indians allied with Metacom burned the books; perhaps they had come to see the Bibles as indicative of English intrusions into their way of life. For them, to destroy the Bible was to destroy the one object that Puritans held dear—the one object from which these English men and women drew justification for nearly all their behavior, including their strategies for undermining Native American traditions. Of the anecdotes that lend validity to this scenario, one involves an Englishman residing somewhere near a band of hostile Narragansetts. This man was said to have had "a strange confidence . . . that whilest he held his Bible in his hand, he [would be] secure from all kinde of violence. . . . the enemy finding him in that posture, deriding his groundless apprehension or folly therein, ript him open, and put his Bible in his belly."[56] Perhaps this man's attackers sought once and for all to return the Word to its true source—the belly from which it emanated. And perhaps this is indicative of a broader Native American hostility to the written word; to put a man's book in his belly was to collapse the mystical distance between the spoken and the written; it was to remove from New England the written word, that peculiar technological innovation that, perhaps more than any other, divided Puritan and Indian.

There is, however, another way to interpret the fate of Eliot's Bibles. For the desecration of corpses and Bibles in the fashion just described was not some uniquely heathen act. During the Wars of Religion, for instance, French Catholics stuffed pages from Protestant vernacular Bibles into the wounds and mouths of Protestant dead. Implied in such acts was a broad, symbolic rebuke to Protestantism: if the Word were to

[54] *Journal of Jasper Danckaerts 1679–1680*, ed. Bartlett Burleigh James and J. Franklin Jameson (New York: Barnes and Noble, 1913), 264.

[55] S. F. Cook, *The Indian Population of New England in the Seventeenth Century* (Berkeley: University of California Press, 1976), 84. The number was surely much lower at the time of the war. This estimate is of the Massachuset population in 1610—the eve of demographic catastrophe that came with initial English settlement.

[56] [Nathaniel Saltonstall,] *A New and Further Narrative of the State of New-England, Being a Continued Account of the Bloudy Indian-War, from March till August, 1676* . . . (London: J. B. for Dorman Newman, 1676), 6–7.

be every Christian's word, so it would also belong to the dead, Satan's vessels.[57] There is a suggestion in all this that what made these vernacular Bibles worthy of such desecration was precisely the language in which they were written—that somehow translation transformed them into something other than repositories for God's Word. Such thinking was not limited to the Catholic world. Aside from officially sanctioned censorship of corrupt Bible translations, English Protestants had engaged in explicit acts of Bible burning during the English civil war. In these acts, there was exhibited little sense that destroying the Bible represented anything like a serious violation of the Word itself—so long as what was destroyed had somehow been perverted. Indeed, as so often is the case with revered objects, corrupted or ersatz versions take on the personas of their corrupters. That is perhaps why ritual burnings of vernacular Bibles and the hanging or burning at the stake of their printers often occurred in unison.[58]

There is much reason to believe that this is why the Eliot Bibles were burned, and that therefore they were burned not by Indians, suspicious of the mystical qualities of print, but by English Puritans who perceived the book as threatening precisely because it was written in a tongue of alleged barbarians that had only recently been represented in print. Perhaps much as Spanish conquistadores destroyed Aztec pictographic texts during the conquest of Mexico, Puritans destroyed these Indian Bibles for a perceived superstitious and pagan content, which could not be scrutinized by the dominant population.[59] Perhaps some Puritans had begun to doubt that those odd configurations of letters Eliot and his assistants so labored over retained their Christian significance. And perhaps, in the minds of some Puritans, King Philip's War was the final proof that in fact they had not and that the words in the Indian Bible did not signify the same things to the Indians that, in English, they had signified to the Puritans.

While it is difficult to know what English combatants thought about the Bible, there is much to suggest that for New England Company officials translation had in fact been a failure. In December 1679, less

[57] Natalie Zemon Davis, *Society and Culture in Early Modern France* (Stanford, Calif.: Stanford University Press, 1975), 157.

[58] Examples of suppressed Bibles are mentioned in Gabriel Peignot, *Dictionnaire critique, littéraire et bibliographique des principaux livres condamnés au feu* . . . (Paris: Chez A. A. Renouard, 1806), 35–38. Puritan Bible burning, though evidently rare, did occur in the 1650s under the aegis of the antinomian Ranters. Gilbert Roulston, *Ranters Bible* (London: J.C., 1650). On book burning in general, see Leo Lowenthal, "Caliban's Legacy," *Cultural Critique* 8 (Winter 1987–88): 5–17.

[59] On destruction of indigenous writings in Mexico, see Serge Gruzinski, *The Conquest of Mexico: The Incorporation of Indian Societies into the Western World, Sixteenth–Eighteenth Centuries*, trans. Eileen Corrigan (Cambridge, England: Polity Press, 1993), 14–15 and passim.

than four years after the end of the war, they undertook to reform the Christianization process in New England. English-language instruction was to be central to their new project. "Wee fully concur," their representatives in the colonies explained, "with your advice as to [the Indians] learning the English Tongue . . . and have given our orders accordingly to Mr. Elyot and others that are their Teachers & Rulers that they endeavour respectively to effect the same."[60] In 1682 these same representatives reported to Robert Boyle, the natural philosopher and governor of the New England Company, that they had "begun to make some allowance to a . . . Mr. Daniel Gookin, who hath entred upon preaching to the Indians at Natick in the English tongue."[61] Gookin, a proponent of English-language evangelism, appeared to be prevailing in the very "praying town" Eliot founded thirty-one years before and the first such town to form a true Puritan church of saints.

Eliot, however, had not been prepared to abandon his translating activities. In 1681 he requested support from Boyle for a second printing of the Massachusett Bible to replace those destroyed in the war. "Until we have Bibles, we are not furnished to cary the Gospel unto ym for we have no means to cary religion thither, saving by the Scripture. This very argument . . . doth continually instigate my heart, to have the Bible printed."[62] Boyle resisted, forcing Eliot to call on Baxter, who in turn wrote Boyle with the following request: "I am desired by Mr. Eliot to solicit you for your consent to the printing of his 2d edition of the whole Bible: It seems they want not money: I hear you are against it. I intreate you to consider that this question is not whether it be most profitable to the present generation, but whether it shall ever be done [because of Eliot's age]."[63] Although by 1685 Eliot had generated adequate funds to support a second printing of the Massachusett Bible, King Philip's War, it would appear, had demonstrated to the financial supporters of Eliot's activities that their investment in Indian-language Bibles had barely paid off. Perhaps it also demonstrated to them that Massachusett was in fact a serious barrier to Christian learning.

Nothing is more indicative of changing assumptions about Massachusett than the growing sense among many observers that the language Indians spoke was incomplete; that Indians' reliance on rhetorical and gestural embellishment was indicative not of a pure heart but

[60] John W. Ford, ed., *Some Correspondence between the Governors and Treasurers of the New England Company in London and the Commmissioners of the United Colonies in America* (London: Spottiswoode, 1896), 59.

[61] Ibid., 68.

[62] Ibid., 66.

[63] N. H. Keeble and Geoffrey F. Nuttall, *Calendar of the Correspondence of Richard Baxter* (Oxford: Clarendon Press, 1991), vol. 2, 251.

of an inferior tongue. Thus the seventeenth-century English traveler John Josselyn could casually link two seemingly contradictory observations about Indian speakers: "Their learning is very little or none, Poets they are as may be ghessed by their formal speeches, sometimes an hour long, the last word of a line riming with the last word of the following line."[64] Indeed, Europeans were increasingly concluding that it was a lack of experience and, in turn, a failure to develop extended vocabularies that left American Indian speakers to resort to more intuitive means of communication. And, as described by one writer, this mode of communication acquired an ominous quality in the decades after King Philip's War. As Cotton Mather observed, "Our Eliot made a tender of the everlasting salvation to [King Philip]; but the monster entertained it with contempt and anger, and, after the Indian mode of joining *signs* with *words*, he took a button upon the coat of the reverend man, adding 'That he cared for his gospel, just as much as he cared for that button.'" In Mather's mind, simile and godlessness went together. King Philip's reply to Eliot's gesture was a sign of what was to come. "The world has heard what a terrible ruine soon came upon that monarch and upon all his people," he concluded.[65] Implied in Mather's statement was the possibility that King Philip's gesture represented some sort of distinct indigenous mode of communication.

Whatever Mather actually meant, there is little doubt that his was a generation without the millennial confidence that had made the Eliot Bible possible. Although a faction among the New England Company commissioners supported a third printing of the Bible, those favoring rapid "Anglicization" ultimately prevailed. In a letter drafted by Mather to be sent to company officials in England sometime before 1710, a group of commissioners made known their conclusion that "the best thing we can do for our Indians is to Anglicise them in all agreeable Instances; and in that of Language, as well as others. They can scarce retain their Language, without a Tincture of other Salvage Inclinations, which do but ill suit, either with the Honor, or with the design of Christianity." Mather even went so far as to conclude that this was the desire of many Indians, who themselves felt that "their Indian Tongue is a very penurious one . . . and the great things of our Holy Religion brought unto them in it, unavoidably arrive in Terms that are scarcely more intelligible to them than if they were entirely English." Mather supported his case with a quote from someone he referred to as "a discreet person whom we lately employd in a visitation of the Indian

---

[64] *John Josselyn, Colonial Traveler,* ed. Paul J. Lindholdt (Hanover, N.H.: University Press of New England, 1988), 97.

[65] Mather, *Magnalia Christi Americana,* 1:566.

Villages," who reported: "'There are many words of Mr. Elliott's forming which they never understood. This they say is a grief to them. Such
a knowledge in their Bibles, as our English ordinarily have in ours, they
seldom any of them have; and there seems to be as much difficulty to
bring them unto a competent knowledge of the Scriptures, as it would
be to get a sensible acquaintance with the English Tongue.' "[66] While
Mather and the other proponents of Anglicization may not have represented the opinion of all the New England Company commissioners or,
for that matter, of the governor himself, it is clear that in the end their
views shaped policy. While for a time the company continued to print
Indian-language textbooks, it did so partly to facilitate English-
language instruction. And by the late 1720s, the company had ceased
printing any Indian-language texts. English was emerging as the official
language of New England.[67]

Language, John Eliot had assumed, was no real barrier to Christianization. All souls could grasp and experience divine truth because all souls
were subjects of the same God. Words were merely the utterances that
harbored that truth, but they in no way determined its meaning. Any
sense that Indian speech lacked certain expressions or that the Indians
themselves lacked certain ideas could be explained as a failure of human communication, which was by nature imperfect and would remain
so until the unified kingdom of God reigned once again on earth. This
thinking rested on the fundamental belief that the confusion of tongues
was reparable and that its repair depended on the transcendence and
power of biblical truths. There was, in this millennialist doctrine, no
tolerance for human difference. While languages may give rise to nations, the universal and divine language that underlay all human
speech would ultimately render those national differences meaningless,
as all of humanity came together as one biblical commonwealth.
    The kind of utopian ambition that made this thinking meaningful in
the mid–seventeenth century had, by the latter part of the century,
come to be associated not so much with Christian renewal as with intol-
erance and confessional conflict. Indeed, the very notion that the confusion of tongues could be remedied would come to be seen as just
another expression of hubris, fanaticism, and spiritual arrogance. As
Anglo-American philosophers tired of the religious zealotry that had
resulted in almost two centuries of unending and bloody religious conflict, some of them began issuing devastating criticism of any doctrine

<hr />

[66] Samuel Sewall, "Letter Book of Samuel Sewall," *Collections of the Massachusetts Historical Society*, 6th ser., 1 (1886): 401–3.
    [67] Kellaway, *The New England Company*, 162–65.

that presupposed the possibility of universal human understanding. The rationale for perhaps the most influential such criticism was that no truth could be understood as innate, and that therefore the connection between language and understanding was not superficial but integral. What one knew, one knew because of the language one spoke. Hence, differences in the world's tongues, far from being mere impediments to global salvation, were instead coming to be understood as indications of profound difference in the nature and order of thought. Far from inviting the restoration of a universal language, the confusion of tongues therefore invited a permanent and irrefutable sense of humility.

CHAPTER IV

The Savage Word

IT IS RARE that an individual can be singled out for shaping an entire field of study. But that was the case with John Locke, whose *Essay Concerning Human Understanding* became the foundation for eighteenth-century Anglo-American language philosophy.[1] With that work, Locke gave new validity to the notion that words were pure convention, contrived and shaped by humans through the centuries, and differing through time and space not because of primordial events or moral failure but because of the uniqueness and diversity of human experience itself. As such, they were entirely arbitrary in their relation to reality. They were not symbols, bearing some intrinsic relation to that which they signified; nor were they signs designated by higher powers. Instead, the "tacit consent" of society established the connection between words and things. There was nothing innate that made words meaningful, and no act of dominance could permanently secure their meaning. It was for this reason, Locke wrote, that the emperor Augustus himself acknowledged "that he could not arbitrarily appoint, what idea any sound should be a sign of, in the mouths and common language of his subjects."[2] Language was at once the result of human

---

[1] One reason for this was that Leibniz's critique of Locke, *Nouveaux essais sur l'entendement*, did not appear in print until 1765. Locke's importance in this context is explored in Hans Aarsleff, "Introduction," and "Leibniz on Locke on Language," in *From Locke to Saussure: Essays on the Study of Language and Intellectual History* (Minneapolis: University of Minnesota Press, 1982), 3–83; and "Locke's Influence," in *The Cambridge Companion to Locke*, ed. Vere Chappell (Cambridge: Cambridge University Press, 1994), 252–89. On Locke's lasting importance as a revisionist logician and rhetorician, see Wilbur Samuel Howell, *Eighteenth-Century British Logic and Rhetoric* (Princeton, N.J.: Princeton University Press, 1971), 264–98, 489–502. Among the many eighteenth-century overtures to Locke the rhetorician, one of the more overt is Thomas Sheridan, *A Course of Lectures on Elocution* (1762; facsimile reprint, Menston England: Scolar Press, 1968), esp. v–xviii. The broader cultural history of the empiricist conception of language is explored in Michel Foucault, *The Order of Things: An Archaeology of the Human Sciences* (New York: Vintage Books, 1973). Also see Murray Cohen, *Sensible Words: Linguistic Practice in England, 1640–1785* (Baltimore: Johns Hopkins University Press, 1977); and Arno Borst, "The History of Languages in the Flux of European Thought," in his *Medieval Worlds: Barbarians, Heretics, and Artists in the Middle Ages*, trans. Eric Hansen (Chicago: University of Chicago Press, 1992), 14–33.

[2] John Locke, *An Essay Concerning Human Understanding*, ed. Peter H. Nidditch (Oxford: Oxford University Press, 1975), III, ii, 8.

agency and yet above individual will; humans created it, yet no individual could render it stable. No individual could establish the sort of immutable and perfect correlation between word and thing that defined an ideal or Edenic tongue. This Lockean doctrine raised the critical question that if words were socially constructed, could morality itself be regarded as a social construct? Further, if the connection between words and reality was entirely arbitrary, what accounted for the human capacity to communicate a range of emotions and feelings that seemed to transcend mere verbiage? Was it possible that such seemingly universal human sentiments were merely conventional? While these were perhaps the most fundamental and lasting problems Locke's argument raised, his position had another implication which proved far less controversial, and far more influential. It made possible a new, strictly rational explanation for the diversity of the world's tongues.

After Locke, Babel was no longer needed to explain the confusion of tongues. A uniform and universal human rationality, applied in different environments and at different times, produced words that reflected the distinct experiences of nations. What underlay this argument were the familiar notions that the human mind is a tabula rasa and that humans everywhere, by nature, possess reasoning capacities that allow them to form their thoughts into words, and to order their words into complete and distinct languages. Language was thus—much like writing, painting, or architecture—a material expression of human genius, as exercised over the centuries in a progressive, evolutionary fashion that revealed in its very form the historical movement of nations. As Locke's later interpreter, the chemist and political radical Joseph Priestley, explained, in the history of architecture, "structures have always been at first heavy, and inconvenient, then useful and ornamental, and lastly real propriety and magnificence have been lost in superfluous decorations . . . and language, being liable to the same influences, hath undergone the same changes."[3] As with any art, language had a history. It experienced periods of growth and improvement, as well as periods of decay and decline. Toward the end of the eighteenth century, the Philadelphia philologist and minister Nicholas Collin described this process succinctly when he wrote that "the languages of nations are fabrics raised from rudiments to various forms and magnitudes, far less by accidents, than by application of thought and speech to the various and growing circumstances of human societies."[4] In

---

[3] Joseph Priestley, *A Course of Lectures on the Theory of Language and Universal Grammar* (1762; facsimile reprint, London: Routledge/Thoemmes Press, 1993), 173.

[4] Nicholas Collin, "Philological View of Some Very Ancient Words in Several Languages," *Transactions of the American Philosophical Society* 4 (1799): 476.

charting the history of language changes, the philosopher thus charted the history of nations.

Locke wrote *An Essay Concerning Human Understanding* in part to further the sorts of educational reforms promoted by latitudinarian theologians and opponents of classical pedagogy. He argued that education ought to begin with experience, privileging the acquisition of factual knowledge over the acquisition of skills, particularly the classical methods of discourse and disputation. His philosophical justification for this assertion came from a vigorous rejection of the doctrine of innateness, or the view that certain ideas precede experience. For Locke, experience as the true source of knowledge was, rightly understood, the only valid foundation for education. In this latter light, the *Essay* was fully consistent with the revisionist educational thinking of Francis Bacon, Dury, Wilkins, and others, thinking that represented a lasting challenge to the classical notion that logic and rhetoric— thought and communication—were separate arts. If for these latter figures the artificiality of this dichotomy lay in its failure to recognize an original and universal tongue—one so perfect in its marriage of form and substance as to make rhetoric superfluous—for Locke it lay in a fundamentally flawed conception of the human intellect. And the central tenet of that flawed conception was that humans had the capacity to grasp the natural essences of things. For Locke this notion was fundamentally mistaken. It assumed that humans could achieve parity with divine understanding. Hence, instead of being rendered irrelevant by a perfect tongue, logic and rhetoric were better understood as unified under the rubric of "understanding," something that denoted not merely the passive reception and assimilation of preordained truths but the moral capacity to distinguish among the possible origins of ideas, to characterize those ideas accordingly, and to communicate those characterizations to others in an intelligible way.

Language, in this scheme, was no mere vessel for preexisting truths that could be given greater acuity and beauty through classical tropes and topoi—or through its own original perfection. It was instead the material of understanding. This meant that the ideas humans convey do not differ from the words that convey them; or, at least for Locke, such a distinction was meaningless and pernicious. It merely empowered those inclined toward formulaic and recondite patterns of thought—patterns generally (if incorrectly) associated with Scholasticism—by compelling people to turn their attention from the natural world, wherein divinity, truth, and beauty lay ready for all to experience, to the artificial world of verbal embellishment and preconceived topics, a world easily controlled by ideologues and potentates. If we are to "speak of things as they are," Locke wrote, "we must allow, that all the art of rhetoric . . . all the artificial and figurative application of words eloquence hath invented, are for nothing else but to insinuate wrong ideas, move the passions, and thereby mislead the judgment."[5]

Locke's search for an alternative rhetoric founded on experience and nature rather than convention and habit was inseparable from a more fundamental desire to establish an epistemological justification for religious tolerance. And that justification came from the claim that although Scripture represented God's Word, it did so in an inherently imperfect medium—the words of mortals. Because experience changed while words remained the same, meaning was, by definition, fluid. This explained how it was that different nations often had similar terms to denote unrelated objects. Such terms were borrowed without a firm sense of their original meaning, allowing an ever greater historical chasm between that original meaning and modern usage. Hence, because even "revealed truths, which are conveyed to us by books and languages, are liable to the common and natural obscurities and diffi-culties incident to words: methinks it would become us to be more careful and diligent in observing the former, and less magisterial, posi-tive, and imperious, in imposing our own sense and interpretations of the latter."[6] Locke was not seeking to cast doubt on the existence of universal truths but was striving to establish the incommensurability of human knowledge—a state of affairs caused by words. Truth exists, is known by God, and can be revealed to humanity. But even revelation will never be full, making perfect human understanding impossible. This meant that when humans analyzed nations other than their own, they could claim no position of absolute knowledge from which to judge such cultures; for any judgment would be marred and imperfect precisely because of the inherent instability of words. All of this amounted, for Locke, to a justification for Christian humility and a plea to the morally righteous to recognize the subordinate and sinful character of *all* humans, to grasp the universal limitations that made understanding human.[7]

[5] Locke, *An Essay Concerning Human Understanding*, III, x, 34. Also, Howell, *Eighteenth-Century British Logic and Rhetoric*, 489–502; and Barbara J. Shapiro, *Probability and Certainty in Seventeenth-Century England: A Study of the Relationships between Natural Science, Religion, History, Law, and Literature* (Princeton, N.J.: Princeton University Press, 1983), ch. 7, esp. 242–43.

[6] Locke, *An Essay Concerning Human Understanding*, III, ix, 23.

[7] My interpretation here relies heavily on John Dunn, *The Political Thought of John Locke: An Historical Account of the Argument of the 'Two Treatises of Government'* (Cambridge: Cam-bridge University Press, 1969), esp. chs. 3 and 4; and "The Claim to Freedom of Con-science: Freedom of Speech, Freedom of Thought, Freedom of Worship?" in *From Per-secution to Toleration: The Glorious Revolution and Religion in England*, ed. Ole Peter Gell,

As part of this broader attack against any absolutist or intolerant Christian doctrine, Locke rejected the possibility that humans had in their meager capacities the power to invent or discover a perfect and universal language. No one, in Locke's mind, "can pretend . . . the perfect reforming the languages of the world, no, not so much as that of his own country, without rendering himself ridiculous."[8] To think otherwise, in Locke's vision, was to think that humans had the potential to achieve perfect knowledge—an impossibility in a moral order secured by the ultimate and immutable superiority of divine knowledge. Locke's position on these matters very much echoed that of Eliot's doubters. Just as these Puritans had lost confidence in the transparency of speech, the translatability of Christian ideas, and the possibility for perfect communication across space, so Locke challenged the notion that anything like a perfect exchange of ideas could be achieved not only through space but also through time—particularly with respect to ideas as abstract as those associated with morality. Such ideas were simply too far removed from common experience or sensation to fully survive translation. It is therefore no wonder that "the terms of our law . . . will hardly find words that answer them in the Spanish or Italian, no scanty languages; much less, I think, could any one translate them into the Caribbee or Westoe tongues."[9] For this reason, "the greatest part of disputes were more about the signification of words, than a real difference in the conception of things."[10] What the inventor of a word meant when he coined a term was lost forever to posterity, being replaced by vague associations, passed through the generations by memorization and imitation, with the result that knowledge existed in a permanent state of opacity.

This notion became integral to a number of eighteenth-century inquiries into the possibility of a natural religion, one in which morality and truth were found not simply in Scripture but also in the natural and innate feelings of individuals. Those feelings, far from reflecting the gulf between divine morality and human character, instead represented the active expression of divine will. What made humans immoral, according to this doctrine, was their willingness to defy conscience—a willingness that eighteenth-century social critics increasingly associated with "civilization," or the refinement of culture. In a

Jonathan I. Israel, and Nicholas Tyacke (Oxford: Clarendon Press, 1991), 171–93. Also see Richard Ashcraft, "Faith and Knowledge in Locke's Philosophy," in *John Locke: Problems and Perspectives*, ed. John W. Yolton (Cambridge: Cambridge University Press, 1969), 194–223.

[8] Locke, *An Essay Concerning Human Understanding*, III, xi, 2.

[9] Ibid., III, v, 8. Also see II, xxii, 6.

[10] Ibid., III, ix, 16.

widely influential exploration of this ideal, the former French military officer and political and religious exile Louis-Lom d'Arce, Baron de Lahontan, constructed a dialogue between himself and a Huron called Adario, the latter offering reasoned challenges to seemingly syllogistic Scholastic logic. Throughout the discussion, published first in 1703 in England (where Lahontan spent his final years, in political exile), Adario challenges the notion that spiritual truths could be known through the Word. "If we take your word for it," Adario remarks, "every period of [the Bible] sprung from the mouth of the Great Spirit. But if the Great Spirit mean'd that his Words should be understood, why did he talk so confusedly, and cloath his Words with an ambiguous Sense?"[11] Why, Adario was asking, would universal truths, spoken by a perfect being, arouse so much confusion and discord? Why would the English have told him that their Bible was the same as the French, and yet their two religions differ as night does from day? For a nonliterate figure reared in nature, it made no sense to assume that universal truths could be transmitted in so fluid a medium as human speech. Indeed, very much like Locke, Adario was suggesting that the true source of murderous conflict among Christians was attributable to language, that limiting medium through which humans were doomed to convey their thoughts.

It is possible that Lahontan drew his inspiration directly from Locke, for he clearly shared Locke's hostility to spiritual arrogance. But similar views had been propagated in Lahontan's native France through the teachings of a group of Jansenist intellectuals who congregated around the Port-Royal abbey outside of Paris. While not completely uniform in their thinking, these dissenting Catholics promoted quasi-Calvinistic reform within the Catholic Church. But perhaps what unified them more than anything was their often rabid hostility to the Society of Jesus, its perceived moral depredations, its alleged hostility to a traditional secular social order, and, above all, its defense of the possibility of worldly salvation. Through the second half of the seventeenth century, the Port Royalists produced an almost unending stream of anti-Jesuit essays and pamphlets, many of which found ready readership in England. Their virulent hostility to the Jesuit order and its often rigid educational methods may explain why the Catholic Port Royalists—who included Antoine Arnauld, Pierre Nicole, and, most famously, Blaise Pascal—

---

[11] *Lahontan's New Voyages to North-America*, ed. Reuben Gold Thwaites (1703; Chicago: A. C. McClurg, 1905), vol. 2, 524. On the publishing history and reception of Lahontan's works, see Gilbert Chinard, "Introduction," in *Dialogues Curieux Entre L'Auteur Et Un Sauvage De Bon Sens* (Baltimore: The Johns Hopkins University Press, 1931). Also see Anthony Pagden's *European Encounters with the New World: From Renaissance to Romanticism* (New Haven, Conn.: Yale University Press, 1993), 120–40.

DIALOGUES

De Monſieur le

BARON DE LAHONTAN

Et d'un

SAUVAGE,

Dans l'AMERIQUE.

Contenant une deſcription exacte des mœurs
& des coutumes de ces Peuples Sauvages.

*Avec les Voyages du même en Portugal & en
Danemarc, dans leſquels on trouve des parti-
cularitez trés curieuſes, & qu'on n'avoit
point encore remarquées.*

Le tout enrichi de Cartes & de Figures.

A AMSTERDAM,

Chez la Veuve de BOETEMAN,

Et ſe vend

A Londres, chez DAVID MORTIER, Li-
braire dans le Strand, à l'Enſeigne d'Eraſme.
M. DCCIV.

Title page from the first French edition of Baron de Lahontan's
*Dialogues de Monsieur le Baron de Lahontan et d'un sauvage dans
L'Amerique* (London, 1704). Courtesy of the John Carter Brown
Library at Brown University.

shared with the Protestant educational reformers a desire to privilege experience over the rehearsed disputation of classical rhetoric and logic. For one of the tenets of the Port Royalists, following Pascal, was the notion that although reason was the way of the elect, it was also a capacity with inherent limits. As such, it was incapable of revealing the way to worldly salvation. This view represented an explicit rejection of much Jesuit doctrine and, as articulated by Pierre Nicole in his *Essais de morale,* apparently captured Locke's interest.[12] During his exile in France, from 1675 to 1679, Locke translated several of Nicole's essays, writings that very much speak to the call for humility present in Adario's voice but a call also integral to Locke's entire philosophical opus. If for Nicole the limits of human knowledge meant that men were best served by deferring to the Catholic Church hierarchy in matters religious and moral, for Locke they meant that although no individual could claim authoritative knowledge of Scripture, some, through rational exploration, could achieve higher levels of understanding.[13] In France, it is clear, such thinking did encourage a reassessment of the stability of language and the nature of the rhetorical arts.

Bernard Lamy, although not a member of the Port-Royal circle, shared the group's general interest in educational reform, particularly their desire to place experience at the core of learning. In pursuit of this ideal, he produced the widely used rhetoric *The Art of Speaking,* which in its popular English edition, first published in 1676, was wrongly attributed to the Port Royalists. In that work, Lamy explained— in terms not at all unlike those employed by Locke—that "custom is the master and sovereign arbiter of all languages. No man can dispute its empire, as being established by necessity, and confirmed by universal consent."[14] Language exists and is given meaning as a matter of

[12] The Jansenist-Jesuit antagonism is treated in Robin Briggs, "The Catholic Puritans: Jansenists and Rigorists in France," in *Puritans and Revolutionaries: Essays in Seventeenth-Century History Presented to Christopher Hill,* ed. Donald Pennington and Keith Thomas (Oxford: Clarendon Press, 1978), 333–54. Perez Zagorin also discusses the anti-Jesuit propaganda of Blaise Pascal and Antoine Arnauld in *Ways of Lying: Dissimulation, Persecution, and Conformity in Early Modern Europe* (Cambridge, Mass.: Harvard University Press, 1990), 154–55. On the seventeenth-century English reception of Port Royalist writings, see Ruth Clark, *Strangers and Sojourners at Port Royal; Being an Account of the Connections between the British Isles and the Jansenists of France and Holland* (Cambridge: Cambridge University Press, 1932), chs. 8 and 15. A more general treatment of English anti-Catholicism in the seventeenth century is John Miller, *Popery and Politics in England* (Cambridge: Cambridge University Press, 1973), esp. ch. 4.

[13] Locke's interest in Nicole and Jansenism is discussed in John Marshall, *John Locke: Resistance, Religion and Responsibility* (Cambridge: Cambridge University Press, 1994), 89–90, 131–38.

[14] Bernard Lamy, *The Art of Speaking: Written in French by Messieurs Du Port Royal,* 2d ed. (London: W. Taylor, 1708), 39. A detailed discussion of Lamy's contributions is found in

habit and consent. The passage of time, however, erodes this relationship, insinuating disparities between a term and its original intended meaning. And mortals, confined as they are within the historical limitations of their own tongues, will forever suffer an imperfect and incomplete understanding of Scripture and all that it may hold within it, including the key to salvation.[15]

The notion that human knowledge is inherently limited may bring to mind some sort of moral relativism. But there is little reason to think that Locke, or any of the figures who immediately influenced and shared his views, entertained what Isaiah Berlin has described as "a doctrine according to which the judgment of a man or a group, since it is the expression or statement of a taste, or emotional attitude or outlook, is simply what it is, with no objective correlate which determines its truth or falsehood."[16] Rather, Locke trusted in the existence of universal natural laws that transcended history and everywhere governed human actions. The problem humans faced was that these laws, because communicated in conventional terms, had grown obscure, suffering the same historical degradation experienced by all ideas communicated in speech. The movement of time, by allowing the original meaning of words to be lost, had thus distorted morality. "In order to rectify these defects," the Locke scholar John Dunn has written, "it is necessary to find some criterion for human morality which is outside history. Hence, the necessity for a law of nature."[17] There was no doubt that such a law existed. It was God's will. The problem that preoccupied eighteenth-century moral philosophers was identifying and defining such a law. As we shall see, this problem was behind much interest not only in Indians generally but also in Native American language. These languages were assumed to possess qualities that made them uniquely valuable for a wider inquiry into the foundation of a natural—and, by definition, moral—social order. As the tongues of allegedly unrefined nations possessing neither the intellectual nor technological innovations that rendered European tongues complex and abstract, they were assumed to be transparent tongues, affording glimpses of that fundamental and universal human nature that had been obscured over time by layers of social refinement and intellectual

Wilbur Samuel Howell, *Logic and Rhetoric in England, 1500–1700* (Princeton, N.J.: Princeton University Press, 1956), 378–82.

[15] An interesting discussion of late seventeenth-century French debates about translation is Michel de Certeau, "L'Idée de traducion de la bible au XVIIème siècle: Sacy et Simon," in *Recherches de Science Religieuse* 66:1 (1978): 73–91.

[16] Isaiah Berlin, *The Crooked Timber of Humanity: Chapters in the History of Ideas* (New York: Vintage Books, 1992), 80.

[17] Dunn, *The Political Thought of John Locke*, 97.

growth. To uncover that nature was also to reveal an alternative aesthetic, shaped by feelings and passion rather than convention and reason.

Imbedded in the notion that words were human inventions was the paradoxical possibility that those words could also limit and shape intellect. Indeed, this was one of Locke's central claims, and it was the basis for his calling for Christian humility. For much like Eliot's financial supporters, he not only doubted that translation could overcome the corrosive effects of history but also raised the possibility that history in fact yielded different ways of thinking. The reason was that the most abstract words arose with only an indirect relation to experience. Their primary origin, Locke argued, lay in the human tendency to apply reasoning faculties to the simplest words, in much the way that natural philosophers might begin analyses with whole numbers. This was the origin, for instance, of general taxa or classificatory terms—terms with no readily apparent foundation in sense experience. Humans invented such words only after applying their reasoning faculties to a confusing array of specific names, in a natural effort to simplify communications.[18] Most of Locke's argument for the growth of verbal abstractions depended on empirical examples or his own observations about human thought. But he pointed the way toward a historical explanation for this process, and this was something his eighteenth-century interpreters made much of. In doing so, they transformed language from an effect to a cause. They showed that beyond simply reflecting the historical gradations that separated nations, language could actually create those gradations. This meant, in effect, that it could create culture.

Perhaps the most important interpreter of Locke in this regard was the French philosopher and priest Étienne Bonnot de Condillac (1715–80), whose *Essai sur l'origine des connoissances humaines* (1746) was published in an English edition in 1756 with the advertisement "a supplement to Mr. Locke's Essay on the Human Understanding." Condillac explained the evolution of language in terms of a series of stages, corresponding to the evolution of mind. This linguistic telos begins with symbols, icons, or pantomimes, designed by humans to embody their ideas but requiring a very limited operation of the mind. Such symbols bore a literal relationship to the object they denoted. Because, Condillac suggested, humans had a natural tendency to make sounds when presented with simple representations of their ideas, especially when those representations suggested things embedded in human memory—things that excited the basest passions of fear and hunger,

---

[18] See, for instance, Locke, *An Essay Concerning Human Understanding*, III, iii.

for example—humans began to associate those symbols with sounds. Hence the birth of words. This is followed by a series of stages, including evocative song and poetic eloquence, whereby rude shouts are transformed into ever more precise and complex speech, ultimately secured through writing. But the   n speech that was abstract and therefore cou   as the result of a basic mental response to sense experi…ce. … ondillac, such verbal forms had their origin in a process Diderot termed "decomposition," an operation that allows humans to assign one sound to many similar objects. Only by decomposing those objects, by identifying and distinguishing their representative and peculiar qualities, did humans embellish their speech with descriptive terms and general categories or taxa.[19] Much like numbers, Condillac suggested, the earliest spoken words were thus symbols that afforded all kinds of intellectual operations that were otherwise not possible. The foundation for these operations was the natural human tendency to categorize and classify things. This tendency transformed language from a collection of merely evocative metaphoric terms, embellished by gesture, song, and poetry, into a collection of signs, governed by a set of grammatical rules, that convey ideas only distantly related to sensation.

Condillac made few connections between this process and the diversity of the world's tongues. He did, however, suggest that in addition to a moderate climate, unique historical circumstances are required for the improvement of language. Most important among them is the birth of great writers, figures able not only to have new thoughts but also to invent new words with which to express those thoughts. Such figures bring a flurry of intellectual activity to a given age, as other thinkers and writers struggle to comprehend their innovations: "It is with languages as with geometrical signs; they give a new insight into things, and dilate the mind in proportion as they are more perfect." The implications here are the very Lockean ones that mind is always subordinate to language and that those nations whose tongues are not improved will by definition be nations whose minds are not improved. People habituated to inferior tongues would suffer a sort of mental impairment and would be incapable of the knowing expression of complex thoughts, even upon learning Latin or other tongues equipped to express such thoughts. Conversely, a person of superior genius forced to operate within the parameters of an unrefined tongue would be unable to rise to the levels of genius known among speakers of his native tongue. Were such a person to join a nation of barbarians, "I apprehend that he may become a genius in regard to those people; but

[19] This is treated in Pagden, *European Encounters with the New World*, ch. 4.

we plainly see that it is impossible for him to equal some of the eminent writers of the age of Lewis XIV." No other conclusion could be reached but that "there can be no such thing as a superior genius, till the language of a nation has been considerably improved."[20]

Such thinking, it should be said, has been almost wholly dismissed by modern theorists. As the American linguist Edward Sapir wrote shortly after World War I, "When it comes to linguistic form, Plato walks with the Macedonian swineherd, Confucius with the head-hunting savage of Assam."[21] There is no correlation, that is, between perceived powers of intellect and the expressive capacities of a given language. What was to be a marginal idea in the twentieth century, however, was dominant in the eighteenth. For virtually all eighteenth-century language philosophy depended on Locke's basic premise: language is the material expression of mind, and mind has a uniform and progressive history. What differentiates people is thus nothing internal but instead something external; it is environment that either hinders or encourages the progress of nations. Extending this reasoning globally, "primitive peoples" could be regarded as living examples of civilized peoples' ancient ancestry. As the New York colonial administrator and physician Cadwallader Colden explained the idea early in the eighteenth century, "We are fond of searching into Remote Antiquity, to know the Manners of our earliest progenitors: if I be not mistaken, the Indians are living images of them."[22] Perhaps even more illustrative of this idea was the comment in 1750 by the French writer Charles Duclos that "those who live a hundred miles from the capital, are a century away from it in their modes of thinking and acting."[23] There was, in this vision, nothing of the post-Darwinian sense that history is about means rather than ends; that it has no ultimate object but rather is an infinite series of contingencies, built not on an overriding rational plan but on immediate circumstances. Instead, history is progressive, uniform, and to a large extent predictable. And language reflects this.

Condillac's hypothesis centered on the individual. It is the individual genius who ultimately improves a nation's language; likewise, it is the

[20] Étienne Bonnot de Condillac, *An Essay on the Origin of Human Knowledge: Being a Supplement to Mr. Locke's Essay on the Human Understanding*, trans. Thomas Nugent (1756; facsimile reprint, Gainesville, Fla.: Scholar's Facsimiles and Reprints, 1971), 288–90.

[21] Edward Sapir, *Language: An Introduction to the Study of Speech* (San Diego: Harcourt Brace, 1921), 219.

[22] Cadwallader Colden, *The History of the Five Indian Nations* (1727, 1747; reprint, Ithaca, N.Y.: Cornell University Press, Cornell Paperbacks, 1964), x.

[23] Quoted in Peter Gay, *The Enlightenment: The Science of Freedom* (New York: Alfred A. Knopf, 1969), 4.

individual speaker who bears the burden of an inferior tongue. This
conception underlay the popular Enlightenment tendency to understand variations in speech in terms of the stages of development and
deterioration among humans themselves: infancy, maturity, and the decline of old age. Hence, we see the frequent comparison of savage
speech with infant babble. In both, some argued, the origins of more
sophisticated language could be found. One author explained that like
children, capable of thinking only in terms of their most immediate
wants, "there may be tribes, who have no words to express time past, or
the time to come" and can only express the basest passions or "whatever they may feel internally." What else could "mere savages and children" express, if they "have very faint ideas of things that are not immediately pressing upon them"? It was the immediacy of their speech,
the apparent impulsive connection between sensation and utterance,
the paltriness of ideas, that distinguished the words of children and
"savages" from those of the civilized.[24]

Similar reasoning could be applied to others as well: the deaf, the
mentally impaired, and the insane. But in such cases, inferior speech
resulted not from any lack of words, but from a failure in understanding—a failure, that is, to interpret what would otherwise be familiar
words. It is one of the more paradoxical aspects of much Enlightenment language theory that language is at once the work of human
intellect and yet can exist, in certain situations, independently of that
intellect. Hence, the case in which speakers utter what they do not
understand. As Locke sought to demonstrate, the act of speaking a
cultivated tongue did not ensure full comprehension.

Locke and Condillac had assumed that what inspired humans to
fashion words was self-interest. Everywhere humans thought, they
thought in terms of satisfying wants, bettering their condition, and
avoiding pain. And they thought in an evolving fashion that allowed
them to move beyond the expression of carnal wants to the expression
of more remote desires. For Locke, this argument for the origin of
speech raised few serious moral concerns. He accepted that humans
were self-interested, but he also accepted the absolute and ultimate
sovereignty of God. This meant that although linguistic meaning was
socially constructed, there was a divine sanction that governed the interactions of men, and hence there was no possibility for any kind of
Hobbesian state of nature. While Condillac appears to have shared this
assumption, he did little to resolve the essential tension of Lockean
language philosophy: that insofar as a moral order depended on lan-

[24] Thomas Gunter Browne, *Hermes Unmasked* (1795; facsimile reprint, Menston, England: Scolar Press, 1969), 57. See also Cohen, *Sensible Words*, 125–26.

guage, it too was constructed. But even more serious, while Condillac did not reject the notion that usage depends on social consent, he nonetheless maintained that individuals of genius are the ultimate source of words. What this suggested was precisely what Locke sought to counter: the possibility that at some level morality itself could be reduced to the will of individual mortals. A far preferable situation, and one that Locke presupposed, was one in which some sort of natural law could be shown to dictate the character of thought and speech. With respect to the growth of language, this meant an explanation that relied entirely on natural processes not reducible in any way to individual power but instead entirely the consequence of a universal human character and the impersonal laws that governed that character. Such an explanation, in addition to liberating human consciousness from the whim of individuals, afforded the first possibility of a truly natural rhetoric based not on human invention but on natural law. By appealing to natural inclinations rather than preordained conventions of eloquence and argument, such a rhetoric promised to be both easier to learn and unbound by cultural difference. It also promised a way to candid speech, or speech that did not conceal the basic emotions and natural sentiments of speakers. Uncovering the parameters of such a rhetoric was the ambition of the young Scottish professor of logic and moral philosophy Adam Smith.[25]

In his efforts to justify this new rhetoric, Smith formulated what might be considered the first truly sociological explanation for the growth of language. Departing sharply from Locke, he presumed no divine presence to maintain a moral order.[26] Rather, he relied entirely on assumptions about human nature, the most important of which was that humans had a natural tendency to coalesce into larger and more inclusive social units. The novelty of Smith's position is at least partly attributable to his central concern. As a "practical moralist," engaged in teaching members of a commercial society how to function in a just and moral fashion, Smith sought to introduce his students to the new rhetoric, a mode of communication that, as we shall see, placed the highest value on candor and made the superficiality and insincerity of the marketplace both unnatural and undesirable.[27] Because it was "nat-

[25] On Smith the rhetorician, see Howell, *Eighteenth-Century British Logic and Rhetoric*, 536–76.

[26] John Dunn, "From Applied Theology to Social Analysis: The Break between John Locke and the Scottish Enlightenment," in *Wealth and Virtue: The Shaping of Political Economy in the Scottish Enlightenment*, ed. Istvan Hont and Michael Ignatieff (Cambridge: Cambridge University Press, 1983), esp. 131–34.

[27] Smith's moral philosophy is treated in Nicholas Phillipson's "Adam Smith as Civic Moralist," in Hont and Ignatieff, *Wealth and Virtue*, 179–202.

ural," Smith assumed he could establish the existence of such a rhetoric from empirical evidence. To do so, he formulated a natural history
of language. That history presupposed the universality of human nature and its predictable expression through time and, for this reason,
one of Smith's early biographers characterized it somewhat derisively as
"conjectural history."[28]

The broad parameters of Smith's natural history of language (which
appeared as "Considerations Concerning the First Formation of Languages," a short work initially published in 1761 and later appended to
editions of Smith's *Theory of Moral Sentiments*) differed little from those
of his predecessors. In a scenario used by Condillac as well, Smith asserted that all language begins after "two savages, who had never been
taught to speak, but had been bred up remote from the societies of
men, would naturally begin to form that language by which they would
endeavour to make their mutual wants intelligible to each other, by
uttering certain sounds, whenever they meant to denote certain objects."[29] Those objects would come to be known by the "particular"
names given them. Words derived from something other than carnal
impulses require greater powers of intellect and are therefore present
only in the tongues of more developed nations. In turn, the more
primitive a people, the fewer abstract terms they would possess.
"Though custom has rendered them familiar to us," numbers, for instance, "express, perhaps, the most subtle and refined abstractions
which the mind of man is capable of forming." Hence, we should not
be surprised to hear of "some savage nations, whose language was capable of expressing no more than the three first numeral distinctions."[30]
The question that led Smith away from earlier Lockean doctrine was,
How did such rudimentary forms evolve into languages with uniform
conjugations and declensions?

For Smith, the answer was not individual genius but the expansion of
social life: small, isolated groups could accommodate a diverse array of
terms—crude verbs—signifying different kinds of action. When natural
social attraction brought two nations together, however, those nations
had no choice but to combine their two tongues into a single, convo-
luted whole. As diverse groups strove to represent their diverse experiences in a single tongue, their vocabularies would expand to the point

[28] Dugald Stewart, "Account of the Life and Writings of Adam Smith, LL. D." in *Adam
Smith: Essays on Philosophical Subjects*, ed. W. P. D. Wightman, J. C. Bryce, and I. S. Ross
(Oxford: Clarendon Press, 1980), 293.

[29] Adam Smith, "Considerations Concerning the First Formation of Languages, and the
Different Genius of Original and Compounded Languages," in *Adam Smith: Lectures on
Rhetoric and Belles Lettres*, ed. J. C. Bryce (Oxford: Clarendon Press, 1983), 203.

[30] Ibid., 214.

of incomprehensibility. A natural process of accommodation and sim-
plification, however, produced a standard set of conjugations, applica-
ble to the diverse experiences of different peoples. The wider a people's social intercourse, that is, the more comprehensive would be their
vocabulary. Nature, however, ensured that this process did not impair
the utility of a given tongue. Hence, as nations grew, so their vocabularies grew more uniform and systematic while the rules governing the
use of those vocabularies grew more numerous and complex. "It may
be laid down for a maxim," Smith wrote, "that the more simple any
language is in its composition, the more complex it must be in its
declensions and conjugations; and, on the contrary, the more simple it
is in its declensions and conjugations, the more complex it must be in
its composition."[31] As disparate groups of people merged and folded
together for political and economic advantage, their languages became
less complex and idiosyncratic. Hence, just as a people's intellectual
development was reflected in the breadth of their vocabularies, so,
Smith was suggesting, was the scope of their social milieu reflected in
the simplicity and uniformity of their verb forms and declensions.

Writing near the time Smith published his "Considerations," Joseph
Priestley made much of this point. There was no doubt in his mind
that nations inclined to expand, whether through commerce or conquest, would be nations whose language would experience concurrent
expansion. Isolated nations, in contrast, would have little incentive to
embellish their tongues. Nothing better illustrated these two diverging
paths than the experience of the Greeks and the contrasting one of the
Hebrews: "The private life and policy of the Hebrews, living under an
absolute monarchy . . . the immediate design of which was to keep
them clear of all connection with neighbouring nations, was too uniform to afford them many opportunities or occasions of enlarging, or
embellishing their language." The Greeks, in contrast, "divided into a
great number of separate communities, perpetually vying with each
other in power, policy, commerce, and arts . . . where not only publick
consultations were held for the general utility of *Greece*, but poems, and
even histories, were recited in publick, could not fail giving particular
attention to their language."[32]

This correlation between social development and language change
was widely accepted in Smith's Scotland, even by authors who utterly
rejected some of his other premises. The most remarkable—and bizarre—such figure was the Scottish jurist and moral philosopher James
Burnett, Lord Monboddo, a reactionary social critic who despised the

---

[31] Ibid., 221–22.
[32] Priestley, *A Course of Lectures on the Theory of Language*, 169–71.

notion that language, or any part of culture, could be reduced to base, organic processes. For Monboddo, such an idea implied that a human moral order would be no different than an animal moral order: both were driven by crude impulses for self-preservation and reproduction. A far preferable alternative, Monboddo argued, was the Platonic notion that language was a latent human faculty that established a clear and immutable distinction between the animal and the human. "It is only civil society," however, "and the close intercourse of men with one another in that society, that bring forth this latent quality by giving him occasion to exercise it."[33] It is not the natural course of history, whereby humans, through rational choice and an immutable desire for happiness, expand and improve their tongues. Rather, it is social and political stability and the concurrent rise of a leisured, literary class that make refined language possible. In this regard Monboddo agreed with Condillac, although the two differed sharply on the matter of the absolute origin of language. On this point he also agreed with Samuel Johnson, who argued that "those who have much leisure to think, will always be enlarging the stock of ideas, and every increase of knowledge, whether real or fancied, will produce new words, or combinations of words."[34]

In his six-volume *Of the Origin and Progress of Language* (1773–92) Monboddo illustrated his claims with facts from contemporary ethnographic tracts, including material about the Huron, selectively drawn from the relations of the seventeenth-century Recollect missionary Gabriel Sagard. Monboddo's purpose was to demonstrate a correlation between crude speech and social fragmentation. The Huron, he asserted, lacked the critical institutions of civil society; they were a nation in which justice was secured not by judges and laws but by individual acts of vengeance. Such a nation, in Monboddo's scheme, would by definition speak an unrefined tongue. With no clear lines of social authority and no clear governmental presence, the Huron "languages can have no standard, or anything fixed and established in the use of them." It is therefore no wonder that "hardly any one village of the Hurons speaks the same language as another; nay two families of the same village do not speak exactly the same language."[35] What this re-

[33] James Burnett, Lord Monboddo, *Antient Metaphysics* (Edinburgh: Bell and Bradfute, 1799), vol. 6, 146.

[34] Samuel Johnson, *Selected Writings*, ed. Patrick Cruttwell (Harmondsworth, England: Penguin Books, 1968), 240. Johnson's linguistic theory is discussed in Alvin Kernan, *Samuel Johnson and the Impact of Print* (Princeton, N.J.: Princeton University Press, 1989), 187–93.

[35] James Burnett, Lord Monboddo, *Of the Origin and Progress of Language* (1773; facsimile reprint, Menston, England: Scolar Press, 1967), vol. 1, 327–28.

flected, in Monboddo's mind, were broader failures in Huron society that inhibited the emergence of a literary class, freed from baser pursuits to apply their imaginative abilities to language. The consequence was that instead of a far-reaching and uniform language, the Huron seemed to speak a mishmash of dialects and patois. The assumption that language change depended upon the actions of individuals served Monboddo's larger goal of establishing that culture has no basis in nature.

Unlike Monboddo, Smith never discussed the ethnological implications of his theory of language refinement, but his greatest work, *The Wealth of Nations* suggests ways in which that theory might have been related to cultural variation. The argument of that work rested in part on the so-called four-stage theory, a model of socioeconomic development in which societies pass through four discrete stages: hunting, pasturage, agriculture, and finally commerce.[36] For Smith, each succeeding stage corresponds to a greater division of labor. Hence, in the most advanced commercial society, the farmer would be "nothing but a farmer" and "the manufacturer, nothing but a manufacturer."[37] Because in such societies individuals depend on others to fulfill specific needs, the variety of social interactions is wide. At the other extreme, "among nations of hunters," however, "the lowest and rudest state of society, such as we find it among the native tribes of North America," there is no significant division of labor. "Every man is a warrior as well as a hunter," with the result that he has few social contacts.[38] Such small, clannish societies of hunters, whose vocabularies refer only to immediate corporeal wants or needs, could be expected to speak a language possessing a narrow vocabulary and little grammatical uniformity. Only in commercial societies—in which labor is specialized and commercial agents are forced to express complex relations and abstract references to the self and others—are there favorable conditions for linguistic refinement.

Similar reasoning explains why one of the final stages of linguistic development is the invention of pronouns and verb conjugations that refer to the self: "I"; "I am"; "I have." As Smith explained in his "Considerations," nothing is more abstract than *I*, "the objects of which it may be predicated, do not form any particular species of objects distinguished from all others." It joins "in its signification the seemingly opposite qualities of the most precise individuality, and the most exten-

[36] On the four-stage theory, see Ronald Meek, *Science and the Ignoble Savage* (Cambridge: Cambridge University Press, 1976).
[37] Adam Smith, *An Inquiry into the Nature and Causes of the Wealth of Nations* (Oxford: Oxford University Press, 1993), 13.
[38] Ibid., 393.

sive generalization."[39] It is the absolute abstraction of *I* that creates difficulties in explaining the first-person singular verb conjugations in general, but in particular the conjugation of the "to be" verb. "I am", for instance, "denotes not the existence of any particular event, but existence in general. It is, upon this account, the most abstract and metaphysical of all verbs; and, consequently, could by no means be a word of early invention."[40] As at once the most abstract and specific of pronouns, it is no wonder that *I* is likely to elude those with the most undeveloped minds—those "first formers of language." Hence, according to Smith, children tend to refer to themselves not by pronouns but by proper names. Lacking any sense of individuality, "a child, speaking of itself, says, *Billy walks, Billy sits,* instead of *I walk, I sit.*"[41] We might therefore conclude that the need for such pronouns existed only in mature societies. For, only in such societies are transactions based not on face-to-face exchanges of concrete, naturally occurring artifacts but on impersonal agreements concerning objects as abstract as money. That is, only in societies in which social and commercial relations depend almost entirely on a man's "word" is there an imperative to identify one's self in a way that is qualitatively different from a proper name. The latter is mere artifice. It is a designation that implies no deeper recognition of one's individuality and one's capacity to bear responsibility for one's own actions. The former, in contrast, suggests full recognition of individuality and personal accountability.

To suggest that self-recognition represented the highest achievements of mind was to suggest not simply that self-consciousness was a phenomenon present only among the most civilized nations; it was also to explain the apparent sincerity and emotional candor so often associated with indigenous speakers. Such speakers, so most theorists assumed, were unable to make ceremony merely ceremonious by distinguishing between a public persona and a private self. They lacked the powers of calculation and manipulation that allowed White orators to turn their speech into duplicitous, Machiavellian rhetoric. That is, they were unable to inspire in audiences emotions and sentiments they themselves did not feel. They were, so the reasoning went, much like the White child raised by Indians, who Noah Webster explained, was "always surprised to find a person saying one thing and meaning another."[42]

This same reasoning explains the frequent refrain among eigh-

---

[39] Smith, "Considerations," 219.

[40] Ibid., 221.

[41] Ibid., 219.

[42] Noah Webster, *A Collection of Essays and Fugitiv* [sic] *Writings on Moral, Historical, Political, and Literary Subjects* (Boston: I. Thomas, 1790), 235.

teenth-century literary critics that the poetic genius, the sheer sublimity, of the ancient poets could never be achieved by poets constrained to think and compose in modern tongues. How was it, the eighteenth-century rhetorician Thomas Gunter Browne asked, "that the oldest writers (such as Homer and Isaiah) were the happiest poets?" The answer was that they were "the youngest talkers—Their art of speech was in an earlier state than our's." And for this reason, "they seized the boldest metaphors.—Every noun, every verb, every adjective, every particle, is or may be used as a metaphor." It was for this same reason that "every child, or savage, may be called a poet—but we in the present times, and partly from ignorance, partly from affectation, have missed the true road to the imagination; and, instead of going boldly through the senses, we have attempted to go through the schools—A dirty, muddy labyrinth."[43]

The result of this schooling was that modern orators had lost the capacity for truly eloquent, emotive speech. Rational understanding and eloquence were inversely proportionate. As nations formulated particular words that corresponded to ever more abstract thoughts, so orators grew less eloquent. "What a Roman expressed by the single word, *amavissem*," Smith explained, "an Englishman is obliged to express by four different words, *I should have loved*."[44] The latter was "constantly confined by the prolixness, constraint, and monotony of modern languages."[45] For Smith, this "prolixness" represented nothing less than an impediment to the expression of sublime emotion. "It ties down many words to a particular situation," he explained, "though they might often be placed in another with much more beauty."[46] The very qualities that made a speaker eloquent, including the use of metaphor, and gesture, were also the qualities lost to the progress and development of human intellect. Modern nations, the Scottish historian and moral philosopher Adam Ferguson explained, demand "records or authorities, relating to any distant transactions" in order to administer to affairs of state and commerce.[47] Such modern factual knowledge was meant to instruct rather than move. We are thus left to conclude that "the language of early ages, is in one respect, simple and confined; in another, it is varied and free: it allows liberties, which, to the poet of

---

[43] Browne, *Hermes Unmasked*, 65–66. The problem is explored in W. Jackson Bate, *The Burden of the Past and the English Poet* (Cambridge, Mass.: Harvard University Press, 1970).

[44] Smith, "Considerations," 224.

[45] Ibid., 226.

[46] Ibid., 224.

[47] Adam Ferguson, *An Essay on the History of Civil Society*, ed. Fania Oz-Salzberger (Cambridge: Cambridge University Press, 1995), 168.

after times, are denied."[48] In addition to rendering language less poetic, the growth of mind left audiences more skeptical, less susceptible
to passionate persuasion. "Our superior good sense," David Hume wrote,
"should make our orators more cautious and reserved than the ancient,
in attempting to inflame the passions, or elevate the imagination of their
audience."[49] Audiences had simply grown too sophisticated not to be
skeptical. And one of the reasons, in the minds of many, was that in place
of natural eloquence, contemporary English-speaking orators spoke
empty speech lacking in true emotion or anything else, for that matter,
that revealed a speakers' sincerest feelings. As the historian Kenneth
Cmiel has put it, there was among eighteenth-century cultural critics "the
sense that *ethos* was giving way to *persona*, or, to use other terms, that
character was disappearing for role playing."[50] Contemporary orators, it
appeared, had become nothing more than puppets. Their attachment to
what they uttered was no more real or sincere than that of marionettes or
actors uttering the superficial and rehearsed lines of the theater. In
contrast, truly great orators, unburdened by the conventions of refined
speech, allowed nothing to intervene between themselves and their
truest sentiments. For this reason, they were able to rise above the rational cognition of their audience and appeal directly to its inner sense, a
sense, so it was increasingly believed, closer to true nature than a rational
faculty shrouded in the accumulated strata of convention and historical
refinement. Such was the kind of oration Europeans so often associated
with the native peoples of America.

Somehow, what Europeans had lost in eloquence, American Indians
seemed to have preserved. Writing in the first decade of the nineteenth century, the Indian agent and diplomat Amos Stoddard noted
that the Indians "speak from nature, and not from education. They
utter what their subject inspires, and never advert to approved models
as their standard." And it is this "language of nature [that] can alone
arrest attention, persuade, convince, and terrify; and such is the language of the Indians."[51] The same sentiment lay behind Noah Web-

---

[48] Ibid., 166.

[49] David Hume, *Essays: Moral, Political, and Literary*, ed. Eugene F. Miller (Indianapolis:
Liberty Classics, 1985), 104.

[50] Kenneth Cmiel, *Democratic Eloquence: The Fight over Popular Speech in Nineteenth-Century
America* (New York: William Morrow, 1990), 27. On the rise of a "new rhetoric," see
Howell, *Eighteenth-Century British Logic and Rhetoric*, esp. chs. 4 and 6; Adam Potkay, *The
Fate of Eloquence in the Age of Hume* (Ithaca, N.Y.: Cornell University Press, 1994); and Jay
Fliegelman, *Declaring Independence: Jefferson, Natural Language, and the Culture of Performance*
(Stanford, Calif.: Stanford University Press, 1993), esp. 28–35.

[51] Amos Stoddard, *Sketches, Historical, and Descriptive, of Louisiana* (Philadelphia: M.
Carey, 1812), 431–32.

ster's comparison of the languages of antiquity, the apocryphal verse of the third-century Scottish bard Ossian, and the speech of Native American orators: "When nations have but few words to express their ideas, they have recourse to figures, to significant tones, looks and gestures, to supply the defect. Hence, the figurative language of the Orientals of antiquity; hence the imagery of the Caledonian Bard [Ossian]; the bold metaphorical language of the American natives, and the expressive tones and gesticulations that attend their speaking."[52]

This Native American talent for eloquent speech, according to Thomas Jefferson, was indicative of the libertarian nature of Indian government. "The principles of [American Indian] society forbidding all compulsion," he explained, "they are to be led to duty and to enterprise by personal influence and persuasion. Hence eloquence in council, bravery and address in war, become the foundations of all consequence."[53] Jefferson's was not a unique interpretation. Expressing a similar view, one of his ideological opponents, the Connecticut Federalist Jedediah Morse, exclaimed, "What civilized nations enforce upon their subjects by compulsory measures, [Indians] effect by their eloquence."[54] Given the state of Indian society, in other words, it made sense to assume, as the Jesuit Father Le Jeune had of the Algonquians, that "all the authority of their chief is in his tongue's end; for he is powerful in so far as he is eloquent."[55] These remarks reverberate with echoes of a Ciceronian republican ideal in which eloquent public speech constituted the sinews of primitive nationhood.[56] In addition, however, the perceived eloquence of Indians was fully in accord with the principles of Lockean language philosophy. Instead of the opaque words of civil society, such peoples uttered transparent words derived not from calculation and politics but from sensation and emotion.

[52] Noah Webster, *Dissertations on the English Language, With Notes Historical and Critical* (Boston: I. Thomas, 1789), 66.

[53] Thomas Jefferson, *Notes on the State of Virginia*, ed. William Peden (New York: Norton, 1972), 62.

[54] Jedediah Morse, *The American Geography; or, A View of the Present Situation of the United States of America* . . . (Elizabethtown, N.J.: Shepard Kollock, 1789), 18. See also De Witt Clinton, "Address before the New York Historical Society on the Iroquois or Six Nations," in William W. Campbell, *The Life and Writings of De Witt Clinton* (New York: Baker and Scribner, 1849), 237–38.

[55] JR, 6:243. See also William Smith, *Some Account of the North American Indians; their Genius, Characters, Customs, and Dispositions, towards the French and English Nations* (London: R. Griffiths, 1754), 40; William Smith, *The History of the Province of New York, from the first Discovery to the Year M.DCC.XXXII* (London: T. Wilcox, 1757), 40; and Benjamin Franklin, "The Savages of North America," in *The Works of Benjamin Franklin*, ed. John Bigelow (New York: Putnam's, 1904), vol. 10, 386.

[56] Cicero, *De Inventione*, trans. H. M. Hubbell (Cambridge, Mass.: Harvard University Press, 1949), 7.

The apparent decline of poetic speech in civilized societies had to do with more than merely the refinement of intellect. Equally significant, in the minds of a number of theorists, was the introduction of writing. Over time, the latter made communication a wholly impersonal, logocentric act. For writing, much like speech, progressed through universal stages that corresponded to the growing capacity of nations for abstract thinking. As William Warburton, perhaps the best-known eighteenth-century historian of writing, explained, "All the barbarous nations upon earth, before the invention and introduction of letters, made use of hieroglyphics, or signs for things, to record their meaning." Consistent with their literal ways of thinking, primitive nations, that is, employed pictures, and later hieroglyphs, that represented their thoughts in a highly literal fashion. As thinking became more complex and abstract, and in turn defied ready representation, writing itself grew more abstract—so abstract, in fact, that it came to represent not things but sounds. There was, Warburton wrote, "a gradual and easy descent, from a picture to a letter."[57] The former, far from arbitrary, was akin to early shouts and screams insofar as it was elicited by immediate experience. The latter was comparable to the most refined speech, bearing only an arbitrary relationship to that which it represented. This evolution, critics concluded, furthered the dilution of a modern poetic voice. As the Dublin rhetorician Thomas Sheridan proclaimed in 1762, "Some of our greatest men have been trying to do that with the pen, which can only be performed by the tongue; to produce effects by the dead letter, which can never be produced but by the living voice."[58]

Beyond simply rendering language mundane, writing aggravated the confusions and misunderstandings perpetuated by the spoken word. By representing speech, writing did not so much provide a connection to posterity as encourage the false notion that such a connection was at all possible. This same criticism had been integral to Locke's views of the Bible. For him, the fact that God's Word was a written word did little to ensure the lasting stability of meaning. Indeed, it was difficult to imagine that meaning could be preserved through the centuries when even authors of one nationality used the same words to mean entirely different things. "This is so evident in the Greek Authors," Locke explained, "that he that shall peruse their writings will find, in almost every one of them, a distinct Language, though the same words."[59]

Lahontan, too, made much of this. Referring to the "infinity of lyes

---

[57] *The Works of the Right Reverend William Warburton* (London: T. Cadell and W. Davies, 1811), vol. 4, p. 131.

[58] Sheridan, *A Course of Lectures on Elocution*, xii.

[59] Locke, *An Essay Concerning Human Understanding*, III, ix, 22.

and fictions" present in Jesuit writing about his own country, Adario observed that "if we see with our eyes that lies are in print, and that things are not represented in paper as they really are; how can you press me to believe the sincerity of your Bible that was writ so many ages ago, and translated out of several languages by ignorant men that could not reach the just sense, or by lyars who have alter'd, interpreted, or pared the words you now read?"[60] Not only was the written word inherently unstable; it also caused familial catastrophe and fostered dissimulation, fakery, and other acts of manipulation. "One bit of paper," Adario reminds his audience, "is enough to ruin a whole family. With a slip of a letter a woman betrays her husband, . . . a mother sells her daughter, and a forger of writing cheats whom he pleases." Far preferable were the ways of Adario and his brethren: "We can do all our business . . . by the help of our hieroglyphics. You know very well that the characters which we draw upon the peel'd trees in our passages, comprehend all the particulars of a hunting or warlike expedition, and that all who see these marks know what they signifie."[61] Adario was suggesting that these symbols, unlike phonetic signs, were transparent; their meaning could never be doubted or manipulated.

It was perhaps the pessimistic assessment of the future of poetry, eloquence, and human creativity more generally that drove Lord Monboddo, and the similarly inclined Jean-Jacques Rousseau, to challenge the Lockean explanation for the origins of language. These figures regarded language less as the result of innovation than of inspiration, arising not out of the rational pursuit of basic needs but from pure emotion. For, Rousseau observed, "it is neither hunger nor thirst but love, hatred, pity, anger, which drew from [people] their first words."[62]

Rousseau's interest in language began with another of the paradoxes implicit in Lockean language philosophy, namely, How could language be a social construct if societies depended on language for their very existence? How could a social construct be a constituent element of society itself? How, that is, could language precede society? This paradox was implicit in all Lockean explanations for the evolution of language, and it was one that Rousseau first dealt with in his *Discourse on the Origins of Inequality*, which initially appeared in 1755. In that essay, Rousseau set out to show that what most philosophers regarded as *natural* laws represented a posteriori assertions. To regard modern, polite society as the fulfillment of natural laws was, in Rousseau's view, to give

---

[60] Thwaites, *Lahontan's New Voyages to North-America*, vol. 2, p. 523.

[61] Ibid., pp. 589–90.

[62] *On the Origin of Language: Jean-Jacques Rousseau; Two Essays: Jean-Jacques Rousseau and Johann Gottfried Herder*, trans. John H. Moran and Alexander Gode (Chicago: University of Chicago Press, 1966).

undeserved legitimacy to a world rife with moral contradictions and, by definition, bearing no relation to any natural state. It is only in a primitive state, a period of human history prior to any sort of calculation or ambition aimed at raising men out of nature, that the laws of nature could be observed. For ultimately what humans willed was not the unfolding of their nature but the countering of it. For Rousseau, in other words, historical development could not be reduced to natural laws. This point was premised on a notion Monboddo may in fact have borrowed from him: language is a latent faculty that humans cultivate as societies grow more elaborate and diverse. Any imperfections in understanding were not, therefore, attributable to universal and natural historical processes and their deleterious effects on language but had to be understood as purely human failings. This was a sharp and deliberate rebuke to the pessimistic Lockean notion that the diversity of tongues was largely natural and inevitable.[63]

By arguing that society preceded language, Rousseau was seeking to prove that man in a natural state was not a speaker but a listener, a silent, self-sufficient being who acted in the best interest not of any artificial division among people—class, nation, race—but in the interest of all humanity. The rational processes of forming analogies, classifying, and decomposing words that Condillac posited, for Rousseau, were far too complex and abstract to be seen as operations brought about simply by some response to bodily needs. In Rousseau's view, humanity would have vanished from the face of the earth had it focused its very limited natural faculties on the formation of abstractions—and, indeed, animals needed no such abstract operations of mind to satiate basic wants and needs. Any natural law, for Rousseau, would therefore have to be founded not on presumptions about the universal operations of a tedious rational capacity but on clear evidence that in a natural state humans are fundamentally moral beings. For Rousseau, nothing about morality, therefore, could be regarded as a construct. Above all, its terms cannot be relegated to mortal language. Morality is natural and inherent, and all that is immoral, including human inequality, can be attributed to failures in the application of uniquely human faculties. Among apes, there is no inequality—other than that between male and female, which the notoriously sexist Rousseau took fully for granted—and so among man in nature, there would be no inequality. The fundamental reason is that primitive humans

[63] On Rousseau's relation to Monboddo, see Arthur O. Lovejoy, "Rousseau and Monboddo," in *Essays in the History of Ideas* (Baltimore: Johns Hopkins University Press, 1948), 38–61; and Robert Wokler, "Apes and Races in the Scottish Enlightenment: Monboddo and Kames on the Nature of Man," in *Philosophy and Science in the Scottish Enlightenment*, ed. Peter Jones (Edinburgh: John Donald Publishers, 1988), 147–48.

have primitive ideas. Man in nature simply lacked the very concepts that permitted the scheming and calculation; the power mongering and avarice; the oppression and manipulation that fostered artificial distinctions among humans. Hence, while Rousseau rejected any "natural" explanation for the origin of language, he very much accepted the Lockean view that language was historical and language change was the result of historical progress—something which, for Rousseau, merely obscured human nature beneath layers of controlling convention.

As he explained in his "Essay on the Origin of Languages Which Treats of Melody and Musical Imitation," published posthumously in 1781, "To the degree that needs multiply, that affairs become complicated, that light is shed, language . . . becomes more regular and less passionate. It substitutes ideas for feelings. It no longer speaks to the heart but to reason. . . . Accent diminishes, articulation increases. Language becomes more exact and clearer, but more prolix, duller and colder."[64] Eloquence, that is, disappears. In contemporary society, humans act not according to their passions but according to the mandates of unnatural and coercive institutions. They are excited not by eloquence but by "arms and cash." As societies became more complex, as human relations became more diverse, as sensation and speech grew more and more estranged, as politics shifted from the art of persuasion to the art of coercion, so did speech become pure affect. Indeed, Rousseau went so far as to conclude that the tongues of modern nations "are made for murmuring on couches," not for communicating with the *people*. Such tongues served conspirators and liars by making words pure convention, entirely detached from natural feeling, and ideally fit for calculation and corruption. In the end, it would be "impossible for a people to remain free" while speaking the polite tongues of Europe.[65] For Rousseau, as Jean Starobinski has put it, "the history of language begins in silence and ends in politics."[66]

The notion that language was socially constructed, as we have seen, was the cause of considerable debate in the eighteenth century. But the related notion that language was historical, and that its history corresponded to the progressive history of mind, was accepted by philosophers as an almost unwavering article of faith. Even Rousseau, who dismissed any organic explanation for the evolution of speech, accepted the notion that the increasing complexity and convolution of

[64] *On the Origin of Language*, 15–16.

[65] Ibid., 72–73.

[66] Jean Starobinski, *Jean-Jacques Rousseau: Transparency and Obstruction*, trans. Arthur Goldhammer (Chicago: University of Chicago Press, 1988), 310.

language was concurrent with the unnatural and pernicious refinement of societies. In this latter regard, too, his disagreement with Locke was not total. For although the two men understood the growth of language in sharply differing ways, they shared the belief that language was an (opaque) medium. To think otherwise—as Eliot did—was for Locke merely to foster religious persecution and, for Rousseau, to bring the dissipation of natural human feelings of love, compassion, and sympathy. For both men, history ultimately made the world's languages impediments to the dissemination of truth. It had rendered the meaning of words eternally imprecise and uncertain; it had introduced a barrier between nations different from that left by the punitive Babel only in its severity. For differences in language not only inhibited the free exchange of ideas but also indicated more fundamental differences in the very faculties that afforded understanding. In the end, the Lockean conception of language provided a philosophical rationale for the seeming futility of translation.

But it also changed the focus of language study from the pursuit of a perfect or universal language to the study of words, or etymology. What in late medieval and early Renaissance language philosophy had provided genealogies of things had come to provide genealogies of thought. By the latter half of the eighteenth century, natural historians had come to regard words as the most reliable artifact for tracing the prehistory of nations. And they engaged in a massive, worldwide project to assemble the world's tongues into a single genealogical map of all peoples. For if words were passed through the generations, then presumably beneath the layers of obfuscation and distortion one could find remnants of earlier usages or, more properly, earlier ages. It was this assumption that compelled the first generation of American antiquaries to undertake the ambitious collection and analysis of America's indigenous tongues.

CHAPTER V

Science of the Vanished

ON FEBRUARY 10, 1786, the American Revolutionary War hero and citizen of France, the Marquis de Lafayette, sent George Washington a list of words along with a request that Washington add corresponding American-Indian words. Lafayette explained that the American words were to be added to others already collected by the German natural historian Peter Pallas and his patron, the empress Catherine the Great of Russia. Impelled to aid the empress more out of diplomatic expediency than any real interest in her project, Lafayette was somewhat embarrassed about asking so grand a figure as George Washington for such a trifling favor. "I beg your pardon, my dear General," he wrote, "for the trouble I give you, but [I] have been so particularly applied to, that I cannot dispense with paying great attention to the business."[1]

Without hesitation, Washington called on two government agents—General Richard Butler, superintendent of Indian affairs in the Ohio country, and Thomas Hutchins, a government geographer working in that region—to supply words for the empress's vocabulary. He explained to Butler that with an American contribution, Catherine's project would "throw light upon the original history of this country and . . . forward researches into the probable connection and communication between the northern parts of America and those of Asia."[2] Beyond this, Washington believed that philosophical proof of the shared lineage of humankind would encourage harmony among nations. By demonstrating "the affinity of tongues" the world over, the empress was promoting "the affinity of nations." She was showing that human difference was merely superficial; that all nations ultimately are of the same origin and are, at some fundamental level, subject to the same set of natural laws. Washington even went so far as to suggest that knowledge of an underlying, original parent language could provide grounds for

---

[1] *The Letters of Lafayette to Washington, 1777–1779*, ed. Louis Gottschalk (Philadelphia: American Philosophical Society, 1976), 311. Lafayette sent the same request to Franklin. See Franklin to Lafayette, April 17, 1787 in *The Writings of Benjamin Franklin*, ed. Albert Henry Smyth (New York: Macmillan, 1906), vol. 9, 569–71.

[2] Washington to Richard Butler, January 10, 1788, in *The Writings of George Washington*, ed. John C. Fitzpatrick (Washington, D.C.: U.S. Government Printing Office, 1931–44), vol. 29, 369. Also, Washington to Hutchins, August 20, 1786, 28:525; Washington to Butler, November 27, 1786, 29:88–89.

a new universal culture. If all people could simply recognize their shared debt to an original tongue, the "assimilation of manners and interests" was not far off. For, if at some level human speech was universal, then it stood to reason that cultural diversity was ultimately anomalous. And a worldwide recognition of this fact "should one day remove many of the causes of hostility from amongst mankind."[3]

Washington was expressing what was for his generation of Americans the primary justification for studying American Indian language: it would permit philosophers to pare away layers of cultural diversity brought by the vagaries of time and to glimpse the ancient past of a peoples with no written record and few surviving antiquities. More than manners, morals, or religion, the analysis of language, this generation of learned Americans assumed, afforded the greatest insight into the ancient American past. In contrast to Locke, however, Washington and his peers seem to have retained much faith in the latitudinarian doctrine that a philosophical or perfect language would bring an end to moral conflict. If, however, for seventeenth-century latitudinarians a universal language was the way to Christian harmony, for the apostles of the American Enlightenment it promised to unify humanity by revealing the singular truth that human creation was unified. For these Americans, words were the stuff of a historical calculus—discreet, easily represented, orderly facts that revealed collective human experience.[4] They were also disappearing.

Of the twenty-nine known Eastern Algonquian languages and dialects, for example, eleven would become extinct by the middle of the nineteenth century, and others would continue to be spoken by only a small handful of elders.[5] The trend was readily apparent to late eighteenth- and early nineteenth-century Euro-American observers, observers who often erroneously assumed a correspondence between the disappearance of a language and the disappearance of a people. This tendency no doubt reflected the more general habit among American writers of mistaking displacement for disappearance. While it is true that language death can be the result of the death of a population, socioeconomic choice and cultural change seem to be far more prevalent causes. Furthermore, because language is not defined by absolute

[3] Washington to Lafayette, January 10, 1788, *Writings of George Washington*, 29:375.

[4] John C. Greene, *American Science in the Age of Jefferson* (Ames: Iowa State University Press, 1984), ch. 14. On other kinds of ethnological activity, see Greene, chapters 12–13, and Clark Wissler, "The American Indian and the American Philosophical Society," *Proceedings of the American Philosophical Society* 86:1 (September 1942): 189–204.

[5] Ives Goddard, "Eastern Algonquian Languages," in *Handbook of North American Indians, Vol. 15: The Northeast*, ed. Bruce Trigger (Washington, D.C.: Smithsonian Institution, 1978), 71.

evolution but is fluid, infinitely adaptable, and in constant flux, the notion that language change and language death were purely post-colonial phenomena seems dubious. It is more probable that the movement of Indian kin groups and refugees before and during the colonial era meant a similar movement of the loci of indigenous languages.[6]

But perhaps reflecting the triumphal feelings that pervaded post-Revolutionary Euro-American culture, there was little sense that Native American nations could possibly survive the expansion of the American Republic. Hence, Thomas Jefferson wrote, "It is to be lamented then, very much to be lamented, that we have suffered so many of the Indian tribes already to extinguish, without our having previously collected and deposited in the records of literature, the general rudiments at least of the languages they spoke." Had someone collected word lists or vocabularies "of all the languages spoken in North and South America, . . . it would furnish opportunities to those skilled in the languages of the old world to compare them with these, now, or at a future time, and hence to construct the best evidence of the derivation of this part of the human race."[7] And it was White Americans' awareness that the opportunity to establish such connections was waning that gave their linguistic activities a sense of urgency.

Historians have associated this urgent quest to preserve disappearing cultural fragments with a Romantic compassion that was more literary than literal. Far from an impulse to relieve suffering, it constituted a quest for sentimental or emotional experience.[8] It would be wrong to suggest that it was this quest alone that inspired Indian language study in the age of Washington and Jefferson, but there was very clearly a sense that something more than mere scientific knowledge was to be gained from understanding the Indian past—a sense, it would appear,

[6] The experiences of Indians during and after the Revolutionary War are explored in James H. Merrell, "Declarations of Independence: Indian-White Relations in the New Nation," in *The American Revolution: Its Character and Limits*, ed. Jack P. Greene (New York: New York University Press, 1987), 197–223. Also see Colin G. Calloway, *The American Revolution in Indian Country: Crisis and Diversity in Native American Communities* (Cambridge: Cambridge University Press, 1995). On language death, see the essays in R. H. Robins and Eugenius M. Uhlenbeck, eds., *Endangered Languages* (Oxford: Berg Publishers, 1991); and Nancy C. Dorian, *Language Death: The Life Cycle of a Scottish Gaelic Dialect* (Philadelphia: University of Pennsylvania Press, 1981).

[7] Thomas Jefferson, *Notes on the State of Virginia*, ed. William Peden (New York: Norton, 1972), 101.

[8] On the emergence of this variant of Enlightenment sociability, see Norman S. Fiering, "Irresistible Compassion: An Aspect of Eighteenth-Century Sympathy and Humanitarianism," *Journal of the History of Ideas* 37:2 (April–June 1976): 195–218. Also see Karen Halttunen, "Humanitarianism and the Pornography of Pain in Anglo-American Culture," *American Historical Review* 100:2 (April 1995): 303–34; and Keith Thomas, *Man and the Natural World: A History of the Modern Sensibility* (New York: Pantheon Books, 1983), ch. 4.

that foreshadowed Romantic interest in ruined and lost cultures. Americans and Europeans were everywhere reaching into other, allegedly simpler worlds to establish the sources of national identity.[9] And remnants of those worlds seemed to be preserved in language. For, the latter is, wrote the philologist Johann David Michaelis, "a kind of archives, where the discoveries of men are safe from any accidents, archives which are proof against fire, and which cannot be destroyed but with the total ruin of the people."[10]

We can see a similar sentiment expressed by the Philadelphia minister and philologist Nicholas Collin, who noted in a 1799 article that "languages are widely scattered and jumbled fragments of a mirror, which when skillfully joined and polished will present instructive pictures of men and things in *pristine times*."[11] It was in part this desire to recover "pristine times" that inspired European philologists to publish dozens of vocabularies, grammars, and comparative philological studies of lost and dying languages in the late eighteenth and early nineteenth centuries.[12]

A typical example of this was *An Analysis of the Gaelic Language* (1778), written by William Shaw, a friend of Samuel Johnson's, best known for challenging the authenticity of James Macpherson's "Ossian" poems. The book attempted to resurrect Gaelic and provide a tool to more effectively introduce Protestantism to Gaelic speakers. Beyond this practical aim, it presented a withering critique of those unwilling to defend and preserve dying languages. Such people were,

[9] Harry Liebersohn, "Discovering Indigenous Nobility: Tocqueville, Chamisso, and Romantic Travel Writing," *American Historical Review* 99:3 (June 1994), esp. 762–63. On the "rage for ruins," see Rose Macaulay, *Pleasure of Ruins*, 2d ed. (New York: Walker and Co., 1966); and Larzar Ziff, *Writing in the New Nation: Prose, Print, and Politics in the Early United States* (New Haven, Conn.: Yale University Press, 1991), esp. ch. 3.

[10] Johann David Michaelis, *A Dissertation on the Influence of Opinions on Language and of Language on Opinions* . . . (1759; reprint, New York: AMS Press, 1973), 13. Another discussion of the European appropriation of the Native-American past in America is Anthony Pagden, "From Noble Savages to Savage Nobles: The Criollo Uses of the Amerindian Past," in his *Spanish Imperialism and the Political Imagination: Studies in European and Spanish-American Social and Political Theory 1513–1830* (New Haven, Conn.: Yale University Press, 1990), 91–116. Also see the essays in Eric Hobsbawm and Terence Ranger, eds., *The Invention of Tradition* (Cambridge: Cambridge University Press, 1983).

[11] Nicholas Collin, "Philological View of Some Very Ancient Words in Several Languages," *Transactions of the American Philosophical Society* 4 (1799): 508.

[12] The connection between the new humanitrianism and the study of language has, to my knowledge, received no sustained treatment. For a discussion of the rise of comparative philology, see Maurice Olender, *The Languages of Paradise: Race, Religion, and Philology in the Nineteenth Century*, trans. Arthur Goldhammer (Cambridge, Mass.: Harvard University Press, 1992), ch. 1 and passim. Also see Benedict Anderson, *Imagined Communities: Reflections on the Origin and Spread of Nationalism*, rev. ed. (London: Verso, 1991), ch. 5.

from Shaw's perspective, encouraging the disappearance of sympathy and compassion. The relics of conquered nations, Shaw explained, fill the mind with "the ardent enthusiasm of inquiry, and a multitude of sorrowful thoughts on the instability of the highest temporal grandeur, which, attended by pleasing melancholy, leaves the mind calmly pensive, and gently perplexed." The sublime encounter with the ruins of ancient Rome, Carthage, or Athens may inspire the intellect, but "when I look back into the former times of Gaël, . . . finding it so much involved in obscurity, or suppressed and obliterated by the policy of a neighbouring monarch, I could sit down and weep over its fall, execrating the policy of usurping invaders, ever destructive of letters, humanity, and its rights." To bear witness to dying and dominated cultures, Shaw was suggesting, was to experience the range and profundity of human emotion lacking in the ordinary lives of men. It was to feel sorrow and compassion, pity and disgrace, all of which inspired a noble desire to recover and preserve what one could of these nations, lest the compassion they elicited be lost forever.[13]

A similar desire to excite natural human compassion lay behind the Orientalist vogue of the late eighteenth and early nineteenth centuries. This quest to recapture the glories of the ancient Near East, so often associated with the Napoleonic conquest of Egypt, in fact began some decades before. Pursuing better understanding of Hindu law, the English jurist and colonial official Sir William Jones made an earth-shattering discovery: Sanskrit, Latin, and Greek were of the same Indo-European linguistic family, and all three were represented in poetry. The implications of this discovery for European conceptions of culture were staggering: after Jones, philosophers could no longer assume that ancient and extinct languages, such as Sanskrit, were necessarily inferior in structure and expressive power to the refined tongues of Europe. No longer could it be so readily assumed that historical progress was the key to linguistic improvement or that the most refined tongues were occidental. For what Jones showed was that Greek and Latin did not evolve in distinct historical trajectories—corresponding to the lives of the Greek and Roman nations—but shared their lineage with languages of the peoples of the Orient. Nothing less was at stake here than the centrality of Europe in the Western map of the world.[14]

---

[13] William Shaw, *An Analysis of the Gaelic Language* (1778; facsimile reprint, Menston, England: Scolar Press, 1972), xi.

[14] See O. P. Kejariwal's interesting discussion, "William Jones: The Copernicus of History," in *Objects of Enquiry: The Life, Contributions, and Influences of Sir William Jones (1746–1794)*, ed. Garland Cannon and Kevin R. Brine (New York: New York University Press, 1995), 102–15. On the orientalist vogue, see Edward Said, *Orientalism* (New York: Vintage Books, 1978), 73–92, and passim; and Thomas R. Trautmann, *Aryans and British India* (Berkeley: University of California Press, 1997), esp. ch. 3.

In a seminal paper delivered in 1786 at a meeting of the Asiatic Society of Bengal, Jones used careful etymological analysis to demonstrate that "the Sanskrit language, whatever be its antiquity, is of a wonderful structure; more perfect than the *Greek*, more copious than the *Latin*, and more exquisitely refined than either, yet bearing to both of them a stronger affinity . . . than could possibly have been produced by accident; so strong indeed, that no philologer could examine them all three, without believing them to have sprung from some common source, which, perhaps, no longer exists."[15] The significance of this statement cannot be overestimated. It rested on an empirical demonstration of the cultural links between East and West—no minor achievement in an age consumed with establishing the shared descent of humankind. But of perhaps even greater significance, Jones offered an empirical challenge to the notion that living European tongues were exceptional and superior.

A related willingness to reject the primacy of European tongues inspired the Reverend Nicholas Collin's proclamation that even the languages of "illiterate modern nations merit great attention." For, he wrote, "some scalping heroes of America may be kinsmen of Alexander, Caesar, and the proudest conquerors of Europe." Collin even went so far as to proclaim that "the classical languages are edifices, whose groundworks were laid in a wilderness, on materials brought from diverse quaries of barbarous tongues; the roots of many classic words may therefore grow in Tartary and Æthiopia." Sharing the growing doubt about the educational value of Latin and Greek—doubt given factual validity by Jones's work—Collin continued: "The classics therefore do not merit the excessive praise for antiquity, so generally bestowed on them but they are very valuable for their ample writings, by which their affinities with each other, and with many other languages can be known."[16]

Jones stimulated a stampede of philologists, seeking to recover and preserve prose and poetry of the ancient languages of the Near East. But for reasons still not fully explained, he was only slowly recognized in the Anglo-American world for his language studies.[17] The attention

[15] William Jones, "The Third Anniversary Discourse: On the Hindu's," *Asiatic Researches* 1 (1799): 422–23.

[16] Collin, "Philological View," 478–79. On the debate over the classics in American education, see Benjamin Rush's essay "An Enquiry into the Utility of a Knowledge of the Latin and Greek Languages . . . ," *American Museum* 5 (1789): 525–35; and Noah Webster, *A Collection of Essays and Fugitiv* [sic] *Writings on Moral Historical, Political, and Literary Subjects* . . . (Boston: I. Thomas, 1790), 4–7. Also see Linda K. Kerber, *Federalists in Dissent: Imagery and Ideology in Jeffersonian America* (Ithaca, N.Y.: Cornell University Press, 1970), 111–18; and Carl Richard, *The Founders and the Classics* (Cambridge, Mass.: Harvard University Press, 1994), ch. 7.

[17] Jones's influence on the philological community is treated in Hans Aarsleff, *The*

he received from Americans was usually for his general ability to balance a professional life with an extraordinary life of learning. It was for this reason that the Philadelphia editor and man of letters Charles Brockton Brown referred to that "learned and accomplished lawyer" as "one of the brightest ornaments of the age."[18]

There were, however, those who recognized and celebrated more specifically Jones's literary achievements. Writing in July of 1819 to commend the Philadelphia linguist Peter Stephen Du Ponceau for his studies of American Indian languages, John Adams asked, "What has become of the Sanskrit Language which Sir William Jones solemnly assures us is more perfect than the Greek?" Answering his own question, Adams suggested precisely why it was that such an observation should be solemn and why it was that Du Ponceau's work was so urgent: "Politicians have extinguished all the records, history's traditions and nations of such remote antiquity on which they could lay their rapacious claws, and we are left to grope in the dark and puzzle ourselves to explain a thousand things which would have appeared very simple if we had . . . the pure light of antiquity."[19] Adams was urging Du Ponceau to follow Jones's model in his study of American languages, lest these languages—and the history contained within them—be lost forever to the designs of a corrupt society. In his gravity of tone, Adams echoed the antiquarian impulse sweeping the American world of letters at this time. To preserve linguistic artifacts was to afford the possibility of empirical historical knowledge, and only such knowledge could be defended from intrusions by the self-interested and corrupt who would write history with regard for only their own interests. Indeed, we might read in Adams's remarks a latent anxiety about increasingly popular pro-slavery arguments that challenged the very foundation of the human sciences in the Enlightenment. Perhaps it was the desire to defend that older, universalizing vision of human nature that gave the American study of Indian language its unique sense of urgency.

No citizen of the young United States embodied that desire more than Thomas Jefferson, who devoted himself to the collection and study of Indian vocabularies for most of his adult life. Repeating in 1816 what

---

Study of Language in England, 1780–1860 (Princeton, N.J.: Princeton University Press, 1967), ch. 4. See also Said, *Orientalism*, 77–79; and Trautmann, *Aryans and British India*, ch. 2 and passim.

[18] Charles Brockton Brown in *The American Review and Literary Journal* 2:3 (1802): 290. On Jones's American reputation, see Robert A. Ferguson, "The Emulation of Sir William Jones in the Early Republic," *New England Quarterly* 52:1 (March 1979): 7.

[19] John Adams to P. S. Du Ponceau, July 5, 1819, the American Philosophical Society Library, APS archives.

Quincy July 5th 1819

Dear Sir

Your favour of 28th June has given me more pleasure than you can imagine; I am delighted to find a Gentleman in America who ever knew Court my friend Court, he was introduced to me in 1778 and I continued to enjoy his friendship till his death, he has mentioned me more than once in his Works, he was a kind of Walking Alexandrian Library and as modest amiable and unassuming as he was learned—

If I remember right he some where says that the Court of Nebuchadnezzar was a kind of Augustan age in Babylon, and I suspect there had been many Augustan ages in the history of this Globe, and of mankind before that of Nebuchadnezzar — and that some of those augustine ages, if you had the history of them, might explain to you the mysterys you find in the Indian languages. What has become of the Chaldean Languages and all its dialects, Phenician Carthaginian fragments only of the Hebrew are preserved, and that was only an obscure dialect of the Chaldean. What has become of the Sanscrit Language which Sir William Jones solemnly assures us is more perfect than the Greek — Politicians have extinguished all the records, Historys Traditions and Nations of such remote Antiquity on which they could lay their rapacious Claws, and we are left to grope in the dark and puzzel ourselves to explain a thousand things which would have appeared very simple if we had have had, the pure light of Antiquity. —

I hope to live to see Mr Heckwelder's account of his Missionary labours among the Indians — and shall ever be his, and yours, sincere Friend and most humble Servant.

John Adams

Peter S Du Ponceau.

Letter from John Adams to Peter Stephen Du Ponceau, 5 July 1819, probably in the hand of Adams's niece, Louisa Catherine Smith. Courtesy of the American Philosophical Society.

he had said many times before, he noted, "During the course of my public life, and from a very early period of it, I omitted no opportunity of procuring vocabularies of the Indian languages."[20] Such vocabularies, Jefferson believed, would provide "the best proof of the affinity of nations which ever can be referred to."[21] It was perhaps symbolic of the larger failure of Jeffersonian Indian policy that Jefferson's own efforts to collect and study these vocabularies met with disaster: at the end of his presidency, most of his vocabularies were lost in transit between Washington and his home in Virginia.[22]

Jefferson's quest for empirical evidence regarding America's ancient history was part of his larger effort to refute the claims of the French natural historian George Louis Leclerk, Comte de Buffon, and other Old World writers who alleged that a hostile American climate left the indigenous population irrational, lacking in sexual ardor, and generally antisocial. Together, these alleged deficiencies left Indians unable to form extended social relations—precisely that which it was assumed would have fostered linguistic refinement.[23] Jefferson and his fellow polemicists countered that the depleted condition of American Indians was a consequence of short-term circumstances—particularly the ravages of colonialism—rather than any inherent and lasting condition, and that if Europeans had actually had any experience with America's indigenous population, they would have discovered unique gifts. Nothing better illustrated this, in Jefferson's mind, than the Native American talent for moving eloquence. And no speech was more representative of this ability than that of the Mingo, Logan, or Soyechtowa. Delivered in 1774 at the close of Lord Dunmore's War—one of the

[20] Jefferson to Peter Wilson, Jan. 20, 1816, in Andrew Lipscomb and Albert Ellery Bergh, *The Writings of Thomas Jefferson* (Washington, D.C.: Thomas Jefferson Memorial Association, 1903–4), vol. 14, 401–3. See also Jefferson to Benjamin Hawkins, August 4, 1787, 6:231; Jefferson to Hawkins, March 14, 1800, 10:161; Jefferson to Dr. John Sibley, May 27, 1805, 11:79; Jefferson to Levett Harris, April 18, 1806, 11:102.

[21] Jefferson, *Notes on the State of Virginia*, 101.

[22] On the loss of his vocabularies see Jefferson to Wilson, in Lipscomb and Bergh, *The Writings of Thomas Jefferson*, 14:402. The longer-term failure of assimilationist policies is perhaps best illustrated by support for forced removal of Indians from ancestral lands. See Bernard Sheehan, *Seeds of Extinction: Jeffersonian Philanthropy and the American Indian* (Chapel Hill: University of North Carolina Press, 1973), ch. 9; and William G. McLoughlin, *Cherokee Renascence in the New Republic* (Princeton, N.J.: Princeton University Press, 1986), esp. ch. 20.

[23] The eighteenth-century debate over the American environment is treated in Gilbert Chinard, "Eighteenth Century Theories of America as a Human Habitat," *Proceedings of the American Philosophical Society* 91:1 (February 1947): 27–57; Ralph N. Miller, "American Nationalism as a Theory of Nature," *William and Mary Quarterly*, 3d ser., 12:1 (1955): 74–95; and Antonello Gerbi, *The Dispute of the New World: The History of a Polemic, 1750–1900*, trans. Jeremy Moyle (Pittsburgh: University of Pittsburgh Press, 1973).

era's many violent frontier confrontations between Indians and Euro-American squatters—Logan's speech came to represent for many elite, White Americans the stoicism, dignity, and eloquence with which Indians responded to the onslaught of white settlers.[24] But it was also, in the minds of its admirers, indicative of the natural eloquence thought to be lacking in modern society. "I may challenge the whole orations of Demosthenes and Cicero," Jefferson ventured, "and of any more eminent orator, if Europe has furnished more eminent, to produce a single passage superior to the speech of Logan."[25] A people with such poetic gifts could not be far removed from the same ancestry claimed by Europeans. But, ultimately, it was not so much this talent for using language that would establish the Indians' humanity. Rather, it was the very nature of their language itself that would do so.[26]

In his earliest philosophical statements about Indian language, Jefferson implied that it not only could reveal the absolute age of the aboriginal nations of America but also could establish their relative age. That is, in addition to revealing the ancient filiations of peoples, language could reveal who was descended from whom. With this argument, Jefferson thought he could prove that the inhabitants of the Americas were not, as Buffon had assumed, the socially degenerate descendants of Asians but, in fact, their progenitors. This was surely his most perverse scientific hypothesis, contradicting virtually all thinking on the matter of American Indian origins. But it served Jefferson's more general quest to demonstrate that Native American ancestry dated back "perhaps not less than many people give to the age of the earth."[27] By dating the lineage of America's indigenous population in this fashion, Jefferson was suggesting that the Americas may not be a "new world" but in fact may be the seat of civilization itself. Jefferson's belief that this could be proved through language study rested on the prevailing eighteenth-century notion that linguistic development reflected mental development.

This thinking reveals itself in the vocabulary lists he circulated among government officials residing near Native American towns. Jefferson arranged the lists, he explained, so that they would exhibit "such objects in nature as must be familiar to every people, savage or civilized."[28] The

---

[24] The reception of Logan's speech is discussed in Edward D. Seeber, "Critical Views on Logan's Speech," *Journal of American Folklore* 60 (April–June 1947): 130–46.

[25] Jefferson, *Notes on the State of Virginia*, 62.

[26] Jefferson's search for the universal and unifying ties of humanity is emphasized by Daniel Boorstin, *The Lost World of Thomas Jefferson* (Chicago: University of Chicago Press, 1948), esp. ch. 2; and Sheehan, *Seeds of Extinction*, ch. 2, esp. pp. 46–47.

[27] Jefferson, *Notes on the State of Virginia*, 102.

[28] Jefferson to Peter Wilson, Jan. 20, 1816, *The Writings of Thomas Jefferson*, 14:402–3.

VOCABULARY.

English	Native	English	Native	English	Native	English	Native
Fire	Assirat	belly	Nesphee	gold		nine hundred	
water	Iske	back	Nhenaase	silver	Osphum	a thousand	
earth	Kitakke	file	Tuski	copper	Mikkojirkininkham	white	
air	Masheim	hubby		a stone	Anaum	black	
wind	Kitikkim	nipple	Niwerkteum	wood	Tahunn	green	
sky	Asarget	thigh	Prim	gun		blue	
sun	Rohu	leg	Whit	a mountain	Otee	yellow	
moon	Nehunke	foot	Not	hill	Thutuhumu	red	
star	Terget	toe	Guild	valley	Estaketitchuhok	good	
light	Oforung	fin	Witrukim	sea	Tahittium	bad	
darkness	Toki	milk		lake	Antumuntakul	large	
day	Niuka	bone	Otullum	pond	Nimafack	small	
night	Opsitke	blood	Whent	river	Tillium	high	
heat	Nette	lue	Lelukhem	creek	Sifu	low	
cold	Tta	death	Napil	a spring	Tofork	broad	
smoke	Kuhuk	food	Munittking	grass	Amkukul	narrow	
cloud	Thunkkuit	meat	Auuu	a tree	Ottuuk	old	
fog	Witain	fat	Puuu	pine	Koruta	young	
rain	Ututtun	lean	Lamwrk	cedar	Whuta	new	
snow	Ututil	bread	Opuru	sycamore		hard	
hail	Hukhanen	Indian-corn	Muthuitu	poplar	Amuhuuk	soft	
ice	Tuutkem	milk	Nununhem	ash	Pakmme	sweet	
frost	Topihuttet	egg	Stuut	elm	Whtchuuttuutu	four	
dew	Aphuuttut	a house		beech	Oththettanikuk	bitter	
rain-bow	Amuthum	the hammock		birch	Withuun	hot	
thunder	Puthikhum	buffalo	Sittuumuuo	maple	Snukhtuumme	cold	
lightning	Ouukiuut	elk	Lutimutur	oak	Witrhutii	dry	
yesterday	Othke	deer	Atdile	chesnut	Suumuuti	wet	
to-day	Kiutke	moose		hicory	Etuimuinye	strong	
to-morrow	—	bear	—	walnut	Khuimuinye	weak	
a day	Kuhu	wolf	Tumme	locust	Umuuk	pretty	
a month	Guuku kuikum	panther	Nuiuuntkuuu	mulberry	Othimuuy	ugly	
a year	Liuhe	wild-cat	Tuhupu	a vine	Chifuukkif	sick	
spring		pole-cat	Aukith	tobacco	Stuule	brave	
summer	Nityum	fox	Sepuut	ivy	Nulukinta	cowardly	
autumn	Sghuuko	monax	Nupuuhitkle	furrow	Guuli	wise	
				one	Siuku	foolish	
				two			

Delaware vocabulary, compiled by Thomas Jefferson in 1792. Courtesy of the American Philosophical Society.

list therefore began with the simplest and most easily sensed objects—fire, water, earth, air, wind—and proceeded through some 280 words of increasing abstraction, concluding with "yes" and "no"—words not founded on any objective sense experience. Jefferson does not, it should be noted, end his list with what Adam Smith took to be the most abstract of terms, the first-person singular pronoun: "I." Rather, the term precedes a series of verb infinitives. Perhaps this is indicative of Jefferson's erroneous belief, widely incorporated in nineteenth-century caricatures of Indian speech, that Indian languages lack the first-person singular conjugation. Such an assumption reflects social and cultural bias rather than any sort of linguistic reality and is consistent with the Enlightenment notion that Indians, like children, are unable to make abstract references to themselves.

Whatever underlying assumptions were imbedded in these lists, their fundamental logic is simple: the more basic and immediate a human experience—heat, cold, etc.—the earlier the invention of corresponding words. And the older the word, the more likely it would be to reveal etymological similarities with the corresponding word in related languages. For instance, the word for "fire," because derived from the Stone Age experience of heat, would bear some etymological resemblance even in the languages of peoples separated by great distances in time and space. As such, it offered the best possibility for revealing ancient human relations. As ideas grew more abstract, so too would the corresponding words show fewer etymological similarities to the same ideas as represented in other tongues. That is, as nations progressed and refined their speech, so would they grow more distinctive in their vocabularies. To trace one nation's descent from another, one would simply follow the etymological similarities from the most to the least primitive terms: the greater the number of similar words used by two nations, the more recent their genealogical filiation.

The notion that etymological comparisons could provide special insight into the ancient American past was not new. Hugo Grotius, among others, had employed comparative etymology in his effort to solve the Indian origins question.[29] What was new, however, was a growing sense that language was peculiarly suited to uncovering the past relations of primitive peoples. Natural historians and philosophers had long assumed that in the absence of a written record or material artifacts, comparisons between the manners, morals, and languages of the

---

[29] Lee Eldridge Huddleston, *Origins of the American Indians: European Concepts, 1492–1729* (Austin: University of Texas Press, 1967), 120 and passim. An eighteenth-century example is James Adair, *Adair's History of the American Indians*, ed. Samuel Cole Williams (1775; reprint, New York: Promontory Press, 1930), 40–77.

peoples of the Americas and those of Asia and the ancient cultures of Europe could reveal shared lineage.[30] But by the middle of the eighteenth century, natural historians had come to doubt the historical stability of manners and morals, and they began suggesting that an ancient past could best be revealed by language alone. Without writing, so they reasoned, it was almost impossible for the "uncivilized" to preserve moral and religious institutions over many generations. While other cultural traits dissolved, the spoken word, in contrast, retained identifiable traces of its origins. One of the more sustained expositions of this view came from the French Jesuit traveler and missionary Father Pierre François Xavier de Charlevoix, a writer who was well known in the Anglo-American world.[31]

Charlevoix recorded his ideas about Indian language study in his *Journal of a Voyage to North America*, a diffuse collection of observations he made while exploring the upper Great Lakes region in the 1720s. Like so many visitors before and after him, Charlevoix was preoccupied with the question of Indian origins. But comparing "manners, customs, religion and traditions of the Americans," he wrote, would only produce "a false light, more likely to dazzle, and to make us wander from the right path, than to lead us with certainty to the point proposed." When applied to nonliterate nations, such comparisons offered no guarantee of accuracy, precisely because those nations had been unable to sustain collective memory. Without writing and other systems for graphically organizing and codifying knowledge, those institutions that depended on memory—law, religion, civil government, family inheritance, and education—could be obliterated by the flux of time. "New events," Charlevoix explained, "and a new arrangement of things give rise to new traditions, which efface the former, and are themselves effaced in their turn. After one or two centuries have passed, there no longer remain any marks capable of leading us to find the traces of the first traditions."[32] The effects of this loss of tradition were all the more pronounced on primitive or "wandering nations" who lived "without

---

[30] See Anthony Pagden, *The Fall of Natural Man: The American Indian and the Origins of Comparative Ethnology* (Cambridge: Cambridge University Press, 1982).

[31] Among the English and American writers who mention Charlevoix are Jonathan Carver, *Travels through the Interior Parts of North America in the Years 1766, 1767, and 1768* (1781; reprint, Minneapolis: Ross and Haines, 1956), 199; Benjamin Smith Barton, *New Views of the Origin of the Tribes and Nations of America* (Philadelphia: Privately printed, 1797), iii; Elias Boudinot, *A Star in the West; or, A Humble Attempt to Discover the Long Lost Ten Tribes of Israel* . . . (Trenton, N.J.: D. Fenton, S. Hutchinson, and J. Dunham, 1816), 90; Albert Gallatin, *Archaeologia Americana: Transactions and Collections of the American Antiquarian Society* 2 (1836): 7.

[32] Pierre François Xavier de Charlevoix, *Journal of a Voyage to North America*, ed. Louise Phelps Kellog (first English ed., 1761; reprint, Chicago: Caxton Club, 1923), vol. 1, 55.

principles, laws, education, or civil government," the very institutions that preserve ancient traditions.[33] There was, in Charlevoix's view, something of a vicious cycle in the information economies of primitive nations: without writing, collective memory was impossible. Without collective memory, the various institutions that allow a nation to resist rapid and capricious change—law, religion, and government—lacked permanence. The writers who had focused their analyses on the comparative study of such institutions, Charlevoix declared, "neglected the only means that remained to come at the truth of what they were in search of; I mean the comparing of languages."[34] For, if nations with weak ties to their pasts were unable to preserve distinctive institutions, they were equally unlikely to experience refinements in their speech. They simply lacked the range of experiences and the socialization required for such refinements. This meant that their languages were, in essence, transparent. Without new ideas, secured by writing, law, and other institutions designed to establish social stability, these tongues did not retain the accruing marks of the ages. They had not, that is, expanded their vocabularies or refined their grammars to such an extent that remnants of ancestral tongues had been lost.

This same reasoning led Noah Webster to conclude that "the wonderful structure of language and its progress from a few simple terms expressive of natural objects, which supplied the wants or effected the senses of unlettered men, thro [sic] a series of ingenious combinations to express new ideas, growing with the growth of the human mind to its highest state of refinement, are yet to be charted and elucidated." And yet it was because of this very process that language could reveal "numerous facts respecting the origin, migration, and intermixture of nations . . . ; and the common origin of all the nations of Europe and those of Asia . . . may be confirmed beyond the possibility of a reasonable doubt by the affinity of their languages."[35] Showing similar views, Samuel Johnson wrote, "I have always difficulty to be patient when I hear authors gravely quoted, as giving accounts of savage nations, which accounts they had from the savages themselves." Without letters, Johnson assumed that such nations could never preserve knowledge about their pasts: "There is no tracing the connection of ancient nations, but by language; and therefore I am always sorry when any language is lost."[36] Johnson was defending a method of historical analysis that presumed a certain permanence in language, even when not codified by writing. It may seem perverse to associate a traditionalist of

[33] Ibid., 56.
[34] Ibid., 54.
[35] *Letters of Noah Webster*, ed. Harry R. Warfel (New York: Library Publishers, 1953), 273.
[36] *The Tour to the Hebrides and the Journey into North Wales*, vol. 5 of *Boswell's Life of Johnson* (Oxford: Clarendon Press, 1950), 224–25.

Johnson's kind with the radical republican Jefferson. But on this point, they agreed: languages bore the imprint of mind. And for ancient nations whose collective intellects were not clouded by abstract thoughts, the correspondence between ideas and speech provided what was assumed to be the most reliable source of historical knowledge, short of written text.

While American students of Indian language were united in their desire to uncover the ancient lineage of the Indians themselves, they were not in harmony regarding precisely what the linguistic evidence revealed. To Jefferson, the fact that native peoples, living on the same land and in close proximity to one another, had formed a multitude of distinct languages meant that America and its peoples were actually quite ancient. The alternative view—and the one that became most widely embraced in the first half of the nineteenth century—was that linguistic diversity in America was merely superficial, and that investigators like Jefferson had mistaken dialects for languages. This difference of interpretation was not just another of the quibbles that occupied American natural historians and philosophers at the time. More than any other such disagreement, it reveals Jefferson's dogged determination to uncover the details of the indigenous American past, and in turn to demonstrate that the "newness" of America and its peoples was a false conjecture of European philosophers.

Although his interest in collecting Indian vocabularies was lifelong, Jefferson's most sustained discussion on the subject came relatively early in his scientific career, with *Notes on the State of Virginia,* first published in 1787. In that work, Jefferson suggested that an abundance of American radicals—or root languages—indicated that the ancestry of American Indian nations had to predate that of the peoples of Asia. Given the striking linguistic variety his forebears had encountered in Virginia, Jefferson deduced that there were "probably twenty" radicals in America "for one in Asia." Such astonishing linguistic diversity, he argued, indicated that the ancestry of the American Indians had to predate that of the primitive peoples of Asia, who spoke only several distinct languages. For, he explained, "a separation into dialects may be the work of a few ages only, but for two dialects to recede from one another till they have lost all vestiges of their common origin, must require an immense course of time." And since so many more such changes appeared to have taken place in America, the conclusion was inescapable: the nations of America were "of greater antiquity than those of Asia."[37] Jefferson's quest to disprove the degenerative effects of the American environment led him to posit the degenerative qualities

---

[37] Jefferson, *Notes on the State of Virginia,* 102.

of culture itself—a perspective that contradicted Lockean language philosophy in the most dramatic fashion. For Jefferson's claim suggested that the natural effects of time were not, as Adam Smith proposed, the coalescence of linguistic groups but the diversification of language. The implication of such a notion was similar to the late medieval view that human nature did not encourage the formation of larger and larger nations, bound by uniformities of speech, but instead encouraged the opposite tendency: the corruption and diversification of language.

Jefferson's chief critic on this matter was the Philadelphia physician and professor of botany Benjamin Smith Barton. A longtime member of the American Philosophical Society, Barton had extended his medical interests to the physiology of race. While studying medicine at the University of Edinburgh in the late 1780s, he wrote a prize-winning dissertation on the subject and edited the Scottish edition of *An Essay on the Causes of the Variety of Complexion and Figure in the Human Species* (1787), a work by Samuel Stanhope Smith, the president of the College of New Jersey, now Princeton. After establishing himself in Philadelphia's scientific circles, Barton set out to demonstrate the empirical validity of Smith's claim that there was a single human species and that race indicated no biological difference but was instead entirely the result of environment. Barton believed that demonstrating this with physical evidence not only would normalize the Native American past but also would refute European claims about the relative infancy of America and its peoples. "In this vast portion of the world," he declared, "we discover the influence of a hand which moulded matter into forms at periods extremely remote: we have good reason to believe as remote as any other parts of the world. The physical infancy of America [was thus] one of the many dreams of the slumbering philosophers of our times."[38] But how exactly was this to be proved?

Barton's key statement on the relation between language and Indian history came in his *New Views of the Origin of the Tribes and Nations of America* (1798), a condensed version of what he had planned to be a massive natural history of America, a work as grand in its evidence and analysis as the one it was to refute—Buffon's massive *Histoire naturelle* (1749–89). Although he pursued an extensive correspondence to gather data for the work, Barton never came anywhere near completing the book. He did, however, venture this brief synopsis of his ethnological findings, most of which he drew from what had, over the years, become an extensive collection of Indian vocabularies. It is worth noting that the form of these vocabularies differed from that of Jeffer-

---

[38] Barton, *New Views*, cviii. For Barton's response to Buffon see p. cvii.

son's vocabularies. Barton appears to have fashioned his vocabulary after that of Peter Pallas's *Linguarium totius orbis vocabularia comparativa*— a work he obtained from Joseph Priestley in the late 1780s and one to which Jefferson gained access only twenty years after he began collecting his own vocabularies.[39] As Pallas had done, Barton placed "God" at the beginning of his vocabulary. This probably indicated the two men's views regarding the language origins controversy. As with Pallas's better-known countryman Gottfried Wilhelm Leibniz, they apparently embraced the older position that language was in essence not conventional, and that words were not related to things in a random fashion. Rather, for Leibniz, and presumably for Pallas and Barton, words were symbols, bearing some underlying, inherent, and divinely sanctioned connection to the things they designated. This view, as we have seen, had significant theological implications. For it suggested that the explanation for the origins of language contained in Genesis was valid. It also suggested that since the oldest known language was the language of Eden, the oldest existing word would have arisen from that place— hence, the name of Adam's teacher, or "God." For Barton, such a scheme may well have been appealing because it was more easily reconciled with the biblical account of creation. Jefferson's argument, in contrast, seemed to imply a passage of time far more extensive than that allowed for by the biblical chronology.[40]

Barton addressed his book directly to Jefferson, more as an act of deference, it would seem, than out of any desire to attack the then vice president's science. He also took great pains to demonstrate his shared belief that there was nothing at all permanent about the Indians' present state; that they were inherently no more degenerate than the peoples of Asia, and that, like all people, they are "susceptible to improvement."[41] But he made no effort to hide his disagreement about the copiousness of American languages. "Nothing is more common," he explained, "than for Indian traders, interpreters, or other persons, to assert, that such and such languages bear no relation to each other: because, it seems, that the persons speaking them cannot always understand one another." Careful comparison, he assured his readers, re-

[39] The details of Barton's receipt of Pallas are discussed in Greene, *American Science in the Age of Jefferson*, 378–79. For details about this addition to Jefferson's library, see E. Millicent Sowerby, *Catalogue of the Library of Thomas Jefferson* (Washington, D.C.: Library of Congress, 1959), vol. 5, 60–63.

[40] On Leibniz, see Hans Aarsleff, "Leibniz on Locke on Language," in *From Locke to Saussure: Essays on the Study of Language and Intellectual History* (Minneapolis: University of Minnesota Press, 1982), 42–83; and "The Study and Use of Etymology in Leibniz," in ibid., 84–100.

[41] Barton, *New Views*, vi.

vealed "that in all the vast countries of America there is but one language."[42] After far more systematic etymological comparison than Jefferson ever attempted in print, Barton concluded that all the American languages could "be referred to one great stock, which I call the language of the Lenni-Lennàpe or Delawares."[43] He even went so far as to say that "we have not discovered in America any two, or more, languages between which we are incapable of detecting affinities . . . either in America or in the old world."[44] According to Barton, Jefferson's principle hypothesis—that the deep-seated differences among American tongues were an indication of their collective antiquity—was thus unfounded.

Perhaps swayed by Barton; perhaps more detached from his dispute with Buffon and his followers; perhaps less comfortable with the biblical implications of his argument, Jefferson eventually did modify his position. In an undated manuscript note in his personal copy of the *Notes*, he acknowledged that it was difficult to conceive of America having been inhabited long enough to produce the vast diversity of tongues he formerly supposed: "The mind finds it difficult to conceive that so many tribes have inhabited [America] from so remote an antiquity as would be necessary to have divided them into languages so radically different." In response to this autocritique, Jefferson offered an alternative explanation, based not on the antiquity of Indian ancestry but on the distinctiveness of Indian psychology. This revision marked a revolutionary moment in Jeffersonian language study: far from revealing a long and dignified history, Jefferson now suggested that America's language geography reflected distinctive qualities of America's indigenous peoples—qualities that made them seem to be victims not so much of imperialism as of their own mental immaturity.

Jefferson's new premise was a familiar one: "The Indians consider it dishonorable to use any language but their own." This was apparent "in their councils with us," where, although "some of them may have been in situations which from convenience or necessity have obliged them to learn our language well, . . . they refuse to confer in it, and always insist on the intervention of an interpreter, tho he may understand neither language so well as themselves: and this fact is as general as our knowledge of the tribes of N. America." Hence, when "a fraction of a tribe

---

[42] Ibid., lxxiv–lxxv.

[43] Ibid., lvi.

[44] *New Views of the Origin of the Tribes and Nations of America*, 2d ed. (Philadelphia: Privately printed, 1798), Appendix, 19. Modern linguists have concluded that Indian groups along the lower Delaware River valley spoke two languages—Munsee and Unami—both of which have been attributed to a proto-Eastern Algonquian language family. See Goddard, "Eastern Algonquian Languages," 72–73.

from domestic feuds has broken off from its main body to which it is held by no law or compact, and has gone to another settlement, may it not be the point of honor with them not to use the language of those with whom they have quarreled, but to have one of their own?" Jefferson was suggesting that a sense of honor and cultural propriety deterred Indians from using the language of their enemies, thereby forcing them to invent entirely new tongues. The consequence of this practice was linguistic diversity rather than refinement, and social division and atomization rather than nation building. Indeed, the alleged crudeness of American Indian language, according to Jefferson, facilitated the practice. Because Indian societies had "use but for few words . . . it would require but a small effort of the mind to invent [new languages] and to acquire the habit of using them."[45]

As with most eighteenth- and early nineteenth-century ideas about Indian language, this one, too, assumed a correlation between mental and linguistic development. A people living in nature, provided for by nature, and with few of the inventions so familiar to the peoples of the civilized West were also a people needing little in the way of linguistic innovation. It was this very point, Jefferson suggested, that may have accounted for Indians' linguistic inventiveness. Rather than the ancient and once-powerful peoples Jefferson initially depicted in his *Notes*, we are now left with a people whose habits of mind bred social discord and linguistic confusion. Such a people, if we extend this reasoning, are less the product of their environment than of distinctive mental deficiencies and cultural biases.

Although Jefferson never doubted that language was the key to the Indian past, his understanding of the relation between language and that past had changed in a profound way. No longer were Indian tongues marked by the same teleological processes of migration and linguistic evolution that appeared to affect all peoples of the globe— albeit at varying rates. Instead, they came together as a pastiche of unresolved conflicts and linguistic innovations facilitated not by intellectual growth but by cultural and intellectual stagnation. Jefferson's dogged insistence that there were in fact many distinct Indian radicals had forced him to recast his image of America's native peoples. Far from a merely noble, if "primitive," people, they had become a peculiarly deficient people, suffering unique effects of historical, cultural, and intellectual stagnation. Instead of epic historical growth, their linguistic diversity merely reflected fundamentally distinct, and inferior, habits of mind. The diversity of languages, according to this model, reflected natural tendencies of humans toward corruption, decadence,

---

[45] Jefferson, *Notes on the State of Virginia*, 282 n. 12.

and depravity. When left to their own devices—when shaped by no superior operations of mind—languages foundered and their speakers grew ever more unable to grasp the universal truths and laws of nature that would allow them to begin the process of social redemption. Instead of coming together as nation-states, those speakers merely degenerated into ever smaller nations without states, or possibly even tribes. Jefferson had come to admit the possibility that language—and implicitly culture as whole—did not experience progressive improvement as a natural result of the movement of time, but that when left to nature, language and culture tended toward entropy.

We might dismiss the issue as a momentary digression that Jefferson never bothered to make public. But if understood in the context of a failing Indian policy—one that foundered on the contradictions between expansionist Jeffersonian land policy and the paternalistic rhetoric of Jeffersonian philanthropy—Jefferson's change of mind makes considerable sense.[46] By suggesting that American Indian language bore the imprint less of antiquity than of inherent intellectual limitations, he was also suggesting his own reasons for a sluggish program of acculturation and assimilation: reformers had to overcome not only centuries of corruption brought by European conquerors but also the Indians' own alleged intellectual deficiencies.

Jefferson's intellectual contortions on the matter of Indian language diversity reflect the power of Barton's argument: as much as he desired to serve his nation by establishing its ancient roots, Jefferson ultimately could not sustain that argument in the face of a contrary biblical account. Perhaps of broader significance, the shift in thinking suggests an emerging crisis in Lockean language philosophy. The notion that language reflected human nature unfolding over time simply could not be sustained in the face of ever more countervailing ethnological knowledge: the diversity of America's tongues implied that human nature had nothing whatever to do with the progressive processes Locke's interpreters described. Indeed, the whole notion that one could come to grasp the ancient human past through a conjectural model of language change was starting to appear hopeless, at best, and downright quixotic, at worst. Such was the perspective of Jefferson's friend in retirement, John Adams. In a series of letters the two men exchanged between 1812 and 1813, they debated the possibility of ever grasping the origins of America's indigenous population.

Adams's skepticism provoked the exchange. After studying the writings of Lafitau and James Adair, and Theodore De Bry's late sixteenth-

---

[46] Reginald Horsman, *Expansion and American Indian Policy, 1783–1812*, 2d ed. (Norman: University of Oklahoma Press, 1992), esp. 156–57.

century engravings, he concluded that on the matter of the Indian's origins, "I shall never know much more of the subject than I do now." The many hypotheses on this unyielding question represented, to Adams, so much confused and unfounded reasoning, and "the immensity of learning profusely expended to support them, have appeared to me, for a longer time than I can precisely recollect, what the Physicians call the *Litteræ nihil Sanantes* [writings correcting nothing]." These hypotheses were, as far as Adams was concerned, ample evidence that anything could be justified regarding the origins of the Indians, and that therefore the pursuit of the matter was of no use to anyone. "Whether serpents teeth were sown here and sprung up Men," Adams wrote or "whether Men and Women dropped from the Clouds upon this Atlantic Island; whether the Almighty created them here, or whether they immigrated from Europe, are questions of no moment to the present or future happiness of Man."[47] What value, Adams was wondering, could there be in a question to which any schoolchild could formulate an answer? Indeed, the whole endeavor smacked of rash hypothesizing so characteristic of an eighteenth century that, for Adams at least, had given rise to a disordered world, adrift in a vast sea of moral uncertainty.[48]

Perhaps nothing better illustrates the depth of Adams's feelings than his caricature of the "system"-building habits of so many eighteenth-century social theorists and moral philosophers. Condillac, Smith, Ferguson, and a host of other philosophers could be included among those who presumed that even without any material record, the dim reaches of the past could be known. What made this so, in their view, was the universality and uniformity of human nature: "I could make a System too. The seven hundred Thousand Soldiers of Zingis, when the whole or any part of them went into battle, they sett up a howl, which resembled nothing that human Imagination has conceived, unless it be the supposition that all the Devils in Hell were let loose at once to set up an infernal scream, which terrified their Enemies and never failed to obtain them Victory. The Indian Yell resembles this: and therefore America was peopled from Asia."[49] Hypotheses on Indian origins, Adams was saying, were ultimately acts of the imagination. They rested on a sort of Platonic reasoning that had no necessary connection to empirical reality.

[47] Lester J. Cappon, ed., *The Adams-Jefferson Letters: The Complete Correspondence between Thomas Jefferson and Abigail and John Adams* (Chapel Hill: University of North Carolina Press, 1959), 308–9.

[48] On Adams's response to post-Revolutionary American society, see Gordon S. Wood, *The Creation of the American Republic, 1776–1787* (Chapel Hill: University of North Carolina Press, 1969), ch. 14.

[49] Cappon, *Adams-Jefferson Letters*, 310.

Adams's polemic was indicative of a more general partisan climate in the early American Republic. It was also indicative of earlier political differences with Jefferson, which had resulted in an almost complete suspension of the two men's friendship for nearly twenty years. Adams's own political affiliation, the Federalist Party, was defined in part by its antagonism toward Jefferson's expansionist land policies, its admiration for English legal institutions, and its patent rejection of the libertarian rhetoric of the French Revolution. During Jefferson's presidency, these political differences broadened to include opposition to almost everything that could conceivably be identified with Thomas Jefferson and his political allies, including their scientific pursuits. Federalist propagandists portrayed Jeffersonian science as fickle, lacking in rigor, and, as one historian has put it, verging on a "senile fixation."[50] This contempt for Jeffersonian science was not merely rhetorical. There was very much a division of labor in early American science, with New England, and its foremost learned society (of which John Adams had been president), the American Academy of Arts and Sciences, tending to focus on astronomical and mathematical sciences, while the primary Jeffersonian institution, the American Philosophical Society, tended to concern itself with natural history and ethnology. Furthermore, the Jeffersonians tended to be more sympathetic to a French science inclined toward abstract materialism and determinism rather than a Baconian natural theology, which saw in scientific pursuits a means to expose, and in turn worship, divine creation. For Jefferson and his circle, exposing the hand of God had never been a primary objective. But for Americans troubled by the course of the French Revolution and the seeming poverty of Enlightenment optimism, this ambition proved increasingly desirable. And, it seems that for Jefferson growing sympathy for this Baconian empiricism created the awkward burden of having to defend claims made for another age.[51]

Jefferson had grown uneasy about the question of Indian origins. In his discussion with Adams, he offers none of the bold hypotheses made in the *Notes*, and in fact sounds rather wary of the whole debate. The diversity of opinion about the historical origins of the American Indians—characterized on the one hand by diffusionist theories that place Indian ancestry with the ancient Israelites, the Tartars, or even one of the sons of Noah, and, on the other hand, by the multiple creationists who defended the notion that racial difference was the result of distinct acts of creation—Jefferson had come to believe, indi-

[50] Kerber, *Federalists in Dissent*, 71.

[51] Ibid., 75–76. Herbert Hovenkamp, *Science and Religion in America, 1800–1860* (Philadelphia: University of Pennsylvania Press, 1978).

cated that the absolute origins of the Indians may be a matter that, like so many others "must receive the same answer, 'Ignoro.' "[52]

Despite this sense of resignation, Jefferson remained convinced that knowledge about America's indigenous population and its lineage was possible, and it was on this point that he formulated his most explicit response to Barton. The reasoning of Barton and others, Jefferson explained to Adams, implied that little of anything could be known. For Barton's insistence that there was one language in all the Americas and, indeed, that all the world's languages shared certain traits seemed to Jefferson like so much anti-intellectual reductionism. If Barton were correct, Jefferson asked, if languages the world over were fundamentally the same, then, "what constitutes identity, or difference in two things?"[53] How, that is, was one to distinguish objects in the world? Such, Jefferson well knew, was the fundamental and formative dilemma of natural history: on what epistemological grounds should taxonomy exist? Should it presume the possibility of some inherent and natural connection between things and their names, such as was the case with the language of Eden? Or should it presume the pure conventionality of words? Nothing less was at stake than the question of whether there was a preexisting, God-given order in nature. For if that were so, then the taxonomy question could be readily solved: a perfect and all-knowing being would allow for no dissonance between word and thing, since to do so would be to allow for limitations on God's knowledge of his own creation. Such thinking fed the ongoing search for the perfect language. If, however, words could never be more than convention, then the possibility of humans ever recovering a perfect language—and, in turn, the possibility of a taxonomy that perfectly represented the order of nature—was nil.[54]

In the end, Jefferson came to accept the latter position, which was consistent with the less optimistic aspects of Lockean epistemology. To follow Barton's reasoning, he concluded, was tantamount to saying that "all things on earth are the same, as consisting of matter," a statement that made meaningless the taxonomic project of natural history. Such reductionism left one to conclude that "all languages may be called the same, as being all made up of the same primitive sounds, expressed by the letters of the different alphabets." But "this gives up the useful

[52] Cappon, *Adams-Jefferson Letters*, 324.

[53] Ibid., 323.

[54] This question fed two centuries of debate in the natural sciences. See M. M. Slaughter, *Universal Languages and Scientific Taxonomy in the Seventeenth Century* (Cambridge: Cambridge University Press, 1982); Michel Foucault, *The Order of Things: An Archaeology of the Human Sciences* (New York: Vintage Books, 1973), ch. 5; and Umberto Eco, *The Search for the Perfect Language* (Oxford: Blackwell, 1995).

distribution into genera and species, which we form, arbitrarily indeed, for the relief of our imperfect memories."[55]

Jefferson's comments indicate a more general concern about the problems such reductionism might pose to the pursuit and organization of knowledge: it could leave all efforts to catalog and chart the natural and human world in a state of semantic confusion. For Americans of the post-Revolutionary era, particularly those who shared Jefferson's initial optimism about the promise of consensual republican politics, the possibility that all knowledge could be reduced to word games, that every man could hold his own opinion depending on how he defined his terms, was repugnant. Indeed, the problem was not simply one for the natural historian or antiquarian: just as natural history, to be effective, had to have conventions of order and taxonomy, so, too, for the science of government: inventing the state was, in a certain sense, not unlike codifying the natural kingdom: both depended on a shared set of assumptions about meaning, identity, and difference.

The problem was acutely apparent to James Madison, writing in *The Federalist* (1788), as he tried to convey to his audience the difficulty of distinguishing between state and federal jurisdiction. In a passage suggestive of Locke's discussion of words, he explained that this political problem was not unlike the scientific problem of distinguishing the faculties of the mind or the kingdoms of nature. All such taxonomic activities suffered the imprecision and uncertainty of human understanding and human speech. The definition of things, he explained, was always limited by "the indistinctness of the object, imperfection of the organ of conception, [and] inadequateness of the vehicle of ideas"—words.[56] It was thus no surprise that, burdened with all these epistemological problems, "the [Constitutional] Convention should have been forced into some deviations from that artificial structure and regular symmetry, which an abstract view of the subject might lead an ingenious theorist to bestow on a Constitution planned in his closet or in his imagination."[57] Both forging a federal constitution and establishing the conventions of etymological study, in other words, depended

[55] Cappon, *Adams-Jefferson Letters*, 323.

[56] James Madison, *The Federalist*, No. 37, in Alexander Hamilton, James Madison, and John Jay, *The Federalist*, ed. Jacob E. Cooke (Middletown, Conn.: Wesleyan University Press, 1961), 237. See also Christopher Looby, "The Constitution of Nature: Taxonomy as Politics in Jefferson, Peale, and Bartram," *Early American Literature* 22:3 (1987): 252–73; Michael P. Kramer, *Imagining Language in America: From the Revolution to the Civil War* (Princeton, N.J.: Princeton University Press, 1992), ch. 4; and Thomas Gustafson, *Representative Words: Politics, Literature, and the American Language, 1776–1865* (Cambridge: Cambridge University Press, 1992), 282–86.

[57] James Madison, *The Federalist*, No. 37, 238.

on reasoned compromise. Madison's remarks were very much informed by the Lockean sense that humanity ought to recognize that
language is the result of social consensus. Only by acknowledging this
fundamental fact, Madison was suggesting, would politicians be able to
establish the semantic conventions—imperfect though they may be—
that could provide a foundation for consensual politics. Only by acknowledging that language is socially constructed, that is, could the
architects of a new government rightly approach their chief task: the
formation of a new language of politics, crafted—as any tool—to suit a
particular application. For every human endeavor rested on the capacity of its participants to agree upon a language. As Jefferson put it,
"Law, medicine, chemistry, mathematics, every science has a language
of its own."[58] And such language was ultimately the result of consent.

In what may reveal the chasm between 1788 and 1813, the respective
years Madison and Jefferson were writing, Madison seems much more
certain about the possibility of formulating a language for the science
of government. "The real wonder is," he wrote, "that so many difficulties should have been surmounted; and surmounted with a unanim-
ity almost as unprecedented as it must have been unexpected." Madison even went so far as to say, "It is impossible for the man of pious
reflection not to perceive in it, a finger of that almighty hand which
has been so frequently and signally extended to our relief in the critical stages of the revolution."[59] For Madison, the relative absence of faction and disagreement at the Constitutional Convention was so remarkable in light of the parade of failure that had, in the past, characterized
such "great councils and consultations," that he could only conclude
that it was the work of divine providence.

Jefferson indicated little or no sense that any such divine guidance
would lead the new nation to consensus about the origins of its aboriginal population. Rather, his sense of resignation suggests a distinct loss
of hope about the possibility of true historical knowledge. Just as was
the case for Madison's students of government, so for Jefferson's natural historians: if they could not agree on the conventions of their disci-
pline, truth would be unattainable. Instead of possessing some underlying, perfect form, the world's languages had become—according to
this view—unrelated social constructs. Implied in this thinking, implied in the notion that specialized languages were needed for specialized knowledge, was the possibility that, as Locke had claimed,
language was in the end opaque and that perfect translation was impossible. Such was to be the conclusion Jefferson reached after aban-

---

[58] Jefferson to Peter Wilson, January 20, 1816, in *The Writings of Thomas Jefferson*, 14:403.
[59] Madison, *The Federalist*, No. 37, 238.

138 CHAPTER V

doning any claims about the relative old age of the New World. In
February of 1825—a little over a year before his death—he wrote to
the Salem Massachusetts lawyer and philologist John Pickering that
Cherokee inflection differed from European grammatical forms so pro-
foundly as to leave one confronted with the disturbing possibility that
"if man came from one stock, his languages did not." Whatever universality there was in human nature, it could never be revealed in language. In this regard, Jefferson was coming to a position analogous to
that of John Locke. Human history would forever be obscured by the
opacity of language. And similarly, no amount of translation could fully
close the gap between speakers of different tongues: "I believe we shall
find it impossible to translate our language into any of the Indian, or
any of theirs into ours."[60]

As the predominant eighteenth-century model for linguistic evolution
came under increasing scrutiny, scholars began to wonder precisely
what it was that the study of etymology revealed. Did it, as Jefferson
initially supposed, reveal the movements of peoples away from a common ancestry? Or did it, as he suggested in his later equivocations,
indicate more about the distinctive character of speakers? These questions ultimately came down to a more general question: to what extent
could language serve philosophy? To what extent could it answer questions about the origins of humanity, the nature of knowledge, and the
uniformity of culture? In the wider world of language study, particularly in England, there was a growing impulse to divorce the scientific
analysis of language from philosophical and theological questions, and
instead pursue cautious, deliberate, empirically verifiable linguistic
truths.

There was also a growing and related sense among students of language that, as seventeenth-century commentators had assumed, the
speaker and the spoken were distinct—that the specific qualities of a
language said nothing about the intellect of the speaker. A supposedly
primitive people did not, that is, necessarily speak a primitive tongue.
This separation of speech from the mind of the speaker was representative of a Romantic particularism—an emphasis on human difference
rather than similarity—that drew the human sciences away from history and toward biology. One result of this intellectual shift was that
what in America had been a marginal idea—that human difference
was fundamental and primordial—acquired new credibility.[61]

---

[60] Mary Orne Pickering, *The Life of John Pickering* (Boston: Privately printed, 1887), 336.
[61] Reginald Horsman, *Race and Manifest Destiny: The Origins of American Racial Anglo-Saxonism* (Cambridge, Mass.: Harvard University Press, 1981), 27 and passim.

CHAPTER VI

An American Poetics

JEFFERSON'S experience as a collector and student of Indian vocabularies was emblematic of the American Founding Fathers' broader experience in the decades after the Revolution. Language, much like the new national government, went from something that would illuminate the common bonds of humanity to something that obscured those bonds. Visions of a new utopian epoch, founded above all on a faith in the unity and uniformity of human nature, gave way to cynicism and a despairing sense that fundamental differences in human nature made the world's cultures incompatible. The possibility that empirical knowledge—in the form of language—could somehow reveal the genetic sinews of humanity gave way to the pessimistic view that language was an opaque medium. Far from revealing the ancient history of nations, it revealed the diverse and conditional vagaries of time. Its value as both an artifact and a medium had become not so much a function of natural forces, exercised gradually over time on human speech, but of accidents of human invention, random in time and place. From something slowly fashioned by the application of thought to experience, language was becoming something invented, and left behind for future discovery. It was, in short, being transformed into something that had no natural connection to its speakers. Language was, once again, bestowed upon nations, not made by them.[1]

While the vast majority of commentators took this to mean that indigenous tongues were important only insofar as they inhibited forced acculturation, some Americans came to see in the essential difference between the languages of the New World and the Old the possibility of a distinct American literary experience. They began to see in Indian tongues the possibility of what might be called an American poetics—something not altogether unlike a structuralist poetics, characterized in this century by Roland Barthes as "a science of the conditions of content, that is to say of forms."[2] The chief proponent of this American poetics was another lawyer-linguist, the Philadelphian Peter Stephen

---

[1] See Kenneth Cmiel, "'A Broad Fluid Language of Democracy': Discovering the American Idiom," *Journal of American History* 79:3 (December 1992): 913–36.

[2] Quoted and translated in Jonathan Culler, *Structuralist Poetics: Structuralism, Linguistics, and the Study of Literature* (Ithaca, N.Y.: Cornell University Press, 1975), 118.

Peter Stephen Du Ponceau, by Thomas Sully (1830). Courtesy of the
American Philosophical Society.

Du Ponceau. Du Ponceau's poetics was not about the actual content of
Indian speech, but about an underlying form which Du Ponceau regarded as unique in the world. Such a poetics seemed to offer fertile
ground for some sort of indigenous American literary movement—
albeit a movement with almost no direct American Indian participation.

If for the early Jefferson language was a reflection of the speaker insofar as it mirrored intellect, for Du Ponceau language was nothing of the sort. It was disembodied, employed by speakers as a matter of historical accident. For Du Ponceau, to study Delaware, for instance, was in no way to study the Delaware themselves. It was, rather, to study an alien artifact born from minds very different from his own and, as such, able to elevate the mundane and legalistic analysis of syntax and linguistic form into the most sublime of literary journeys. For Du Ponceau, that is, language was poetry. But more important, it was American poetry. Du Ponceau was first and foremost an American cultural booster, seeking grounds for the kind of indigenous aesthetic experience that could bring international distinction to American arts and letters. In this regard his ambition was not altogether different from Jefferson's. Both men were seeking to refute the notion propagated among European philosophers that American nature somehow made a rich and refined American culture impossible. Indeed, in the early part of the nineteenth century, this quest unified the Creole inhabitants of the New World. Remarking on Du Ponceau's philological studies, the Salem lawyer and linguist John Pickering compared his labors to those of the Mexican Jesuit Francisco Javier Clavigero, to whom "subsequent writers, both in our own country and in Europe, have been much indebted, not only for the correction of errours which had been successfully propagated respecting [American] languages, but also for a refutation of the unfounded opinions of eminent naturalists and philosophers respecting the degeneracy of the animal and other productions of this continent."[3] Du Ponceau sought to contribute to this labor. But his purpose was as much to counter theories of New World degeneracy as it was to discover the matter for a New World literary experience. This ambition led him to embrace the strikingly modern view that language is something whose structure and expressive power has no necessary relation to the condition of its speakers. For Du Ponceau, the lack of civility that seemed to pervade American Indian societies had no bearing whatever on the fundamental character of American Indian languages. These were the work of other peoples and other ages. And in their underlying structure Du Ponceau believed he found something of a beauty and majesty unknown in tongues elsewhere in the world.

Born to a Catholic family on the Protestant Isle of Ré, France, in 1760, Peter Du Ponceau showed an early aptitude for languages, learning

---

[3] John Pickering, "Introductory Observations," in reprint of Eliot's *Indian Grammar Begun*, in *Collections of the Massachusetts Historical Society* 9 (1822): 226.

entire French and Latin grammars by the age of five.[4] He learned English, Danish, German, and some Greek by the time he reached his late teens. After a short period studying for the priesthood at Bressuire in Poitou, Du Ponceau left for Paris, where he became a student and assistant of the theologian and philosopher Antoine Court de Gébelin. A friend of Franklin, a Freemason, and a propagandist for the American revolutionary cause, Court de Gébelin invited Du Ponceau to act as his secretary while he completed his great opus, *Monde primitif* (1744–96). Along with Pallas's *Linguarium totius orbis vocabularia comparativa* (1786–89) and the Abbé Lorenzo Hervás y Panduro's *Catálogo de las lenguas de las naciones conocidas* (1800–5), the work was to be among the era's major efforts to catalog and classify the world's languages. And much like these other works, Court de Gébelin's had the latitudinarian purpose of revealing an underlying universal language.

Despite overtures from Court de Gébelin, Du Ponceau chose to leave Paris to follow Friedrich Wilhelm August Heinrich Ferdinand, Baron von Steuben, to America. A bankrupt member of the German nobility, the baron was seeking financial salvation through service to the patriot army, and in 1777 he asked Du Ponceau to join him as an English-speaking aide-de-camp.[5] Du Ponceau's decision to go to America seems to have had little to do with any heartfelt desire to help the cause of republicanism. "I shall not set up the vain pretension of having come to this country for the sake of freedom, or of a republican government," he later explained. "My most anxious desire was that of traveling; . . . and to make the confession complete, I must add that the glitter of military service did not contribute a little to confirm my resolution."[6] Having grown up the son of a military officer, Du Ponceau was well aware that military distinction could earn him lifelong financial security and elevated social status. Ill health, however, cut short his service, and instead of returning to France, in July of 1781 Du Ponceau chose to become a citizen of Pennsylvania. Soon thereafter, his rare

[4] Biographical details on Du Ponceau are from James L. Whitehead, ed., "The Autobiography of Peter Stephen Du Ponceau," *Pennsylvania Magazine of History and Biography* 63:2 (April 1939): 189–227; 63:3 (July 1939): 311–43; 63:4 (October 1939): 432–61; 64:1 (January 1940): 97–120; 64:2 (April 1940): 243–69; William A. Tieck, "In Search of Peter Stephen Du Ponceau," *Pennsylvania Magazine of History and Biography* 89:1 (January 1965): 52–78; Murphy D. Smith, "Peter Stephen Du Ponceau and His Study of Languages: A Historical Account," *Proceedings of the American Philosophical Society* 127:3 (1983): 143–79.

[5] On Steuben, see Charles Royster, *A Revolutionary People at War: The Continental Army and American Character, 1775–1783* (Chapel Hill: University of North Carolina Press, 1979), 213.

[6] Whitehead, "Autobiography of Peter Stephen Du Ponceau," 63:4 (October 1939): 446–47.

language skills earned him a post in the office of the new American Confederation's secretary of foreign affairs, Robert Livingston, and this position gave him access to the legal profession. Du Ponceau soon distinguished himself as one of the young nation's premier international lawyers and legal scholars.[7]

Du Ponceau showed little serious interest in American Indian culture during the early decades of his life in America. In the one anecdote in which he claims to have first encountered an Indian, however, he reveals a Romantic reverence for indigenous speech that was fully in keeping with humanitarian sentiment of the times. While stationed at Valley Forge in the spring of 1778, he remembered hearing "a French fashionable song," sung by a "supernatural voice . . . melodious and in perfect good taste." The sound suggested to him the Comédié Italienne far more than the Indian he saw before him. Du Ponceau conversed with the man in French and learned that he was a Christian Abanaki called Niaman-Rigounant, who had joined the rebel army during the invasion of Canada. "I parted with him with much regret," Du Ponceau recalled, "and I never saw him since."[8] There could hardly have been a more typical example of the eighteenth-century sentimental characterization of the Indian voice: melodious in song; grave and sober in speech, a voice of passion, a voice able to inspire a listener's feelings and evoke distant recollections and emotions. This aestheticization of the indigenous voice was typical of Du Ponceau's relationship to Indian culture more generally. It was a relationship founded on the sort of detached Romantic compassion that lay behind the antiquarian vogue of the late eighteenth and early nineteenth centuries. This compassion was directed not so much toward the relief of suffering as toward the recovery of a lost society whose once great culture appeared to survive only in ephemeral fragments of language. For Du Ponceau appears to have been convinced—much as Jefferson had been—that modern Indian culture was anachronistic and that it could not coexist with a dominant Euro-American culture. But, in contrast to Jefferson, his interest in preserving something of that dying culture was not philosophical; it was not for purposes of answering questions about the unity of creation. Rather, it was almost purely aesthetic.

Du Ponceau's chief struggle, however, had less to do with the nature of his inquiry than with patronage for his linguistic research. "I am mortified," he proclaimed to Jefferson in 1817, "as well as astonished

---

[7] On Du Ponceau's legal career, see Kurt H. Nadelmann, "Peter Stephen Du Ponceau," *Pennsylvania Bar Association Quarterly* 24 (1953): 248–56.

[8] Whitehead, "Autobiography of Peter Stephen Du Ponceau," 63:2 (April 1939): 221–23.

that so much knowledge respecting the language of the aborigines of our country should be possessed at the furthermost end of Europe, while we know so little."[9] The reason was simply that Du Ponceau and his fellow philologists had to work for their livings. They could claim none of the gentlemanly independence or patronage that allowed Europeans to devote their lives to arcane pursuits. In a letter to the German philologist J. S. Vater, he complained, "We are going on in this country with researches on the Indians and their languages; but unfortunately, we are all professional men, who have our business to attend to." In America "every man . . . lives by his labour, with few exceptions, & there are not enough of rich men to encourage scientific investigations."[10] Du Ponceau's fellow lawyer John Pickering also lamented the fact that "the avocations of business" and "those studies which are necessary in aiding the education of my children" would keep him from the study of Indian language.[11] But Pickering clearly shared Du Ponceau's sense that something was to be gained for the nation by the study of these languages. "If . . . we have any ambition to maintain our proper rank in that great community [of learned nations]," he wrote in 1822, "it is very clear that we must qualify ourselves for that station by pursuing the same objects and making the same acquisitions which the other members of it do. Nations, like individuals, must not expect to have their character taken for just what they themselves assert it to be, but they must establish a solid and lasting reputation by their acts, as an individual must by his conduct in private life."[12]

Du Ponceau's promotion of things American was by no means limited to the study of indigenous tongues. His enthusiasm for that subject seems restrained in comparison to his argument that the English language itself could survive and thrive only in the New World. In an address to the Pennsylvania Library in 1834, he announced that English in Great Britain suffered a constant barrage of corrupting influences, while in America "there is . . . no Gaelic or Cimbro-Celtic, no highland or lowland Scotch, no Yorkshire, Lancashire or Somersetshire Jargon, but every where a uniform idiom." Furthermore, Americans had to travel a far distance to encounter the insidious influences of foreign tongues. British English "has already begun to be corrupted, and will so continue, until the old English tongue shall have been merged into some other." In America, though, "it will be preserved

[9] Du Ponceau to Jefferson, December 11, 1817, in American Philosophical Society History and Literature Committee Letterbook, vol. 1, p. 66, APS Archives.

[10] History and Literature Committee Letterbook, 3: 6–7.

[11] Mary Orne Pickering, *The Life of John Pickering* (Boston: Privately printed, 1887), 281.

[12] Ibid., 324.

pure . . . and it will, as long as it lasts, remain an English branch of an English stock." Du Ponceau went on to explain that it was the duty of Americans to defend the English language against such impurities and deterioration so that "we should hold up a mirror to Great Britain, in which she might see her beautiful language reflected in its purity, and free from the barbarisms which of late years she has too easily suffered to be introduced into it."[13] Protected from the pollutants of non-English speech and vulgar dialects, Du Ponceau was suggesting, American English could be more genuinely English than that of the English themselves. He conspicuously disregards other languages spoken in America, no doubt assuming that along with Old World ways, they, too, would be abandoned at the New Nation's shore. And American Indian speech, however glorious and refined he may have thought it to be, posed no threat to American English. For Du Ponceau, Indian language was to America what physical antiquities were to Europe— pleasing remnants of vanished ages.

With little private wealth to support scientific investigation, well-connected Americans increasingly turned to the federal government for support. This is precisely what Albert Gallatin, the Swiss-born former secretary of the U.S. Treasury, did when he undertook his own comprehensive classification of Indian languages. Du Ponceau, however, warned his occasional correspondent that dependence on the state could jeopardize the integrity of the nation's learned institutions: "The government are thus making a monopoly of science, those who would have corresponded with literary societies and literary men and given them information on the subject of the Indians and their languages; will now consider themselves as bound to reserve all their treasures for the national work, and keep their lips closed to everybody else." Government involvement would only open the way for politics to "interfere with the patrimony of science."[14] If the government directed scientific research, Du Ponceau suggested, there would be a danger of removing science from the hands of disinterested investigators and placing it, instead, in those of politicians and others unlikely to abandon their political objectives for the disinterested pursuit of knowledge. "The government surely cannot think of executing by themselves the plan which you have conceived," he wrote Gallatin. "The honor which properly belongs to them," as it does with any great patron, "is that of having originated the idea and caused it to be executed."[15]

[13] Peter Stephen Du Ponceau, *A Discourse on the Necessity and the Means of Making our National Literature Independent of That of Great Britain* . . . (Philadelphia: Pennsylvania Library, 1834), 35–36.
[14] History and Literature Committee Letterbook, 3:50.
[15] Ibid., 47. On government and science in this period, see A. Hunter Dupree, *Science*

Du Ponceau's concerns about patronage bespeak a more fundamental dilemma: the study of obscure and dying languages was just the kind of arcane avocation critics had come to associate with an exclusive, aristocratic world of learning. It was such learning that James Fenimore Cooper ridiculed with the character Obed Bat, M.D., in *The Prairie* (1824), a novel best known as the one in which the beloved Natty Bumppo meets his end. Cooper's treatment of Bat—or the Latinized "Battius," as he preferred to be called—is laced with satiric contempt for the doctor's constant references to Latinate nomenclature, understood by none but himself; his effete, bumbling manner; and his unflappable obsession with useless learning. So consumed is Battius with his trifling scientific activities that in the face of an Indian attack he remains oblivious to all but his botanical frolic. Much like Prospero himself, Battius displays a naive confidence that his books—rather than the hard-won survival instincts of Natty Bumppo—would be the source of his salvation.

Showing similar suspicions of impractical knowledge, in 1826 the New Hampshire senator Daniel Webster dismissed out of hand the study of Indian language. Aside from a firm conviction that Indian tongues were "the rudest forms of speech," Webster was certain that "there is as little in the languages of the tribes as in their laws, manners, and customs worth studying or worth knowing."[16] Webster was apparently not the only American to possess such opinions. In an 1820 review of *A Discourse on the Religion of the Indian Tribes of North America* by Samuel Foster Jarvis, the reviewer—probably John Pickering—justified his own digressions on Indian language by acknowledging that some might wonder "of what use it is to examine the structure of languages in which there is not literature to compensate us for our labours?" For the very field of philology had been founded on the assumption that language study was a means to an end: a means to improved knowledge of foreign-language texts. Pickering could put forth no such justification for the study of American Indian languages. What he did say, however, was that "if we wish to study human speech as a science, just as we do other science, . . . these neglected dialects of our own continent certainly do offer to the philosophical inquirer some of the most

in the Federal Government: A History of Policies and Activities(Cambridge, Mass.: Harvard University Press, 1957), chs. 2 and 3. On the struggle for patronage of the arts and sciences during the Early Republic, see Joseph J. Ellis, *After the Revolution: Profiles of Early American Culture* (New York: Norton, 1979); and Neil Harris, *The Artist in American Society: The Formative Years, 1790–1860* (New York: George Braziller, 1966).

[16] George Ticknor Curtis, *Life of Daniel Webster* (New York: D. Appleton, 1870), vol. 1, 260.

curious and interesting facts of any language with which we are acquainted."[17]

Du Ponceau and his colleagues found themselves resorting to a combination of Romantic inspiration and natural theology to justify their interest in Indian languages. In his preface to a Delaware grammar, compiled by the Moravian missionary, David Zeisberger, Du Ponceau acknowledged that beyond improved communications between nations, the practical benefits of philology were difficult to identify. "Thus much is certain," however, "that no science more powerfully excites that desire of knowledge which is inherent in our nature, and which, no doubt, was given to us by the Almighty for wise purposes."[18] In notes he wrote to accompany an edition of Eliot's Massachusett grammar, Du Ponceau indicated that his interest in the grammar and in the whole comparative study of language had little to do with social utility. He was bringing Eliot's grammar to light not so much to inspire some sort of apostolic revival as to energize the minds of men. The comparative study of language, of the sort that would be afforded by works such as Eliot's, he explained, "is the study of man through that noble faculty, which distinguishes him from the rest of the animal creation; the faculty of 'holding communication from soul to soul'; an earnest, as I might say, and a foretaste of the enjoyments of celestial life." To those who have said that "metaphysicks is vanity," Du Ponceau offered the following reply: "The ignorant . . . can never succeed in eradicating from the breast of immortal man, 'This pleasing hope, this fond desire / This longing after something unpossessed,' which so powerfully impels him to search into every thing that may throw light on his physical and moral existence. 'Tis the Divinity that stirs within us.' "[19]

Some years later, in his presidential address to the newly formed American Oriental Society, Pickering reminded his listeners that "the question will again be coldly asked—of what utility is this [philological] knowledge? To which the answer," he allowed, "must ultimately be— because a *natural* desire for such knowledge has been implanted in man by his creator for wise purposes . . . and no man is willing to

[17] [John Pickering,] "Review of *A Discourse on the Religion of the Indian Tribes of North America* . . ., by Samuel Foster Jarvis," *North American Review* 11:3 (July 1820): 113.

[18] Peter Stephen Du Ponceau, "The Translator's Preface" to "A Grammar of the Language of the Lenni Lenape or Delaware Indians. Translated from the German Manuscript of the Late Rev. David Zeisberger," *Transactions of the American Philosophical Society* 3 (1830): 76.

[19] Peter Stephen Du Ponceau, "Notes and Observations on Eliot's Indian Grammar," *Collections of the Massachusetts Historical Society* 9 (1822): ii.

throw aside, as useless, these and a thousand other particulars of the
past generations of his race, although he cannot demonstrate their
direct applicability to any common purpose that would in popular language be denominated practically *useful*."[20] To yield to the human desire to know was, in the end, to yield to divine will. It was to worship
God by looking to his creation in nature. "God has revealed himself to
mankind in two ways," Du Ponceau wrote, "by his sacred writings, and
by the works of nature, constantly open before us; and it is the privilege as well as the duty of man to study both to the advancement of
[God's] glory."[21] As if to openly dissent from their Enlightenment predecessors, Du Ponceau and Pickering disclaimed any broader social or
political importance for their linguistic interests. Instead, they ap-
pealed to natural theology, or the old Christian idea that the human
drive to understand was the result not of blind self-interest but of a
divine imperative to worship God through both his works and his
Word. And, consistent with Romantic language philosophy, this justification for studying language implied that languages were not social
conventions but ancient endowments. And hence, to dismiss any language, no matter who its speakers, was to dismiss a component of a
larger divine design.

In addition to revealing a signature American Romantic dilemma—
the conflict between commerce and culture—skepticism about the
utility of Indian-language study also reflected the peculiar place of language study in a broader world of learning. The American poet could
find legitimacy in defending and articulating a national idiom; the
physical scientist could find it in provisioning industry. But the student
of language had the peculiar burden of serving neither purpose in any
obvious way. All he could hope to do was convince others that a divine
imperative to pursue knowledge inspired such painstaking, meticulous,
and arcane pursuits as the analysis of disappearing indigenous tongues.
For it was only through the controlled pursuit of linguistic facts that
language became sublime. The peculiar position of this kind of learning was further reflected in the methodological variance among students of language in the 1820s.[22]

As Du Ponceau understood it, the study of language could take three
forms. The first, he explained to Albert Gallatin, was "*Phonology.*" This
approach involved studying the relationship between sounds and signs.
The second, "*Etymology,*" had been the predominant mode of studying

[20] John Pickering, "Address at the First Annual Meeting," *Journal of the American Oriental
Society* 1 (1843): 59.

[21] Du Ponceau, "Notes and Observations on Eliot's Indian Grammar," ii.

[22] This theme is dealt with in both Ellis, *After the Revolution*, and Harris, *The Artist in
American Society.*

American Indian language. "Its object is the comparison of the *words*, singly, of different languages, tracing their filiation," a method Du Ponceau had little use for.[23] As he once explained to Thomas Jefferson, "The study of language has been too long confined to mere 'word hunting' for the sake of finding affinities of sound."[24] Last, Du Ponceau explained that he preferred the approach of a group of Revolutionary-era French social theorists and philosophers, the Idéologues, who, aside from their opposition to Napoleon and their admiration for American political institutions, remained—in the face of the Revolutionary cataclysm—without apology dedicated to the universalist and determinist traditions of an early French Enlightenment. What this meant was that they disavowed the various forms of irrationalism that came to pervade so much post-Revolutionary culture in favor of the doctrine that rational human nature was universal and that history unfolded as the result of a natural human quest to identify and satisfy needs. The Idéologues' interest in language reflected this position. Far from seeking to uncover the grand course of human history by uncovering etymological filiations, they sought to uncover the distinct cognitive responses humans had to their various environments. And these cognitive processes were identifiable not in words—the focus of most Anglo-American language study—but in structure. To put it in modern terms, the Idéologues believed that mind structures languages. Hence, if one seeks to know the ordering principles behind human thought, one must identify those principles in the order of language. Instead of merely comparing words and identifying etymological correlations, Du Ponceau explained, "*Idéology* . . . compares the grammatical forms and syntax of the different idioms."[25] For the Idéologues, the purpose of such comparison was ultimately the discovery of a universal grammar of the sort that seventeenth-century universal language theorists had thought could bring to philosophy the kind of certainty that numbers brought to mathematics. However, such a universal grammar was valuable to them not so much because it could bring an end to specific moral and theological arguments but because it could, as the historian Keith Baker has written, "establish the basis for a rational social order."[26] By grasping the workings of mind, the Idéologues assumed they could

[23] Du Ponceau to Gallatin, April 2, 1826, Gallatin-Du Ponceau Correspondence, Albert Gallatin Papers, New York Historical Society.

[24] Du Ponceau to Jefferson, Feb. 17, 1817, History and Literature Committee Letterbook, 1:61.

[25] Du Ponceau to Gallatin, April 2, 1826, Gallatin-Du Ponceau Correspondence.

[26] Keith Baker, *Inventing the French Revolution: Essays on French Political Culture in the Eighteenth Century* (Cambridge: Cambridge University Press, 1990), 17. Also George Lichtheim, "The Concept of Ideology," *History and Theory* 4:2 (1965): 164–70; and Emmet

fashion a new moral code consistent with innate patterns of cognition. What mattered to them was thus not the diverse experience of humans—something indicated by the diversions in their vocabularies— but an underlying mode of cognition. And, in contrast to vocabulary, grammar was not contingent on historical and cultural change. Rather, it was rooted in the very structures of mind. Albert Gallatin articulated this doctrine when he wrote that "though new words have been introduced and others become obsolete, though languages have been polished and adorned, the grammatical forms remain the same as they were four hundred years ago, and have been found sufficient for the communication of new ideas and of all that may have been added to our knowledge."[27]

Idéology, Du Ponceau explained to Gallatin, "allows me to muse and dream more than any other [approach to language study], and its *approchements* and inferences are highly attractive." The other branches of philology, while valuable for generating facts and examining "minutely into details," did not afford the same kind of intellectual stimulation Du Ponceau sought for his private time. Furthermore, while "the want of . . . minute examinations may often lead me into errors, . . . I cannot afford time to pursue details as much as I would wish and [jurisprudence] takes up too much of my attention to allow of it."[28] *Idéology*, Du Ponceau was saying, was precisely the kind of self-contained intellectual exercise that would make possible a balance between professional obligation and personal cultivation.

Though he shared the Idéologues' interest in the structure of thought, Du Ponceau departed from their doctrine in one significant way: he rejected the notion that beneath the diverse grammars of the world there could be found a single, original grammar. Apparently Court de Gébelin had been seeking such a "primitive" grammar at the time of Du Ponceau's association with him, and it was an ambition Du Ponceau later denounced as "impossible."[29] Much like Locke, Du Ponceau had no use for the notion that vestiges of an original Edenic language could be identified in existing tongues. "The poet Dante," Du Ponceau explained, "in one of his Visions of Paradise, tells us of a conversation that he had with Adam, the Father of mankind. He asked him what had become of the language which he spoke in the garden of Eden? 'It has perished,' answered the patriarch; 'everything that is hu-

---

Kennedy, "'Ideology,' from Destutt de Tracy to Marx," *Journal of the History of Ideas* 40:3 (July–September 1979): 353–68.

[27] Albert Gallatin, "A Synopsis of the Indian Tribes of North America," *Archaeologia Americana: Transactions and Collections of the American Antiquarian Society* 2 (1836): 207.

[28] Du Ponceau to Gallatin, May 4, 1826, Gallatin-Du Ponceau Correspondence.

[29] Whitehead, "Autobiography of Peter Stephen Du Ponceau," 64:2 (April 1940): 261.

man must perish; heaven alone shall last forever.'" It was thus "in vain . . . to seek for traces of [the primitive language] anywhere. The languages of Memphis, Babylon and Carthage . . . have perished, and the written memorials of them that still remain, mock the science of Philologists."[30] For Du Ponceau, the notion that some sort of foundational universal grammar or language could be found smacked of the kind of conjecture and uninformed hypothesis Adams had attacked. There was, in Du Ponceau's position, however, a different moral conundrum. If language could not be reduced to anything universal, was the same true of thought itself? Were human patterns of cognition as varied as language itself? This conclusion was almost inescapable. For only by abandoning a progressive, teleological, and universal conception of culture—one that makes culture entirely a reflection of mental progress—could Du Ponceau defend his central claim: namely, that in the organization of Indian languages there was a special beauty.

Writing of the Delaware language, he explained that "the manner in which words are compounded [and] the great number and variety of ideas which [Delaware] has the power of expressing in one single word; particularly by means of the verbs; all these stamp its character for abundance, strength, and comprehensiveness of expression." Quite simply, Du Ponceau was seeing beauty and elegance of expression where few had seen it before: not in indigenous eloquence but in the very structure and form of indigenous languages themselves. And this was not merely a superficial matter: Delaware and other American Indian languages ought not "be divested, even in the imagination, of the admirable order, method, and regularity, which pervade them." For "a simple language may be, perhaps, unmethodical; but one which is highly complicated and in which the parts of speech are to a considerable degree interwoven with each other, I humbly conceive, never can."[31] Whatever might be said of American Indians' social lives and physical conditions, Du Ponceau insisted, their languages were the stuff of grammatical genius.

In his 1819 "Report" as corresponding secretary of the American Philosophical Society's Historical and Literary Committee, Du Ponceau explained that his explorations of Zeisberger's Delaware grammar, his correspondence with the Moravian missionary John Heckewelder, and his study of available sources on American Indian language had all led him to conclude the following: first, "that the American languages in general are rich in words and in grammatical forms, and that in their

---

[30] Du Ponceau, *Discourse*, 35.

[31] Peter S. Du Ponceau, "Report of the Corresponding Secretary . . . ," *Transactions of the Historical and Literary Committee of the American Philosophical Society* 1 (1819): xxvii.

complicated construction, the greatest order, method and regularity prevail"; second, "that these complicated forms . . . appear to exist in all those languages, from Greenland to Cape Horn"; and third, "that these forms appear to differ essentially from those of the ancient and modern languages of the old hemisphere."[32] They were, that is, uniquely American. Further, such a "rich, copious, expressive" linguistic form "would rather appear to have been formed by philosophers in their closets, than by savages in the wilderness."[33]

The four Old World forms, the "asyntactic," the "analytic," the "synthetic," and the "mixed," Du Ponceau argued, all lacked the American "polysynthetic" tongue's capacity to combine many ideas into a single word. They did not, that is, reflect so efficient, so concise, and so elegant a cognitive mode. Further, because each word could represent only a single thought, the "asyntactic," tongues spoken in China had "great deficiency of grammatical forms." Chinese words, in Du Ponceau's mind, were thus akin to Chinese script: they were not morphemes or root words, modified by inflections of some kind, but were fixed units of meaning. The "analytic" languages, which included English, Icelandic, Danish, Swedish, and German, "possess . . . grammatical forms, sufficient to express and connect together every idea to be communicated by means of speech, but . . . those forms are so organized, that almost every distinct idea has a single word to convey or express it," making them particularly taxing on speakers' memories. "Synthetic" languages, including Latin, Greek, and the Slavic languages, were those "in which the principal parts of speech are formed by a synthetical operation of the mind, and in which several ideas are frequently expressed by one word." And last, the fourth variety: "The French, Italian, Spanish and Portuguese, with their various dialects, in which conquest has in a great degree intermingled the modes of speech of the second and third class, would together form a . . . 'mixed'" class of languages.[34]

It is doubtless no coincidence that the languages closest in form to those of America—the "synthetic"—are the ones Europeans associated with the beginnings of civilization. It is also significant that Du Ponceau finds in them merely a less effective way of combining ideas into single words and, in turn, a less ingenious structure. For Du Ponceau ultimately held that the inventors of American Indian languages had

[32] Ibid., xxiii.

[33] Ibid., xxvi.

[34] Peter S. Du Ponceau and Rev. John Heckewelder, "A Correspondence Between the Reverend John Heckewelder of Bethlehem, and Peter S. Du Ponceau, esq. . . . ." *Transactions of the Historical and Literary Committee of the American Philosophical Society* 1 (1819): 400–401.

devised the most effective system known anywhere in the world for combining ideas into discrete units of speech. And for Du Ponceau, this was the result of superior intellect. He thus explained, "To me it would appear that the perfection of language consists in being able to express much in a few words; to raise at once in the mind by a few magic sounds, whole masses of thoughts which strike by a kind of instantaneous intuition." So powerful did Du Ponceau find the effect of this that he concluded that such languages "must be the medium by which immortal spirits communicate with each other; such, I should think, were I disposed to indulge in fanciful theories, must have been the language first taught to mankind by the great author of all perfection."[35]

What could be more perfect, and therefore closer to divinity, than a single Delaware word *Wulamalessohalian*," which signified "thou who makest me happy"? "How delighted would be Moore, the poet of the loves and graces, if his language, instead of five or six tedious words slowly following in the rear of each other, had furnished him with an expression like this, in which the lover, the object beloved, and the delicious sentiment which their mutual passion inspires, are blended, are fused together in one comprehensive appelative term?"[36] That a seemingly degraded nation spoke so perfect a tongue could mean only one thing: that there was no "necessary connexion between the greater and lesser degree of civilization of a people, and the organization of their language."[37]

"Alas!," Du Ponceau wrote Heckewelder in July 1816, "if the beauties of the [Delaware] language were found in the ancient Coptic, or in some ante-diluvian Balylonish [*sic*] dialect, how would the learned of Europe be at work to display them in a variety of shapes and raise a thousand fanciful theories on that foundation! What superior wisdom, talents and knowledge would they not ascribe to nations whose idioms were formed with so much skill and method! But who cares for the poor American Indians? They are savages and barbarians and live in the woods; must not their language be savage and barbarous like them?" Such was the preposterous reasoning of "those pretended philosophers who court fame by writing huge volumes on the origin of human language."[38] The ultimate absurdity of this work, to Du Ponceau and the rest of the American philological community, was its utter failure to build from facts and experience. "How shameful it is," John

[35] Ibid., 417.
[36] Ibid.
[37] Ibid., 399.
[38] Ibid., 384.

Pickering remarked, "that while others are rambling among the thorns and briers of the Indian thickets in search of facts, those lazy fellows should loll in their armchairs and cut out an Indian language or Indian manners, according to their own pattern, with as little hesitation or doubt as if they had explored everything themselves! I am tired of such reveries."[39]

European philosophers, Du Ponceau explained, formulate theories "without knowing, perhaps, any language but their own, and the little Latin and Greek that they have been taught at college. You would think, when you read their works, that they had lived in the first ages of the creation and . . . know exactly what words were first uttered when men began to communicate their ideas to each other by means of articulated sounds." It was no wonder that they had the hubris to "tell you how the various parts of speech, in perfect, regular order, were successively formed, and with a little encouragement, they would, I have no doubt, compile a Grammar and Dictionary of the [original] primitive language."[40] For Du Ponceau, this was indicative of the a priori reasoning behind eighteenth-century theories of linguistic refinement. "It is a pity, indeed," he continued, "that the Delawares, the Wyandots and the Potawatamies, with languages formed on a construction which had not been before thought of, come to destroy their beautiful theories." What was an American such as himself to do with evidence that disproved Old World orthodoxy? "Are we to suppress the languages of our good Indians, or to misrepresent them, that the existing systems on Universal Grammar and the origin of language may be preserved? No . . . we shall on the contrary, I hope, labour with all our might to make them known."[41] Du Ponceau was offering himself, his subject matter, and his fellow researchers as foils for the traditions of Enlightenment language study: with access to American Indian speech, he was suggesting to Heckewelder, the two of them would be able to topple the dominant, hierarchical, and Eurocentric Enlightenment philosophy of language.

Du Ponceau saved his most cutting attack for his fellow jurist Monboddo. Although he questioned Monboddo's all too trusting use of Father Sagard—and his near total lack of firsthand experience with the peoples of America—what he most objected to was Monboddo's claim that Huron was a uniquely unrefined tongue. In a biting rhetorical flourish, he asked Heckewelder to "suppose that a Huron or a Dela-

---

[39] Mary Pickering, *The Life of John Pickering*, 311.
[40] Du Ponceau and Heckewelder, "A Correspondence . . . ," 384.
[41] Ibid., 384–85.

ware . . . in the pride of pompous ignorance" were to follow "Lord Monboddo's course of reasoning, he will say: 'The English is the most imperfect language upon earth, for its words have no kind of analogy to each other. They say, for instance, *a house*, and the things that belong to a house they call *domestic.* . . . What belongs to a *king* is royal; to a *woman*, feminine; to a *ship*, naval; to a *town*, urban; to the *country*, rural. Such another irregular, unmethodical dialect never existed, I believe, on the back of the Great Tortoise [North America]!!' "[42] On what grounds, Du Ponceau was asking, could Monboddo rightly judge the Huron, or any other language, for that matter, to be inferior? Surely it was not on his secondhand evidence. Nor was it the a priori assumption that a people with weak social ties were by necessity bound to speak a crude language.

Du Ponceau even went so far as to suggest that European philosophers of language simply could not assimilate knowledge that undermined their sense of cultural superiority. For this reason, "it has been easier to ascribe the beautiful organization of [American] languages to stupidity and barbarism" than to admit that, in the end, philosophers know little about American languages, much less the origin or development of all languages. Both were equally distant from their experience. In a sense, here, Du Ponceau was accusing previous philosophers of failing to adjust their theories to fit the facts; failing, that is, to admit that the entire eighteenth-century evolutionary model for language development was founded on untested premises. He explained to Heckewelder that its proponents—particularly Dr. Adam Smith, its "pre-eminent" proponent—have "set themselves to work in order to prove that those admirable combinations of ideas in the form of words, which in the ancient languages of Europe used to be considered as some of the greatest efforts of the human mind, proceed in the savage idioms from the absence or weakness of mental powers in those who originally framed them."[43] They have thus theorized that "savage nations . . . express many ideas in a single word, because they have not yet acquired the necessary skill to separate them from each other by the process of analysis, and to express them simply."[44]

For all its conviction, Du Ponceau's was a lonely voice. Few were prepared to abandon Enlightenment orthodoxy regarding the correlation between civilization and linguistic refinement, and fewer still were prepared to disassociate the growth of reasoning faculties with the civil-

---

[42] Ibid., 385–86.
[43] Ibid., 418.
[44] Ibid., 398.

izing process. Few, that is, had come to doubt the correlation between poetic speech and mental backwardness. More influential, and more typical, were the views of Du Ponceau's German contemporary, the philologist and philosopher of language Wilhelm von Humboldt, brother of the geographer and statesman Alexander. Humboldt refused to accept Du Ponceau's claims for the mental powers behind indigenous American speech. For him, reason was the sole mark of civility. And a refined capacity to reason was both a cause and an effect of the most precise languages—precise because of their rule-bound and systematic inflection. In Humboldt's view, Greek, for instance, preserved the totality and nuance of an original idea or word by affording every distinct idea an equally distinct and readily classified unit of speech. The American languages, in contrast, do not "carry the free imprint of every material idea, the absolute fixity, and the character that immediately indicates to the ear that the thing presents itself with several relations, such as we find it in the Greek and Sanskrit languages."[45] In other words, instead of evoking in the mind a precise idea of the object, instead of leaving a very limited space between the signifier and the notion it conveyed, Delaware speech communicated ideas through often ambiguous imagery. Humboldt had thus taken the perceived metaphoric tendencies of American languages to represent—as they had for most previous observers—imprecision and crudeness of thought. But, much like Du Ponceau, he did not take for granted the notion that this poetic form was the result of delayed historical growth. Indeed, his very interest in North American tongues grew out of the broader philosophical problem of relating language difference to historical change. In a letter to John Pickering, Humboldt expressed his desire to explain whether the peculiarities of American languages "appertain to a certain train of thought and intellectual individuality altogether peculiar to the American nations, or rather, whether that which distinguishes them proceeds from the social state, from the degree of civilization in which those people happen to be who speak them." Did the distinctive quality of American languages reflect a different structure of mind, or did they, as previous theorists assumed, simply reflect cultural and social stagnation? Whichever was the case, Humboldt clearly embraced the view that the beauty of American tongues was a function of the limited mental power that went into their creation. They were beautiful because they were crude. "It has seemed to me," he continued, "that the character of the American languages is per-

[45] Quoted and translated by Hans Aarsleff in "Introduction" to *Wilhelm von Humboldt: On Language,* trans. Peter Heath (Cambridge: Cambridge University Press, 1988), lxii. The original letter is Vater to Du Ponceau, September 2, 1827, APS Archives.

haps that through which all languages in their origin must at some time have passed."[46]

Du Ponceau would have none of this. Writing in the preface to Zeisberger's Delaware grammar, he complained that "a learned member of the Berlin Academy of Sciences, in an ingenious and profound dissertation on the forms of languages, . . . admits that those of the American Indians are rich, methodical," and, of greatest importance, "artificial in their structure." Their form, that is, did not result from natural processes or circumstances but from purely human invention. Nonetheless, he continued, Humboldt would not allow American languages "to possess what he calls genuine grammatical forms, because, says he, their words are not inflected like those of the Greek, Latin, and Sanskrit, but are formed by a different process," and, as it turned out, a much cruder process called by Humboldt "agglutination." This involved grouping words into larger units of meaning without applying any real logical or formal principles. The result is not elegance and beauty but something that merited "an inferior rank in the scale of languages." Du Ponceau saw no valid justification for this hypothesis; it was simply a matter of ignoring the facts. If Humboldt were to look at Zeisberger's grammar, instead of supposedly simplistic and haphazard "agglutination," he would find "in the conjugations of the Delaware verbs, those inflected forms which he justly admires" in the Indo-European tongues. For Du Ponceau, the views of Humboldt were appalling enough to be compared to those of frontier Indian haters, "disposed to disparage every thing that belongs to the American Indians." And, he warned, "this feeling, when once entertained, knows no bounds, and men, in other respects gifted with judgments and talents, feel its influence unperceived."[47]

Du Ponceau's refusal to accept a correlation between civilization and linguistic refinement was in some sense a reflection of his own cultural milieu. As the product of Europe's cultural provinces, he sought for those provinces a reputation for worthy literary inquiry. He sought, that is, to counter the assumption that culture could never flourish in America. In the end, this provincial quest led Du Ponceau to foreshadow modern linguists' rejection of any correlation between a language's expressive potential and the social, cultural, or racial background of its speakers. Indeed, Du Ponceau would have found little

[46] Mary Pickering, *The Life of John Pickering*, 302.

[47] Du Ponceau, "The Translator's Preface," 77–78. The most suggestive treatment of Du Ponceau's dispute with Humboldt is in Aarsleff's "Introduction" to *On Language*, lxi–lxiv.

fault with Edward Sapir's conclusion that "all attempts to connect particular types of linguistic morphology [or form] with certain correlated
stages of cultural development are vain. Rightly understood, such correlations are rubbish."[48]

[48] Edward Sapir, *Language: An Introduction to the Study of Speech* (San Diego: Harcourt
Brace, 1921), 219.

Conclusion

FEW WHITE Americans shared Peter Du Ponceau's determination to find an indigenous American poetics; fewer still were inclined to see in the languages of Native Americans anything particularly artful. More typical were the views of Lewis Cass, a former superintendent of Indian affairs for the Michigan Territory. In a review of the publication on which Du Ponceau and Heckewelder collaborated—*Transactions of the Historical and Literary Committee of the American Philosophical Society*—he ridiculed Du Ponceau's claims, writing that far from revealing any inherent beauties, the Wyandot dialect of Huron, for instance, "is harsh, guttural, and undistinguishable; filled with intonations, that seem to start from the speaker with great pain and effort . . . , and its acquisition is universally considered upon the frontier as a hopeless task." As for the alleged polysynthetic form of American languages, Cass saw little to be envied in a language that contained words such as *Machelemuxowagan*. "It is idle to talk of such words," he explained. "Every language may have as many, as the most ecstatic philologist could require." What ultimately made the languages of North America distinct, Cass claimed, was precisely that which almost every Enlightenment theorist attributed to them: namely, the imprint of inferior minds. "The range of thought of our Indian neighbors," he observed, "is extremely limited. Of abstract ideas they are almost wholly destitute. They soon forget the past, improvidently disregard the future, and waste their thoughts, when they do think, upon the present. The character of all original languages must depend, more or less, upon the wants, means, and occupations, mental and physical, of the people who speak them, and we ought not to expect to find the complicated refinements of polished tongues, among those of our Indians."[1] For Cass—who, as secretary of war during much of Andrew Jackson's presidency, implemented the Indian Removal Act of 1830 and prosecuted a series of government insurgencies against southern Indian groups—such thinking provided a convenient justification for a new government Indian policy. And that policy presumed that the solution to Indian-White conflict was not forced assimilation but forced separation. The differences of mind between Europeans and Native Americans were, in Cass's view, too profound to be overcome through translation—a view that had long been held by opponents of bilingual Indian education.[2]

[1] [Lewis Cass], *North American Review* 22 (1826): 74–79.
[2] On removal see Francis Paul Prucha, *The Great Father: The U.S. Government and the*

In the heat of the religious awakening that swept the North American colonies during the first half of the eighteenth century, David Brainerd, Presbyterian missionary to Delaware and Mahican, wrote that one of the difficulties of conveying "divine truths to the Understandings of the Indians, was the defectiveness of their language, the want of terms to express and convey Ideas of spiritual things." Brainerd had concluded that the absence of words for "Lord, Saviour, Salvation, Sinner, Justice, Condemnation, Faith, Repentance, Justification, Adoption, Sanctification, Grace, Glory, Heaven" was indicative of the broader weaknesses of the indigenous mind. "What renders it much more Difficult to convey divine truths to the Understandings of these Indians," he explained, "is, that there seems to be no foundation in their minds to begin upon, I mean no Truths that may be taken for granted as being already known."[3] Those truths that Christians had assumed to be imbedded in the natures of all humans—whether or not they were able to articulate them—appeared to be absent from the Native American soul. In this assertion, Brainerd anticipated the view that differences in language represented differences not so much in experience as in human nature. Perhaps the best-known eighteenth-century proponent of this view was the Neapolitan intellectual and opponent of Enlightenment universalism Giambattista Vico: "How is it that there are as many different vulgar tongues as there are peoples? To solve it, we must here establish this great truth: that . . . peoples have certainly by diversity of climates acquired different natures, . . . so and not otherwise there have arisen as many different languages as there are nations."[4] More than merely transcending environmental differences, translation would have to transcend fundamental differences in human nature. What this meant, for some commentators, was the transcending of fundamental and entrenched differences of mind.

Noah Webster, for instance, concluded that "nations, in a savage state, or which have not been accustomed to metaphysical disquisitions, have no terms to communicate abstract ideas, which they never entertained; and hence the absurdity of attempting to christianize savages."[5] One Scottish visitor to the United States, writing in the late

---

American Indians (Lincoln: University of Nebraska Press, 1984), vol. 1, part 2; and Ronald M. Satz, *American Indian Policy in the Jacksonian Era* (Lincoln: University of Nebraska Press, 1975). Also Michael Paul Rogin, *Fathers and Children: Andrew Jackson and the Subjugation of the American Indian* (New York: Knopf, 1975).

[3] David Brainerd, *Mirabeli Dei inter Indicos, or the Rise and Progress of a Remarkable Work of Grace* . . . (Philadelphia: Wm. Bradford, [1746]), 228–29.

[4] Giambattista Vico, *The New Science*, trans., Thomas G. Bergin and Max H. Fisch (Ithaca, N.Y.: Cornell University Press, 1968), 148.

[5] Noah Webster, *A Collection of Essays and Fugitiv* [sic] *Writings on Moral, Historical, Political, and Literary Subjects* (Boston: I. Thomas, 1790), 225.

1830s, arrived at the same conclusion after interviewing a Seneca: because certain complex emotions and ideas seemed alien to Native American consciousness, "translation is accomplished only by means of paraphrases, some of them of a very awkward character, and which, after all that can be done, do not suggest to the Indian the same emotions or ideas which the English words call up in the Anglo-American mind."[6] Indeed, as part of a more general argument against Lockean epistemology, Coleridge claimed that if words were purely expressions of experience, the vocabularies of Europe's peasant population would not differ from that of the savage tribes of the world. As it was, however, "if the history of the phrases in hourly currency among our peasants were traced, a person not previously aware of the fact would be surprized at finding so large a number, which three or four centuries ago were the exclusive property of the universities and the schools; and at the commencement of the Reformation had been transferred from the school to the pulpit, and thus gradually passed into common life." Such, in Coleridge's view, was the only way to explain how the peasant vocabulary—consisting of all sorts of abstractions related to morality and metaphysics—could so transcend its material surroundings. That words resulted not from natural impulses but from creative or imaginative operations of mind raised a critical problem, however—one that became all the more troubling if, as was the case with Du Ponceau, one presupposed differences not just in environment but also in fundamental structures of mind: "The extreme difficulty, and often the impossibility, of finding words for the simplest moral and intellectual processes in the languages of uncivilized tribes has proved perhaps the weightiest obstacle to the progress of our most zealous and adroit missionaries. Yet these tribes are surrounded by the same nature, as our peasants are; but in still more impressive forms; and they are, moreover, obliged to *particularize* many more of them."[7] They are, that is, obliged not so much to resort to metaphors and similes, of the sort that was so widely thought to make their speech eloquent, as to resort to proper names that have only parochial powers of evocation. For Coleridge, there was no necessary connection between a lack of civilization and poetic speech. Poetry—much like language itself—is pure invention, but invention born not out of necessity so much as out of creative imagination. And the capacity of some nations to create poetic speech was, in the end, a result of their distinct natures.

In American writing, few passages better reflect this kind of thinking

[6] George Combe, *Notes on the United States of North America During a Phrenological Visit in 1838–39–40* (Philadelphia: Carey and Hart, 1841), vol. 2, 87.

[7] Samuel Taylor Coleridge, *Biographia Literaria*, ed. James Engell and W. Jackson Bate (Princeton, N.J.: Princeton University Press, 1983), vol. 2, 54.

than Thoreau's tribute to the language of the Abenaki. Although he had "found so many arrowheads" for him to be fully convinced that "the Indian was not the invention of historians and poets," he had to hear that "purely wild and primitive American sound . . . that issued from the wigwams of this country before Columbus was born." It was through language alone that Thoreau could commune not only with the original inhabitants of his nation but also with his nation's past. For Indian language—fixed and unchanging—was for Thoreau, much as it had been for Jefferson, Washington, and Barton, the last remaining tie to the ancient-history of the country. Upon hearing the Abenaki of Maine, he wrote, "I felt that I stood . . . as near to the primitive man of America, that night, as any of its discoverers ever did."[8] It was in delivering their ancient words that, in Thoreau's mind, native peoples distinguished themselves from Whites. "The fact is, the history of the white man is a history of improvement, that of the red man, a history of fixed habits or stagnation."[9] In contrast to Jefferson, for Thoreau this was no simple matter of environmental difference. Rather, it was a matter of the "essential and innate difference between man and man."[10] And that difference was never more apparent to Thoreau than when he heard Abanaki speech. "There can be no more startling evidence" that the Indians are "a distinct and comparatively aboriginal race than to hear this unaltered Indian language."[11]

It was this Romantic notion that language difference was indicative of profound differences in nature that justified for many the deliberate elimination of Indians' languages. For only by being liberated from their impaired tongues, so the reasoning went, could Indians achieve mental parity with Americans of European descent. "In the present state of those people," Albert Gallatin wrote in 1836, "no greater demand need be made on their intellectual faculties, than to teach them the English language; but this so thoroughly, that they may forget their own."[12] And fourteen years earlier, the Reverend Jedediah Morse wrote in a report on Indian affairs that "after a few generations, it is hoped, the English language will take the place" of all Indian tongues. "As fast as possible," he urged his readers, "let Indians forget their own languages, in which nothing is written, and nothing of course can be preserved, and learn ours, which will at once open to them the whole field

---

[8] *The Writings of Henry David Thoreau* (Boston: Houghton, Mifflin, 1887–1900), vol. 3, 184–85.
[9] Ibid., 8:235–36.
[10] Ibid., 8:235.
[11] Ibid., 3:184.
[12] Albert Gallatin, "A Synopsis of the Indian Tribes of North America," *Archaeologia Americana: Transactions and Collections of the American Antiquarian Society* 2 (1836): 159.

of every kind of useful knowledge."[13] In support of this goal, Morse argued against the publication of any texts in Native American tongues. To print such texts, he feared, would simply secure the confusion of tongues that impeded the cultural assimilation of America's indigenous population. He shared Noah Webster's sentiment that only a single "national language is a band of national union."[14]

The possibility that linguistic difference corresponded to differences in human nature—or the fundamental architecture of mind—begged another question: To what degree did differences in language correspond to fundamental differences in human biology? To what degree, that is, was there a correlation between language and race? Few Americans argued for any direct correlation, but in their efforts to reconcile the Mosaic account of creation with vast diversity among humans, some did move in that direction. One of them was the Hartford Congregational minister and theologian Horace Bushnell. Bushnell's interest was not so much in racializing language as it was in resurrecting a more literal and consensual reading of the Bible—something made difficult by the evident profundity of differences in language. In this spirit, he argued that the confusion of tongues would have been meaningless had it not resulted in the complete disappearance of any pre-Babel universal tongue. For, it would have represented a merely temporary punishment and one that humans could presumably control by reconstructing a universal language. Such would seem to offer no real inhibition to human hubris; indeed, for Bushnell, an insidious scientific spirit merely encouraged this attitude. "When our modern ethnologists undertake, as they say, in behalf of the scriptures, to establish the unity of the human race, by tracing all human languages to some common source, through a comparison of terms, or names, found in them all," he wrote, "they would seem to controvert the authority of the scriptures."[15] There was nothing in Scripture, Bushnell was contending, to suggest the possible survival of an original and universal tongue. In the world's languages, in other words, there was no proof of any common lineage. Whatever similarities there may be between tongues could easily be explained as random examples of cultural borrowing, especially since such similarities were by far exceptions to the rule.

Given the absence of any evidence of an original, universal tongue, Bushnell acknowledged two possible ways to explain the linguistic di-

[13] Jedediah Morse, *A Report to the Secretary of War of the United States, of Indian Affairs* . . . (New Haven, Conn.: S. Converse, 1822), 357.

[14] Noah Webster, *Dissertations on the English Language, with Notes Historical and Critical* (Boston: I. Thomas, 1789), 397.

[15] Horace Bushnell, *God in Christ: Three Discourses, Delivered at New Haven, Cambridge, and Andover* . . . (Hartford, Conn.: Brown and Parsons, 1849), 14.

versity of the globe: "the existence of races originally distinct," or "a miracle."[16] That is, the globe's different languages either were distinct signatures of different races or they were remnants of some biblical miracle—some sort of divine moment—that left humans with as many tongues as types of peoples. The argument bears a striking resemblance to that of the mid-eighteenth-century Scottish historian and multiple creationist Henry Home, Lord Kames, who claimed that there had been two creations. The first created humanity itself. The second was the fall of Babel, which created distinct races by scattering humans across the globe and leaving their natures to be shaped by the world's distinct environments. Language and race were therefore correlates, whatever the initial nature of creation.[17] This was a possibility Bushnell did not dismiss: whatever the nature of the original creation, some second, miraculous occurrence had diversified humanity into fundamentally different races. Hence, while Bushnell was not willing to go so far as to assert that multiple creations had given rise to a multitude of tongues, he nonetheless implied that linguistic difference corresponded to something far more profound than different levels of social or mental development. It corresponded, he implied, to profound and primordial human difference.

Bushnell's attitude reflected a growing American willingness to approach linguistic knowledge not as a way to reinforce assumptions about the unity of creation but as a way to assert the peculiarity and distinctiveness of the North American population. This thinking was in fact an extension of Du Ponceau's reasoning: if American Indian languages were cultural inheritances, then it stood to reason that they corresponded to other more profound distinctions. Even the painter and ethnographer George Catlin found himself unable to adhere to the idea that Indian tongues had a shared ancestry. "I do not believe," he explained in his *North American Indians*, "that the languages of the North American Indians can be traced to one root or to three or four, or any number of distinct idioms; nor do I believe all, or any one of them, will ever be fairly traced to a foreign origin."[18]

It was perhaps this possibility, more than simply the recondite character of linguistic knowledge, that made the study of Indian languages so difficult for American philologists to justify. If indigenous American languages could not be reduced to a single, indigenous idiom of some sort, then there was little in them that could be appropriated by White

---

[16] Ibid., 16.

[17] Henry Home, Lord Kames, *Sketches of the History of Man: in Four Volumes*, 2d ed. (Edinburgh: W. Strahan and T. Cadell, 1778).

[18] George Catlin, *North American Indians*, ed. Peter Mathiessen (1832–39; reprint, New York: Penguin Books, 1989), 466.

Americans. For if, in fact, what was primordial about American tongues was not so much their collective polysynthetic character but the various and differing characteristics that made the Algonquian languages distinct from the Iroquoian tongues, then perhaps the true Romantic fact about America was that it was a place of many and different nations— nations whose lineage could not be demonstrated and whose varying experiences offered little consolation to those seeking something that could be identified as distinctly American. Beyond this, however, American philologists faced another dilemma, and that was the absence in the United States of any organic connection between the White population, its language, and the land. For American Romantics, the choice was to celebrate some sort of indigenous poetics of the kind Du Ponceau was seeking to uncover or to sustain the liberal enlightenment view that language was pure social convention. To claim—as European nationalists had begun to do—that language, race, and nation were one, was to claim that the American nation was no nation at all. Indeed, this position had special appeal to racist defenders of slavery, some of whom openly dismissed the possibility that language could ever establish the unity of human creation. In an ironic twist, one such figure, who shared Du Ponceau's doubts about universal language, employed those doubts in defense of racist multiple creationism. The perverse Josiah Nott wrote that the "almighty in his wisdom has peopled our vast planet from many distant centres, instead of one, and with races or species originally and radically distinct." This being the case, what relevance could the story of Babel have to the world's ethnological landscape? For Nott, the answer was simple: "The absurdity of the argument so often reiterated, that the diversity of languages commenced at the building of Babel is obvious, for, according to the Bible itself, different tongues existed before Babel."[19] Not only did this prove that there was no necessary connection between the fall of Babel and the diversity of human tongues, it also suggested that human diversity predated the fall of the tower. Far from some sort of second creation that corresponded to the division of the globe's peoples by tongues, racial diversity, in the minds of figures like Nott, was part of an original, divine creation.[20] Far from reflecting mere differences in mind or hu-

[19] Josiah Nott, *Two Lectures on the Connection between the Biblical and Physical History of Man* . . . (1849; facsimile reprint, New York: Negro Universities Press, 1969), 5, 63. Kenneth Greenberg points out that in fact few defenders of slavery were prepared to defend polygenesis. See *Masters and Statesmen: The Political Culture of American Slavery* (Baltimore: Johns Hopkins University Press, 1985), 89–102.

[20] Among the studies that treat the emergence of a racial conception of human difference in the United States are William Stanton, *The Leopard's Spots: Scientific Attitudes Toward Race in America, 1815–1859* (Chicago: University of Chicago Press, 1960); and

man experience, differences embodied in the early modern conception of nationhood, language had come to reflect differences in race.

The European Romantic era witnessed a vigorous effort to extend this reasoning with assorted claims that in the ancient genius expressed in a people's tongue lay the ultimate proof that national and racial boundaries dated to the time of creation, and were therefore one. From the old Babel in which language and nation were one, European nationalists shifted to a new Babel in which race and nation were one. To speak a distinct national tongue was to express a collective national identity based on an organic and shared inheritance. The notion— defended by Du Ponceau—that a downtrodden nation could speak an extraordinary tongue was anathema to this view. The German philosopher J. G. Fichte proclaimed that in the genius of his nation's tongue lay the source of an overall superiority of mind and culture. In a public address delivered in Berlin less than a decade into the nineteenth century, he proclaimed, "Men are formed by language far more than language is formed by men."[21] This was because the collection of traditional ideas and ancestral emotions embodied in words imposed on speakers a sort of collective memory. For in each word of the German language, Fichte argued, lay an idea or experience unique to the German inventor of that word. To speak German was therefore to give oneself over to the mental processes of all those Germans who had, over time, given form to their language. Speaking German, in other words, bound the speaker to a national past because, quite literally, language embodied that past. The only way, however, for a tongue to retain such comprehensive historical content was for its speakers to defend it against the intrusions of conquerors and weaker races. In doing this, Fichte claimed, his nation had not simply expressed a sort of familial unity of descent and purpose; it had also secured for itself a cultural imperative for racial superiority; it had ensured that speakers of true German—of the original and pure Teutonic tongue—were superior to those other Teutonic peoples who had long ago begun to speak bastardized tongues—that had lost any correspondence to their nation's original greatness. Only the German "speaks a language which has been alive ever since it first issued from the force of nature, whereas the other Teutonic races speak a language which has movement on the surface only but is dead at the root."[22] Similar views were

---

George M. Frederickson, *The Black Image in the White Mind: The Debate on Afro-American Character and Destiny, 1817–1914* (Middletown, Conn.: Wesleyan University Press, 1987), esp. chs. 2–5.

[21] J. G. Fichte, *Addresses to the German Nation*, trans. R. F. Jones and G. H. Turnbull (1807–8; reprint, Chicago: Open Court Publishing, 1922), 55.

[22] Ibid., 68.

not at all unknown in the United States, but they tended to focus less on language than on more diffuse kinds of inheritances—a collection of largely imagined cultural traits that tended to fall under the Anglo-Saxon rubric.[23]

When, in the early nineteenth century, Europeans came to observe the New Nation, they brought with them Old World assumptions about the congruence of language and nation. In applying these assumptions to the United States, one writer in particular depicted a nation where minority tongues of any kind would disappear—not as they had in Europe, because of the alleged brilliance of the dominant tongue, but because of the will of the people. Unlike the nations of Europe, which were created by language, the American nation, it appeared, was creating its own idiom, an idiom with no place for the minority tongues of Indians.

That writer, Alexis de Tocqueville, explained that in democracies "the majority lays down the law about language as about all else." And that majority had no interest in tradition or convention. Rather, it shaped its speech strictly according to its needs: "Now the majority is more interested in business than study, in trade and politics than in philosophical speculation or fine writing. Most of the words coined or adopted for its use will bear the marks of these habits; they will chiefly serve to express the needs of industry, the passions of politics, or the details of public administration." The consequence of this habit was nothing less than the debasement of meaning. With new words forever being invented, and old words being reinvented to express the whim and fashion of the majority, there was nothing to ensure the connection between words and their original significance. Knowledge, as Jefferson had feared, would become nothing more than words; nothing more than signs with a random and fluid connection to reality. "Since there is no accepted judge, no permanent court to decide the meaning of a word," Tocqueville observed, "the phrase is left to wander free . . . , leaving the reader to guess which is intended."[24]

Europe's aristocratic nations had avoided this kind of semantic mayhem precisely because they had the kinds of overreaching, authoritarian institutions needed to define and preserve a national tongue. "In Aristocratic ages," such as the one that—in Tocqueville's mind—maintained a fragile hold on Europe in the 1830s, "when each nation

---

[23] See Reginald Horsman, *Race and Manifest Destiny: The Origins of American Racial Anglo-Saxonism* (Cambridge, Mass.: Harvard University Press, 1981).

[24] Alexis de Tocqueville, *Democracy in America*, ed. J. P. Mayer (Garden City, N.Y.: Anchor Books, 1969), 478–80.

likes to stand apart from the rest and have its own peculiar physiognomy, it often happens that several peoples of a common origin become much estranged from one another, so that . . . they do not speak in the same way." This situation was made all the more prevalent by Europe's class structure. Elites—determined to distinguish themselves not only from the aristocracy of other nations but also from the intrusions of the uneducated, unrefined rabble—established a standard, refined tongue for their nations, and that tongue functioned as a benchmark language in which the correspondence between words and ideas would be secure. But when "men are no longer held to a fixed social position, when they continually see one another and talk together, when castes are destroyed and classes change and merge, all of the words of a language get mixed up too. Those which cannot please the majority die; the rest form a common stock from which each man chooses at random." For this reason, "in the New World there are no dialects, and in the Old they are vanishing."[25] A democratic society would be a single-language society.

[25] Ibid., 480.

Select Primary Sources

Barton, Benjamin Smith. *New Views of the Origin of the Tribes and Nations of America.* Philadelphia: Privately printed, 1797.

Bartram, William. *Travels of William Bartram.* Edited by Mark Van Doren. Paperback ed. New York: Dover, 1955.

Baxter, Richard. *Reliquiæ Baxterianæ: or, Mr. Richard Baxters narrative of the most memorable passages of his life and times.* London: T. Parkhurst et al., 1696.

Brainerd, David. *Mirabeli Dei inter Indicos, or the Rise and Progress of a Remarkable Work of Grace. . . .* Philadelphia: Wm. Bradford, [1746].

Brerewood, Edward. *Enquiries Touching on the Diversity of Language and Religion through the Chief Parts of the World.* London: John Bill, 1614.

Browne, Thomas Gunter. *Hermes Unmasked.* 1795. Facsimile reprint, Menston, England: Scolar Press, 1969.

Bushnell, Horace. *God in Christ: Three Discourses, Delivered at New Haven, Cambridge, and Andover. . . .* Hartford, Conn.: Brown and Parsons, 1849.

Cappon, Lester J., ed. *The Adams-Jefferson Letters: The Complete Correspondence between Thomas Jefferson and Abigail and John Adams.* Chapel Hill: University of North Carolina Press, 1959.

Charlevoix, Pierre François Xavier de. *Journal of a Voyage to North America.* 2 vols. Edited by Louise Phelps Kellog. First English ed., 1761. Reprint, Chicago: Caxton Club, 1923.

Colden, Cadwallader. *The History of the Five Indian Nations.* 1727, 1747. Reprint, Ithaca, N.Y.: Cornell University Press, 1964.

Columbus, Christopher. *The Four Voyages of Christopher Columbus.* Edited by J. M. Cohen. London: Penguin Books, 1969.

Comenius, Jan Amos. *A Reformation of Schooles, Designed in Two Excellent Treatises. . .* 1642. Facsimile reprint, Menston, England: Scolar Press, 1969.

Condillac, Étienne Bonnot de. *An Essay on the Origin of Human Knowledge: Being a Supplement to Mr. Locke's Essay on the Human Understanding.* Translated by Thomas Nugent. 1756. Facsimile Reprint, Gainesville, Fla.: Scholar's Facsimiles and Reprints, 1971.

Cortes, Hernan. *Hernan Cortes: Letters from Mexico.* Edited and translated by Anthony Pagden. New Haven, Conn.: Yale University Press, 1986.

Du Ponceau, Peter S. "English Phonology." *Transactions of the American Philosophical Society* 1 (1818): 228–64.

———. "Report of the Corresponding Secretary . . ." *Transactions of the Historical and Literary Committee of the American Philosophical Society* 1 (1819): xvii–xivi.

———. "Notes and Observations on Eliot's Indian Grammar." In reprint edition of Eliot's *Indian Grammar Begun.* Collections of the Massachusetts Historical Society, 2d ser., 9 (1822): 223–42.

————. "The Translator's Preface" to "A Grammar of the Language of the Lenni Lenape or Delaware Indians. Translated from the German Manuscript of the Late Rev. David Zeisberger." *Transactions of the American Philosophical Society* 3 (1830): 65–96.

————. *A Discourse on the Necessity and the Means of Making Our National Literature Independent of That of Great Britain* . . . Philadelphia: Pennsylvania Library, 1834.

————. *Mémoire sur le système grammatical des langues de quelques nations indiennes de l'Amérique du nord.* Paris: Pihan de la Forest, 1838.

Du Ponceau, Peter S., and Rev. John Heckewelder. "A Correspondence between the Reverend John Heckewelder of Bethlethem, and Peter S. Du Ponceau, esq. . . ." *Transactions of the Historical and Literary Committee of the American Philosophical Society* 1 (1819): 355–448.

Dury, John. *The Reformed School and the Reformed Library Keeper.* 1651. Facsimile reprint, Menston, England: Scolar Press, 1972.

Eliot, John. *The Day Breaking, If Not the Sun-Rising of the Gospell with the Indians in New England.* London: Fulk Clifton, 1647.

————. *The Glorious Progress of the Gospel amongst the Indians in New England.* London: Edward Winslow, 1649.

————. *The Christian Commonwealth: Or, The Civil Policy of the Rising Kingdom of Jesus Christ.* London: Livewell Chapman, 1659.

————. *A Further Account of the Progress of the Gospel amongst the Indians of New England.* . . . London: John Macock, 1660.

————. "Learned Conjectures." In Thomas Thorowgood. *Jewes in America, or Probabilities that those Indians are Judaical, made more probable by some additionals to the former conjectures,* 1–27. London: H. Brome, 1660.

————. *The Indian Grammar Begun: or, An Essay to Bring the Indian Languages into Rules.* . . . Cambridge, Mass.: Marmaduke Johnson, 1666.

————. *The Indian Primer: or, the Way of Training Up Our Indian Youth in the Way of God.* Cambridge, Mass.: Marmaduke Johnson, 1669.

————. *The Logick Primer: Some Logical Notions to Initiate the Indians in the Knowledge of the Rule of Reason.* 1672. Reprint, Cleveland: Burrows Brothers, 1904.

————. "Letters from Rev. John Eliot of Roxbury to Hon. Robert Boyle." *Collections of the Massachusetts Historical Society,* 1st ser., 3 (1794): 177–88.

————. "Letters of John Eliot, the Apostle." *Proceedings of the Massachusetts Historical Society* 17 (1879–1880): 245–53.

————. *John Eliot and the Indians, 1652–1657: Being Letters Addressed to Rev. Jonathan Hanmer of Barnstaple, England.* Edited by Wilberforce Eames. New York: Adams and Grace Press, 1915.

————, trans. *Mamusee Wunneetapanatamwe Up-Biblum God.* Cambridge, Mass.: Marmaduke Johnson, 1663.

Eliot, John, and Thomas Mayhew Jr. *Tears of Repentence: Or, a Further Narrative of the Progress of the Gospel amongst the Indians.* London: Peter Cole, 1653.

Ferguson, Adam. *An Essay on the History of Civil Society.* Edited by Fania Oz-Salzberger. Cambridge: Cambridge University Press, 1995.

Fichte, J. G. *Addresses to the German Nation.* Translated by R. F. Jones and G. H. Turnbull. 1807–1808. Reprint, Chicago: Open Court Publishing, 1922.

Force, Peter, comp. *Tracts and Other Papers, Relating Principally to the Origin, Settlement, and Progress of the Colonies in North America.* 4 vols. Washington, D.C.: Peter Force, 1836.

Ford, John W., ed. *Some Correspondence between the Governors and Treasurers of the New England Company in London and the Commissioners of the United Colonies in America . . . between the Years 1657–1717, to Which Are Added the Journals of the Rev. Experience Mayhew.* London: Spottiswoode, 1896.

Gallatin, Albert. *Archaeologia Americana: Transactions and Collections of the American Antiquarian Society* 2 (1836).

Grotius, Hugo. *On the Origin of the Native Races of America. . . .* Edited by Edmund Goldsmid. Edinburgh: Privately published, 1884.

Hakluyt, Richard. *Divers Voyages Touching the Discovery of America and the Islands Adjacent unto the Same.* London: T. Woodcocke, 1582.

———. *The Principall Navigations Voiages and Discoveries of the English Nation. . . .* London: T. Woodcocke, 1582.

Harriot, Thomas. *A Brief and True Report of the New Found Land of Virginia.* 1590. Reprint, New York: Dover, 1972.

Harrison, William. *The Description of England.* Edited by Georges Edelen. Ithaca, N.Y.: Cornell University Press, 1968.

Heckewelder, John. "An Account of the History, Manners, and Customs, of the Indian Nations, Who Once Inhabited Pennsylvania and the Neighbouring States." *Transactions of the Historical and Literary Committee of the American Philosophical Society* 1 (1819): 3–347.

Hennepin, Louis, *A New Discovery of a Vast Country in America. . . .* 1698. Edited by Reuben Gold Thwaites. Chicago: A. C. McClurg, 1903.

Humboldt, Wilhelm von. *On Language: The Diversity of Human Language-Structure And Its Influence on the Mental Development of Mankind.* 1836. Translated by Peter Heath. Cambridge: Cambridge University Press, 1988.

Hume, David. *Essays: Moral, Political, and Literary.* Edited by Eugene F. Miller. Indianapolis: Liberty Classics, 1985.

Jameson, J. Franklin, ed. *Narratives of New Netherland, 1609–1664.* New York: Charles Scribner's Sons, 1909.

Jefferson, Thomas. *The Writings of Thomas Jefferson.* 20 vols. Edited by Andrew Lipscomb and Albert Ellery Bergh. Washington, D.C.: Thomas Jefferson Memorial Association, 1903–4.

———. *Notes on the State of Virginia.* Edited by William Peden. New York: Norton, 1972.

Johnson, Samuel. *Selected Writings.* Edited by Patrick Cruttwell, ed. Harmondsworth: Penguin Books, 1968.

Joutel, Henri. *A Journal of the Last Voyage Perform'd by Monsr. de la Sale, to the Gulph of Mexico. . . .* London: A. Bell, 1714.

L'Estrange, Hamon. *Americans, no Jewes, or Improbabilities that the Americans are of that race.* London: Henry Seile, 1652.

Laet, Johannes de. *L'Histoire du Nouveau Monde ou Description des Indes Occidentales.* . . . Leyden: Bonaventura and Abraham, 1640.

Lafitau, Joseph François. *Customs of the American Indians Compared with the Customs of Primitive Times.* 2 vols. 1724. Edited by William N. Fenton and Elizabeth L. Moore. Toronto: Champlain Society, 1974–1977.

Lahontan, Baron de. *Lahontan's New Voyages to North-America.* 2 vols. 1703. Edited by Reuben Gold Thwaites. Chicago: A. C. McClurg, 1905.

Lamy, Bernard. *The Art of Speaking: Written in French by Messieurs Du Port Royal.* 2d ed. London: W. Taylor, 1708.

Lawson, John. *A New Voyage to Carolina.* 1709. Reprint, Chapel Hill: University of North Carolina Press, 1967.

Lescarbot, Marc. *The History of New France.* 3 vols. 1612. Edited and translated by W. L. Grant. Toronto: Champlain Society, 1907–1914.

Levett, Christopher. *A Voyage to New England, Begun in 1623 and Ended in 1624.* London: E. Brewster, 1628.

Locke, John. *An Essay Concerning Human Understanding.* Edited by Peter H. Nidditch. Oxford: Oxford University Press, 1975.

Mather, Cotton. *Magnalia Christi Americana; or, The Ecclesiastical History of New England.* . . . 2 vols. 1852. Reprint, New York: Russell and Russell, 1967.

Monboddo, James Burnett, Lord. *Of the Origin and Progress of Language.* 6 vols. 1773. Facsimile reprint, Menston, England: Scolar Press, 1967.

Morse, Jedediah. *A Report to the Secretary of War of the United States, of Indian Affairs.* . . . New Haven, Conn.: S. Converse, 1822.

Pickering, John. Review of Heckewelder and Du Ponceau, *Transactions of the History and Literature Committee. North American Review* 9 (1819): 155–87.

———. "Introductory Observations" to reprint ed. of Eliot's *Indian Grammar Begun. Collections of the Massachusetts Historical Society,* 2d ser., 9 (1822): 223–42.

———. Review of Adelung's *Uebersicht aller bekannten Sprachen und iher Dialekte. North American Review* 14 (1822): 128–44.

———. "Indians" and "Remarks on the Indian Languages of North America." *Encyclopedia Americana* 6 (1831): 581–600.

———. "Address at the First Annual Meeting." *Journal of the American Oriental Society* 1 (1843): 1–60.

Powicke, F. J., ed. "Some Unpublished Correspondence of the Rev. Richard Baxter and the Rev. John Eliot, 'The Apostle to the American Indians,' 1656–1682." *Bulletin of the John Rylands Library* 15:1–2 (1931): 138–76, 442–66.

Priestley, Joseph. *Rudiments of English Grammar.* 1761. Facsimile reprint, Menston, England: Scolar Press, 1969.

———. *A Course of Lectures on the Theory of Language and Universal Grammar.* 1762. Facsimile reprint, London: Routledge/Thoemmes, 1993.

Purchas, Samuel. *Hakluytus Posthumous, or Purchas His Pilgrimes.* . . . 5 vols. London: Henrie Fetherstone, 1625–26.

Quaife, Milo Milton, ed. *The Western Country in the Seventeenth Century: The Memoirs of Antoine Lamoth Cadillac and Pierre Liette.* New York: Citadel Press, 1962.

Quinn, David B., ed. *New American World: A Documentary History of North America.* 5 vols. New York: Arno Press, 1979.

Sagard, Gabriel. *The Long Journey to the Country of the Hurons.* 1632. Edited by George M. Wrong and translated by H. H. Langton. Toronto: Champlain Society, 1939.

Saltonstall, Nathaniel. *A New And Further Narrative of the State of New-England, Being a Continued Account of the Bloudy Indian-War, from March till August, 1676.* . . . London: J. B. for Dorman Newman, 1676.

Shaw, William. *An Analysis of the Gaelic Language.* 1778. Facsimile reprint, Menston: Scolar Press, 1972.

Shepard, Thomas. *The Clear Sun-shine of the Gospel breaking forth upon the Indians in New England.* London: John Bellamy, 1648.

Smith, Adam. *Adam Smith: Essays on Philosophical Subjects.* Edited by W. P. D. Wightman, J. C. Bryce, and I. S. Ross. Oxford: Clarendon Press, 1980.

———. *Adam Smith: Lectures on Rhetoric and Belles Lettres.* Edited by J. C. Bryce. Oxford: Clarendon Press, 1983.

Stoddard, Amos. *Sketches, Historical, and Descriptive, of Louisiana.* Philadelphia: M. Carey, 1812.

Thoreau, Henry David. *The Writings of Henry David Thoreau.* Boston: Houghton, Mifflin, 1887–1900.

Thorowgood, Thomas. *Jewes in America, or, Probabilities that the Americans are of that Race.* London: T. Slater, 1650.

Thwaites, Reuben Gold, ed. *The Jesuit Relations and Allied Documents: Travels and Explorations of the Jesuit Missionaries in New France, 1610–1791.* 73 vols. Cleveland: Burrows Brothers, 1896–1901.

Tyndale, William. *Expositions and Notes.* Edited by H. Walter. Cambridge: Cambridge University Press, 1849.

Webster, Noah. *Dissertations on the English Language, with Notes Historical and Critical.* Boston: I. Thomas, 1789.

———. *A Collection of Essays and Fugitiv [sic] Writing on Moral, Historical, Political, and Literary Subjects.* Boston: I. Thomas, 1790.

———. *Letters of Noah Webster.* Edited by Harry R. Warfel. New York: Library Publishers, 1953.

Whitehead, James L., ed. "The Autobiography of Peter Stephen Du Ponceau." *Pennsylvania Magazine of History and Biography* 63:2 (April 1939): 189–227; 63:3 (July 1939): 311–43; 63:4 (October 1939): 432–61; 64:1 (January 1940): 97–120; 64:2 (April 1940): 243–69.

Whitfield, Henry. *The Light Appearing More and More towards the Perfect Day.* London: John Bartlet, 1651.

———. *Strength Out of Weaknesse: Or, a Glorious Manifestation of the Further Progress of the Gospel among the Indians of New England.* London: John Blague, 1652.

Wilkins, John. *An Essay Towards a Real Character and a Philosophical Language.* 1668. Facsimile reprint. Menston: Scolar Press, 1968.

Williams, Roger. *A Key into the Language of America.* Edited by John J. Teunissen and Evelyn J. Hinz. 1643. Reprint, Detroit, Mich.: Wayne State University Press, 1973.

Winslow, Edward. *The Glorious Progress of the Gospel, amongst the Indians in New England.* London: Hannah Allen, 1646.

Wood, William. *New England's Prospect.* Edited by Alden T. Vaughan. 1634. Reprint, Amherst: University of Massachusetts Press, 1977.

Select Secondary Sources

The following works deal with the study and use of language, and have been particularly important for my own analysis. I have discussed writings that address related issues and themes in the footnotes.

Aarsleff, Hans. *The Study of Language in England, 1780–1860.* Princeton: Princeton University Press, 1967.

―――. *From Locke to Saussure: Essays on the Study of Language and Intellectual History.* Minneapolis: University of Minnesota Press, 1982.

Allen, D. C. "Some Theories of the Growth and Origin of Language in Milton's Age." *Philological Quarterly* 28:1 (January 1949): 5–16.

Anderson, Benedict. *Imagined Communities: Reflections on the Origin and Spread of Nationalism.* Rev. ed. London: Verso, 1991.

Andresen-Tetel, Julie T. "Images des langues américaines au XVIIIe siècle." In *L'Homme des lumieres et la decouverte de l'autre,* edited by D. Droixhe et Pol-P. Gossiaux, 135–45. Brussels: Editions De L'Universite De Bruxelles, 1985.

―――. *Linguistics in America, 1769–1924.* London: Routledge, 1990.

Barber, Charles. *The English Language: A Historical Introduction.* Cambridge: Cambridge University Press, 1993.

Bauman, Richard. *Let Your Words Be Few: Symbolism of Speaking and Silence among Seventeenth-Century Quakers.* Cambridge: Cambridge University Press, 1983.

Bauman, Richard, and Joel Sherzer, eds. *Explorations in the Ethnography of Speaking.* 2d ed. Cambridge: Cambridge University Press, 1989.

Borst, Arno. *Der Turmbau von Babel: Geschichte der Meinungen über Ursprung und Vielfalt der Sprachen und Völker.* 6 vols. Stuttgart: Hiersemann, 1957–63.

―――. *Medieval Worlds: Barbarians, Heretics, and Artists in the Middle Ages.* Translated by Eric Hansen. Chicago: University of Chicago Press, 1992.

Boyarin, Jonathan, ed. *The Ethnography of Reading.* Berkeley: University of California Press, 1993.

Bragdon, Kathleen Joan. "'Another Tongue Brought In': An Ethnohistorical Study of Native Writings in Massachusett." Ph.D. diss., Brown University, 1981.

Brennan, Gillian. "Patriotism, Language, and Power: English Translations of the Bible, 1520–1580." *History Workshop Journal* 27 (Spring 1989): 18–36.

Burke, Peter. *The Art of Conversation.* Ithaca, N.Y.: Cornell University Press, 1993.

Burke, Peter, and Roy Porter, eds. *The Social History of Language.* Cambridge: Cambridge University Press, 1987.

―――. *Language, Self, and Society: A Social History of Language.* Cambridge, Mass.: Polity Press, 1991.

Bynack, V. P. "Noah Webster's Linguistic Thought and the Idea of an American National Culture." *Journal of the History of Ideas* 45:1 (January–March 1984): 99–114.

Calvet, Louis-Jean. *Linguistique et colonialisme: Petit traité de glottophagie.* Paris: Éditions Payot, 1974.

Certeau, Michel de. "L'Idée de traduction de la bible au XVIIème siècle: Sacy et Simon." *Recherches de Science Religieuse* 66:1 (1978): 73–92.

Certeau, Michel de, Dominique Julia, and Jacques Revel. *Une politique de la langue: La Révolution française et les patois.* Paris: Éditions Gallimard, 1975.

Cheyfitz, Eric. *The Poetics of Imperialism: Translation and Colonization from The Tempest to Tarzan.* New York: Oxford University Press, 1991.

Chomsky, Noam. *Cartesian Linguistics: A Chapter in the History of Rationalist Thought.* New York: Harper and Row, 1966.

Cmiel, Kenneth. *Democratic Eloquence: The Fight over Popular Speech in Nineteenth-Century America.* New York: William Morrow, 1990.

———. "'A Broad Fluid Language of Democracy': Discovering the American Idiom." *Journal of American History* 79:3 (December 1992): 913–36.

Cohen, Murray. *Sensible Words: Linguistic Practice in England, 1640–1785.* Baltimore: Johns Hopkins University Press, 1977.

Cornelius, Paul. *Languages in Seventeenth- and Eighteenth-Century Imaginary Voyages.* Geneva: Librarie Droz, 1965.

Driver, Harold E. *Indians of North America.* 2d ed. Chicago: University of Chicago Press, 1969.

Durkacz, Victor Edward. *The Decline of the Celtic Languages: A Study of Linguistic and Cultural Conflict in Scotland, Wales, and Ireland from the Reformation to the Twentieth Century.* Edinburgh: John Donald, 1983.

Edwards, John. *Multilingualism.* London: Routledge, 1994.

Fabian, Johannes. *Language and Colonial Power: The Appropriation of Swahili in the Former Belgian Congo, 1880–1983.* Cambridge: Cambridge University Press, 1986.

Febvre, Lucien, and Henri-Jean Martin. *The Coming of the Book: The Impact of Printing, 1450–1800.* Translated by David Gerard. London: Verso, 1990.

Feidelson, Charles, Jr. *Symbolism and American Literature.* Chicago: University of Chicago Press, 1953.

Fliegelman, Jay. *Declaring Independence: Jefferson, Natural Language, and the Culture of Performance.* Stanford, Calif.: Stanford University Press, 1993.

Formigari, Lia. "Language and Society in the Late Eighteenth Century." *Journal of the History of Ideas* 35:2 (April–June 1974): 275–92.

Foster, Michael K. "On Who Spoke First at Iroquois-White Councils: An Exercise in the Method of Upstreaming." In *Extending the Rafters: Interdisciplinary Approaches to Iroquoian Studies*, edited by M. K. Foster, J. Campisi, and M. Mithun, 183–207. Albany: State University of New York Press, 1984.

Foucault, Michel. *The Order of Things: An Archaeology of the Human Sciences.* New York: Vintage Books, 1973.

Gagnon, François-Marc. *La Conversion par l'image: Un aspect de la mission des Jésuites auprès des Indiens du Canada au XVIIe siècle.* Montréal: Les Éditions Bellarmin, 1975.

Goddard, Ives. "Eastern Algonquian Languages." In *Handbook of North American Indians. Vol. 15, The Northeast*, edited by Bruce Trigger, 70–77. Washington, D.C.: Smithsonian Institution, 1978.

———, ed. *Handbook of North American Indians. Vol. 17, Languages.* Washington, D.C.: Smithsonian Institution, 1996.

Goddard, Ives, and Kathleen J. Bragdon. *Native Writings in Massachusett*. Philadelphia: American Philosophical Society, 1988.

Gray, Edward G., and Norman Fiering, eds. *The Language Encounter in the Americas, 1492–1800*. New York: Berghahn Books, forthcoming.

Greenberg, Joseph. *Language in the Americas*. Stanford, Calif.: Stanford Universiaty Press, 1987.

Greenblatt, Stephen J. "Learning to Curse: Aspects of Linguistic Colonialism in the Sixteenth Century." In *First Images of America*, edited by Fredi Chiappelli, vol. 1, 561–80. Berkeley: University of California Press, 1976.

Greene, John C. *American Science in the Age of Jefferson*. Ames: Iowa State University Press, 1984.

Gruzinski, Serge. *The Conquest of Mexico: The Incorporation of Indian Societies into the Western World, Sixteenth–Eighteenth Centuries*. Translated by Eileen Corrigan. Cambridge, England: Polity Press, 1993.

Guice, Stephen A. "The Linguistic Work of John Eliot." PhD. diss., Michigan State University, 1990.

Gura, Philip F. *The Wisdom of Words: Language, Theology, and Literature in the New England Renaissance*. Middletown, Conn.: Wesleyan University Press, 1981.

Hall, David D. *Worlds of Wonder, Days of Judgement: Popular Religious Belief in Early New England*. New York: Knopf, 1989.

Hanzeli, Victor E. *Missionary Linguistics in New France: A Study of Seventeenth- and Eighteenth-Century Descriptions of American Indian Languages*. The Hague: Mouton, 1969.

Harris, Roy, and Talbot J. Taylor. *Landmarks in Linguistic Thought: The Western Tradition from Socrates to Saussure*. London: Routledge, 1989.

Haugen, Einar. "Dialect, Language, Nation." *American Anthropologist* 68:4 (August 1966): 922–35.

Heath, Shirley Brice, and Richard Laprade. "Castilian Colonization and Indigenous Languages: The Cases of Quechua and Aymara." In *Language Spread: Studies in Diffusion and Social Change*, edited by Robert L. Cooper, 118–147. Bloomington: Indiana University Press, 1982.

Hobsbawm, E. J. *Nations and Nationalism since 1780: Programme, Myth, Reality*. Cambridge: Cambridge University Press, 1990.

Hovdhaugen, Even, ed. *. . . and the Word Was God: Missionary Linguistics and Missionary Grammar*. Münster: Nodus Publikationen, 1996.

Howell, Wilbur Samuel. *Logic and Rhetoric in England, 1500–1700*. Princeton, N.J.: Princeton University Press, 1956.

———. *Eighteenth-Century British Logic and Rhetoric*. Princeton, N.J.: Princeton University Press, 1971.

Hudson, Nicholas. *Writing and European Thought, 1600–1830*. Cambridge: Cambridge University Press, 1994.

Jones, R. F. *The Triumph of the English Language: A Survey of Opinions Concerning the Vernacular from the Introduction of Printing to the Restoration*. Stanford, Calif.: Stanford University Press, 1953.

Kamensky, Jane. *Governing the Tongue: The Politics of Speech in Early New England*. New York: Oxford University Press, 1997.

Karttunen, Frances. "Nahuatl Literacy." In *The Inca and Aztec States 1400–1800: Anthropology and History*, edited by George A. Collier, Renato I. Rosaldo, and John D. Wirth, 395–417. New York: Academic Press, 1982.

Kernan, Alvin. *Samuel Johnson and the Impact of Print*. Princeton, N.J.: Princeton University Press, 1989.

Klor de Alva, J. Jorge. "Language, Politics, and Translation: Colonial Discourse and Classical Nahuatl in New Spain." In *The Art of Translation: Voices from the Field*, edited by Rosanna Warren, 143–62. Boston: Northeastern University Press, 1989.

Knowlson, James. *Universal Language Schemes in England and France, 1600–1800*. Toronto: University of Toronto Press, 1975.

Kramer, Michael P. *Imagining Language in America: From the Revolution to the Civil War*. Princeton, N.J.: Princeton University Press, 1992.

Land, Stephen K. *The Philosophy of Language in Britain: Major Theories from Hobbes to Thomas Reid*. New York: AMS Press, 1986.

Leahey, Margaret. J. "'To Hear with My Eyes': The Native Language Acquisition Project in the 'Jesuit Relations.'" Ph.D. diss., Johns Hopkins University, 1991.

Lepore, Jill. "Dead Men Tell No Tales: John Sassamon and the Fatal Consequences of Literacy." *American Quarterly* 46:4 (December 1994): 479–512.

Lockridge, Kenneth. *Literacy in Colonial New England: An Enquiry into the Social Context of Literacy in the Early Modern West*. New York: Norton, 1974.

Looby, Christopher. "The Constitution of Nature: Taxonomy as Politics in Jefferson, Peale, and Bartram." *Early American Literature* 22:3 (1987): 252–73.

Lowenthal, Leo. "Caliban's Legacy." *Cultural Critique* 8 (Winter 1987–88): 5–17.

Mannheim, Bruce. *The Language of the Inka since the European Invasion*. Austin: University of Texas Press, 1991.

Markley, Robert. *Fallen Languages: Crises of Representation in Newtonian England, 1660–1740*. Ithaca, N.Y.: Cornell University Press, 1993.

Martin, Henri-Jean. *The History and Power of Writing*. Translated by Lydia G. Cochrane. Chicago: University of Chicago Press, 1994.

Mignolo, Walter. *The Darker Side of the Renaissance: Literacy, Territoriality, and Colonization*. Ann Arbor: University of Michigan Press, 1995.

Morgan, John. *Godly Learning: Puritan Attitudes Towards Reason, Learning and Education, 1560–1640*. Cambridge: Cambridge University Press, 1986.

Murray, David. *Forked Tongues: Speech, Writing, and Representation in North American Indian Texts*. Bloomington: Indiana University Press, 1991.

Nida, Eugene A. ed. *The Book of a Thousand Tongues*. Rev. ed. London: United Bible Societies, 1972.

Olender, Maurice. *The Languages of Paradise: Race, Religion, and Philology in the Nineteenth Century*. Translated by Arthur Goldhammer. Cambridge, Mass.: Harvard University Press, 1992.

Ong, Walter J. *Ramus, Method, and the Decay of Dialogue*. Cambridge, Mass.: Harvard University Press, 1958.

———. *The Presence of the Word: Some Prolegomena for Cultural and Religious History*. New Haven, Conn.: Yale University Press, 1967.

————. *Orality and Literacy: The Technologizing of the Word.* 1982. Reprint, London: Routledge, 1988.

Ormsby-Lennon, Hugh. "Nature's Mystick Book: Renaissance *Arcanum* into Restoration Cant." In *Secret Texts: The Literature of Secret Societies,* edited by Marie Mulvey Roberts and Hugh Ormsby-Lennon, 24–96. New York: AMS Press, 1995.

Padley, G. A. *Grammatical Theory in Western Europe, 1500–1700: The Latin Tradition.* Cambridge: Cambridge University Press, 1976.

————. *Grammatical Theory in Western Europe, 1500–1700: Trends in Vernacular Grammar.* Cambridge: Cambridge University Press, 1985.

Pagden, Anthony. *The Fall of Natural Man: The American Indian and the Origins of Comparative Ethnology.* Cambridge: Cambridge University Press, 1982.

————. *European Encounters with the New World: From Renaissance to Romanticism.* New Haven, Conn.: Yale University Press, 1993.

Pilling, James Constantine. *A Bibliography of the Algonquian Language.* Washington, D.C.: U.S. Government Printing Office, 1891.

Potkay, Adam. *The Fate of Eloquence in the Age of Hume.* Ithaca, N.Y.: Cornell University Press, 1994.

Prickett, Stephen. *Words and The Word: Language, Poetics and Biblical Interpretation.* Cambridge: Cambridge University Press, 1986.

Rafael, Vicente L. *Contracting Colonialism: Translation and Christian Conversion in Tagalog Society under Early Spanish Rule.* Ithaca, N.Y.: Cornell University Press, 1988.

Robins, R. H. *A Short History of Linguistics.* Bloomington: Indiana University Press, 1967.

Romaine, Suzanne. *Language in Society: An Introduction to Sociolinguistics.* Oxford: Oxford University Press, 1994.

Salmon, Vivian. *The Study of Language in Seventeenth-Century England.* Amsterdam: John Benjamins, 1979.

————. "Missionary Linguistics in Seventeenth Century Ireland and a North American Analogy." *Historiographia Linguistica* 12 (1985): 321–49.

Sapir, Edward. *Language: An Introduction to the Study of Speech.* San Diego: Harcourt Brace, 1921.

Schreyer, Rüdiger. "Linguistics Meets Caliban, or The Uses of Savagery in Eighteenth-Century Theoretical History of Language." In *Papers in the History of Linguistics,* edited by Hans Aarsleff et al. Amsterdam: John Benjamins, 1987.

Shapiro, Barbara J. *Probability and Certainty in Seventeenth-Century England: A Study of the Relationships between Natural Science, Religion, History, Law, and Literature.* Princeton, N.J.: Princeton University Press, 1983.

Shell, Marc. "Babel in America; or, The Politics of Language Diversity in the United States." *Critical Inquiry* 20:1 (Autumn 1993): 103–27.

Slaughter, M. M. *Universal Languages and Scientific Taxonomy in the Seventeenth Century.* Cambridge: Cambridge University Press, 1982.

Smith, Murphy D. "Peter Stephen Du Ponceau and His Study of Languages: A Historical Account." *Proceedings of the American Philsophical Society* 127:3 (1983): 143–79.

Smith, Nigel. *Perfection Proclaimed: Language and Literature in English Radical Religion, 1640–1660*. Oxford: Clarendon Press, 1989.

Sorenson, Arthur P., Jr. "Multilingualism in the Northwest Amazon." *American Anthropologist* 69:6 (1967): 670–82.

Steiner, George. *After Babel: Aspects of Language and Translation*. Oxford: Oxford University Press, 1975.

Stock, Brian. *The Implications of Literacy: Written Language and Models of Interpretation in the Eleventh and Twelfth Centuries*. Princeton, N.J.: Princeton University Press, 1983.

Street, Brian V., ed. *Cross-cultural Approaches to Literacy*. Cambridge: Cambridge University Press, 1993.

Tambiah, S. J. "The Magical Power of Words." *Man* 3:2 (June 1968): 175–208.

Watts, Pauline M. "Hieroglyphs of Conversion: Alien Discourses in Diego Valades's *Rhetorica Christiana*." *Memorie Domenicane* 21 (1991): 1–29.

Weigand, Hermann J. "The Two and Seventy Languages of the World." *Germanic Review* 17:4 (1942): 241–60.

Winship, George Parker. *The Cambridge Press, 1638–1692: A Re-examination of the Evidence Concerning the Bay Psalm Book and the Eliot Indian Bible . . . .* Philadelphia: University of Pennsylvania Press, 1945.

Wogan, Peter. "Perceptions of European Literacy in Early Contact Situations." *Ethnohistory* 41:3 (Summer 1994): 407–29.

Wolff, Philippe. *Western Languages, AD 100–1500*. Translated by Frances Partridge. London: World University Library, 1971.

Zagorin, Perez. *Ways of Lying: Dissimulation, Persecution, and Conformity in Early Modern Europe*. Cambridge, Mass.: Harvard University Press, 1990.

Index

Note: Page numbers in bold type indicate illustrations.

Dunn, John, 93

Du Ponceau, Peter Stephen, 7, 118, **140**, 159, 165, 166; admiration for Indian speech of, 143; on classification of languages, 152; compared to Bushnell, 164; compared to Locke, 150; and compassion for Indians, 143; contrasted with Enlightenment language philosophers, 148; critique of Humboldt, 157; critique of Monboddo, 154–55; critique of Smith, 155; defense of language study, 147; on Delaware (language), 151, 153; education of, 141–42; on English language, 144–45; on Enlightenment language philosophy, 153–55; on etymology, 148–49; on government and science, 145; on *Idéology*, 149, 150; on language of Eden, 150–51; and the law, 143; modernity of, 141, 157–58; as national booster, 141, 144–45; natural theology of, 148; on patronage for language studies, 143–44; and Romantic language philosophy, 148; on structure of Indian languages, 151–55; on superior beauty of Indian languages, 151–55

Dury, John, 43, 71, 87

Eastern Algonquian languages, 15; extinction of, 113

Edmundson, Henry, 67

Elias, Norbert, 4

Eliot, John, 45, 48, 54, 55, 111; Bible and, 57–58; and censoring of *A Christian Commonwealth*, 77–78; conversion methods of, 64–65; on Hebrew, 68–69; and Indian conversion narratives, 73–75; and Indians as uncorrupted, 58; in King Philip's War, 78; on logic, 70; Massachusett grammar of, 147; on Massachusett (language), 66; and Massachusetts Bay Company, 63; millennialism of, 56–58; New England Company and, 74; political philosophy of, 56–58, 60–62; and praying towns, 62; preaching of described, 76; on printed Massachusett, 66–67; Ramism and, 72–73; and second edition of Massachusett Bible, 81; struggles for donations of, 62–63, 81; as teacher of reading, 52; as translator, 58–62, 66–67; on universal

language movement, 68–69; and the Word, 60–62

eloquence. *See* natural eloquence

English language instruction (of Indians), 48–49, 80–81, 82–83, 162–63

etymology, 138, 148–49. *See also* Jefferson

The Federalist, 136–37

Federalist Party, 134

Ferguson, Adam, 104–5, 133

Fichte, Johann Gottlieb, 166–67

Fifth Monarchy Men, 69

Fludd, Robert, 69

French Revolution, 134

fur traders, 30, 31–32, 33

Gallatin, Albert, 145, 148, 150, 162

Gébelin, Antoine Court de, 142

German, 166–67

Goddard, Ives, 52–53

Gookin, Daniel, 81

Grafton, Anthony, 10

Greek, 116, 118, 156. *See also* classical languages

Green, Samuel, 64

Gregory, Saint, 5

Grotius, Hugo, 22–23, 124

Harriot, Thomas, 13

Harvard College, 70, 72

Hebrew, 47, 53, 68–70

Heckewelder, John, 7, 151, 153

Hennepin, Louis, 13

Hervás y Panduro, Abbé Lorenzo, 142

Hooker, Thomas, 62

Howes, Edward, 49

Humboldt, Wilhelm von, 156–57, 166

Hume, David, 105

Huron (tribe), 30

Hutchins, Thomas, 112

Idéologues, 149–50. *See also* Du Ponceau

Indian languages, **17**; absence of Christian terms in, 35–37, 160; and conversion narratives, 73–74; degree of difference between, 14–15; as derived from Greek or Latin, 25–26; as derived from Hebrew, 24–25; destruction of, 162–63; as difficult to learn, 47, 53; diversity of, 10–15; early explanations for diversity of, 21–23; as exceptional in